India-Korea Dialogue for a 21st Century Partnership

Published by Academic Foundation
in association with

Indian Council for Research on
International Economic Relations,
New Delhi

India-Korea Dialogue for a 21st Century Partnership

Editors

CHOONG YONG AHN & PRAVAKAR SAHOO

ACADEMIC FOUNDATION
NEW DELHI

ACADEMIC FOUNDATION

First published in 2012
by

ACADEMIC FOUNDATION
4772-73 / 23 Bharat Ram Road, (23 Ansari Road),
Darya Ganj, New Delhi - 110 002 (India).
Phones : 23245001 / 02 / 03 / 04.
Fax : +91-11-23245005.
E-mail : books@academicfoundation.com
www.academicfoundation.com

in association with:

Indian Council for Research on International Economic Relations
(ICRIER), New Delhi.
www.icrier.org

Cataloging in Publication Data--DK
Courtesy: D.K. Agencies (P) Ltd. <docinfo@dkagencies.com>

India-Korea dialogue for a 21st century partnership / editors,
Choong Yong Ahn, Pravakar Sahoo.
p. cm.
Contributed articles.
ISBN 13: 9788171889204
ISBN 10: 8171889204

1. India--Foreign economic relations--Korea. 2. Korea--Foreign economic relations--India. I. An, Ch' ung-yŏ ng. II. Sahoo, Pravakar.

DDC 337.540519 23.

Typeset by Italics India, New Delhi.
Printed and bound in India.

Contents

Section II
India-Korea Bilateral Economic Cooperation

Section III
Global Security Challenges: Role for India-Korea Cooperation

List of Tables and Figures

Tables

Figures

About the Editors/ Contributors

Editors:

Choong Yong Ahn is a distinguished Professor of Graduate School of International Studies at Chung-Ang University, Korea. He is also a Foreign Investment Ombudsman at Korea Trade and Investment Promotion Agency. He is also currently the member of the Presidential Council on National Competitiveness and a Member of Regulatory Reform Commission in South Korea. While on leave from Professorship of Economics, Chung-Ang University, he had also served as the President of the Korea Institute for International Economic Policy (KIEP) from 2002 to 2005, Chair of the APEC Economic Committee, and Chair of Board, Choheung Bank. He has maintained a keen interest in public policy, serving in positions such as Consultant to the World Bank, UNIDO Chief Technical Advisor to the Economic Planning Unit of Malaysia to design Malaysia's industrial master plan, and has been the President of several academic societies in Korea including Korea International Economics Association, Korea Econometric Society, Korean Society of International Trade, Korea Development Economics Association, etc. Since receiving his Ph.D from Ohio State University in 1972, Dr. Ahn has published many articles in prestigious international journals and also published a few books.

Pravakar Sahoo is an Associate Professor at Institute of Economic Growth (IEG), Delhi University, India. Prior to joining IEG as Associate Professor (February 2009), he was working as senior fellow in Indian Council for Research on International Economic Relations

(ICRIER), New Delhi. During last 13 years of teaching and research experience, he has worked and published more than 40 research papers in national and international journals such as *Journal of International Trade and Economic Development, Journal of Policy Modeling, Journal of Developing Areas, Journal of Asian Economics, Journal of Asia Pacific Economies, International Economic Journal, Singapore Economic Review, Journal of Economic Policy Reforms, Economic and Political Weekly* etc. on issues related to macroeconomics, development economics, international trade & investment, regional cooperation, infrastructure and FDI. He has carried out projects and acted as a consultant to various national and international agencies including Ministry of Finance and Commerce, Government of India, Asian Development Bank, Asian Development Bank Institute (ADBI), Indo-Sastri Canadian Institute, Indira Gandhi Open University (IGNOU), Korea Institute for International Economic Relations (KIEP) and East West Center, USA. Further, he teaches macroeconomics to high-level government officials and policy makers like Indian economic service and Indian statistical service officers.

Contributors:

Tamal Bandyopadhyay is a Deputy Managing Editor with Mint, India's second largest read financial daily, brought out by HT Media Ltd. in association with The Wall Street Journal. He writes a weekly column on banking and finance every Monday (Banker's Trust) and moderates Mint's panel discussions across Indian cities on critical, contemporary financial and economic issues. An MA in English literature, Tamal started his career as a trainee journalist with Times of India, the country's biggest publication house. In his 25-year career, he worked with three national financial dailies besides Mint. They are The Economic Times, Financial Express and Business Standard. He closely follows developments in international finance and financial markets in India.

Choongjae Cho is an associate research fellow and leader of Southeast and South Asia team at Korea Institute for International Economic Policy (KIEP). He holds a Ph.D in Economics from Hankuk University of Foreign Studies. He was a researcher of Daewoo Economic Research Institute and Lotte Economic Research Institute. He has also worked for The Seoul Economic Daily as a reporter. He is an expert in Indian Economy and is interested in service-led economic growth in India. He has published number of journal articles on Indian economy and co-authored some books on Indian economy and economic cooperation between India and Korea.

Changsu Kim is a Senior Research Fellow at the Korea Institute for Defense Analyses (KIDA), Seoul. Since he joined the Institute in 1985, Dr. Kim has served on such posts as Chief of Japan Studies Division, Chief of Regional Military Affairs Division, Chief of US Studies Division, Chief of International Conflict Studies Division, and Director of the Center for Security and Strategy. In 2007, he served as Special Assistant to the Minister for Policy at the ROK Ministry of National Defense. And from December 2008 to March 2009, he was a NIDS Fellow at the National Institute for Defense Studies, Tokyo, Japan. From 1995 to 2002 and again from 2006 to 2008, Kim was the Editor-in-Chief for *The Korean Journal of*

Defense Analysis (KJDA). He graduated from the Hankuk University of Foreign Studies in Seoul in 1977 and received his MA and Ph.D in Political Science from the University of Cincinnati in 1981 and 1985, respectively.

Joon-Kyung Kim is Professor at the Korea Development Institute (KDI) School of Public Policy and Management. He served as Senior Vice President of KDI and Secretary to the President in Financial Policy. He was also an Assistant Professor at Virginia Tech; Visiting Professor at Columbia University and a World Bank Consultant. His recent research has focused on Sino-Korean economic integration, on restructuring and institutional reforms in Korea's financial and corporate sectors, and on the role of organizations in Korea's economic development. His has written number of research articles on Korean Economy. Kim has a Ph.D in Economics from the University of California at San Diego, and a B.S. in Computer Science and Statistics from the Seoul National University.

Rajiv Kumar is currently Secretary General of Federation of Chambers of Commerce and Industry (FICCI). Before moving to FICCI, he was the Director & Chief Executive of the Indian Council for Research on International Economic Relations (ICRIER), one of India's leading independent economic policy think tanks. He is a member of many important bodies such as Central Board of Directors of the State Bank of India, Telecom Regulatory Authority of India, India Brand Equity Foundation (IBEF) Board of Trustees, and also on the Board of Directors for the United States-India Educational Foundation (USIEF). He was a member of the National Security Advisory Board for two years until October 2008. Dr. Kumar was a Professor at the Indian Institute of Foreign Trade (1987-1989); worked in the Government of India from 1989 to 1995, first in the Bureau of Industrial Costs and Projects, Ministry of Industry (1989-1991) and then as Economic Adviser in the Department of Economic Affairs, Ministry of Finance (1991-1995). He worked at the Asian Development Bank, Manila, for nearly 10 years (1995-2005) and was the Chief Economist at the Confederation of Indian

Industry, New Delhi during 2004-2006. He has a D.Phil in Economics from Oxford University and has several books and publications to his credit. He is also an active columnist.

Chang-Ho Kwag has a Ph.D degree in Economics from the University of Texas at Austin, USA (1991). He worked as a Research Fellow in the Investment and Finance Research Institute from 1991 to 1994. In 1994, he joined the POSCO Research Institute (POSRI) as a Research Fellow. He worked for the Korean Government as Counselor for the Prime Minister of the Republic of Korea in the year 2000, and also advised the Korea Fair Trade Commission from 2001 to 2003. Now, as Director of POSRI heading the Center for Global Research, he is doing in-depth research on global steel industry, steel consuming industries and FDI environments in some major countries like China and India. He is also deeply involved in mapping of POSCO Global Strategy. He has published several papers in renowned international journals and every year participates as a speaker in about 4-5 international conferences on steel and steel making raw materials.

Suresh P. Prabhu is an Ex-Federal Cabinet Minister of Industry, Energy, Environment and Forests, Chemicals and Fertilizers, Heavy Industry & Public Enterprises of the Government of India. He was the Member of Parliament, India from 1996-2009. During his tenure as MP, he chaired very important committees such as, Parliamentary Forum on Environment; Parliamentary Maritime Group; Co-operative Forum of Parliamentarians, Parliamentary Standing Committee on Ministry of External Affairs; and was also a member of important parliamentary bodies such as Public Accounts Committee; Joint Parliamentary Committee to draft Women's Reservation Bill; Parliamentary Standing Committee on Finance and Member, Consultative Committee for the Ministry of Commerce & Industry.

Ajay Shankar is former Secretary to the Government of India, Department of Industrial Policy and Promotion. He joined the Indian Administrative Service in 1973. He has rich and varied experience in the Central and State governments in industrial promotion, the energy sector and urban management and development. As Secretary, Department of Industrial Policy & Promotion, he played a critical role in putting together the stimulus packages at the time of the global economic crisis. Prior to that, he was Principal Adviser in the Planning Commission looking after the water, sanitation and environment and forest sectors as well as provision of rural infrastructure through the Bharat Nirman Programme. As Joint Secretary/Additional Secretary in the Ministry of Power, he played a key role in preparation and enactment of the Electricity Act, 2003 and the rules and policies under the Act.

Narendra Sisodia is the former Director General of the Institute for Defence Studies and Analyses, New Delhi. He was earlier Secretary in the Ministries of Finance and Defence, Government of India and Vice-Chancellor of University of Udaipur. Mr. Sisodia graduated from St. Stephens' College Delhi and obtained a Master's Degree from Harvard University, USA, where he was a Mason Fellow. He joined the Indian Administrative Service in 1968 and served in several key economic and national security assignments at the State and Central government level. In the Government of India, he served as Joint Secretary, Ministry of Defence from 1988-1994. As Additional Secretary in the National Security Council Secretariat, he was a member of the Task Force on Reforming the Management of Defence. He has been the Convener of Indian Pugwash Society and a member of the India-China Eminent Persons' Group.

Foreword

India and the Republic of Korea have shared a close relationship since the establishment of formal diplomatic ties in 1973. Today the two countries have a comprehensive economic and strategic partnership. As the 3rd and 4th largest economies in Asia, the two countries are also playing an increasing role in the global economy.

The last three and a half decades have seen many high-level exchanges and signing of crucial agreements leading to continuous strengthening of bilateral relations. However, trade and investment between India and Korea are relatively low compared to the size and structural complementarities of the two economies. This is due to several tariff and non-tariff barriers and remaining bilateral issues between the two countries.

Against this backdrop, the signing of the India-Korea Comprehensive Economic Partnership Agreement (CEPA) on 7th August 2009 has been an extremely welcome step. This Agreement has provisions for substantial reduction of both tariffs and non-tariff barriers which is taking India-Korea economic relations to a higher level by facilitating greater trade, investment and cooperation in a number of areas.

In the academic domain, the Indian Council for Research on International Economic Relations (ICRIER) in collaboration with the Seoul Forum for International Affairs (SFIA) has been engaged in a Track II dialogue since the late 1990s to improve mutual understanding through interaction among scholars, industry representatives, and policy-practitioners on contemporary issues relating to Indo-Korean relations. The focus of the discussions is on relevant political, economic and strategic issues that India and the Republic of Korea face as members of the dynamic Asian economy and of contemporary international society. The discussions also address prospects for greater bilateral cooperation.

This volume edited by Choong Yong Ahn and Pravakar Sahoo brings together important policy relevant research papers presented by eminent scholars and policy makers at the 9th dialogue held in Seoul in May 2010. This is a comprehensive volume which includes papers on India and the Korea and the global economic crisis, India-Korea bilateral economic cooperation, and India-Korea cooperation in the context of global security challenges.

We hope that this volume will contribute to the knowledge base on India-Korea relations and help scholars and policy makers in enhancing India-Korea relations.

Parthasarathi Shome
Director & Chief Executive
Indian Council for Research on
International Economic Relations

Dalchoong Kim
President
The Seoul Forum for
International Affairs

Message

The rapidly evolving economic and security dynamics in the Asia-Pacific and the East Asia regions in the 21st century call for greater cooperation between India and Korea which enjoy deep cultural affinity between their peoples and significant historical commonalities. No wonder our two countries established a "Strategic Partnership" since January 2010 when President Lee Myung-bak had visited India. This partnership was cemented through an economic understanding by way of the Comprehensive Economic Partnership Agreement (CEPA). The visit of the President of India, Smt. Pratibha Devisingh Patil to RoK in July 2011 has added to the strategic dimension of the bilateral relationship.

This important partnership between two influential members of the global community, the challenges they face and the opportunities for their future cooperation, need constant study, analysis and documentation. The compilation of the excellent and well-researched papers presented at the 9th India-Korea Dialogue undertaken by the Indian Council for Research on International Economic Relations (ICRIER) would add to the body of available information and deserves deep appreciation. I must compliment both ICRIER and Seoul Forum for International Affairs (SFIA) for offering academic support to the evolving India-Korea partnership in a regional as well as global context.

India and Korea learnt lessons from the Asian Financial Crisis of 1997-98 and were able to face the global convulsions of 2007-08 more confidently than many other countries. Both India and RoK have consistently argued against protectionism and advocated greater capital flows, sustainable development and effective regulatory framework for the financial sectors. CEPA and India's partnership with ASEAN and East Asia Summit need to be seen in the larger perspective of our *"Look-East Policy"*.

It is appropriate that the scholarly contributions have not been confined to trade and investment spheres alone but have dwelt on the global security challenges also. In my view, the partnership between our two countries has now matured and has acquired considerable substance wherefrom it is poised to take on global challenges with confidence. It is in this context that I should particularly commend the inclusion of a section on 'Global Security Challenges: Role for India-Korea Cooperation', which covers a wide gamut of strategic issues including terrorism, piracy and safety of sea-lanes on which India and Korea can cooperate.

The publication, *'India-Korea Dialogue for A 21st Century Partnership'* by co-editors Pravakar Sahoo and Choong Yong Ahn is a timely effort as it not only identifies various strands of the bilateral relationship between India and Korea, but places the emerging strands into a coherent and broader vision for the years to come.

S.R. Tayal

Ambassador of India to Republic of Korea

Message

I would like to express my heartfelt congratulations on the publication of *India-Korea Dialogue for a 21st Century Partnership* by Indian Council for Research on International Economic Relations (ICRIER). The publication brings together the papers presented at the 9th Indo-Korea Dialogue held at Seoul in 2010. This track-two dialogue has regularly been organized by ICRIER in collaboration with the Seoul Forum for International Affairs (SFIA) since the late 1990s. Indeed, Korea-India Dialogue has proved to be a significant initiative to consolidate our bilateral ties. Discussions and debates held in the Forum have played an important role in promoting a truly multi-faceted relationship between the two countries.

Korea and India share a long standing traditional friendship. Over the years, this friendship has evolved into a comprehensive economic partnership and more recently into a strategic partnership reinforced by economic and political imperatives.

Our cooperation continues to expand and deepen in all areas of bilateral relations, with frequent exchange of high-level visits, growing trade and investment ties and increasing people to people contacts.

It is on the economic and commercial front that Korea-India relations have made the most notable progress. Our trade and investment relations reached a new high when our two countries signed Korea-India Comprehensive Economic Partnership Agreement (CEPA). The implementation of CEPA has unlocked the potential of the two economies and contributed to phenomenal growth of bilateral trade and investment. However, we believe that even the current impressive bilateral trade and investment figures do not reflect the true commercial potential of the two countries. The entrepreneurs of our countries with the active support of our respective governments are determined to realize the untapped potential in trade and investment. The prospect of cooperation in areas such as construction and infrastructure, nuclear and renewable energy, ICT industry, shipbuilding, defense, chemical industry, etc. hold great promise.

The State Visit of President of Republic of Korea Mr. Lee Myung-bak to India in January 2010 was an important milestone that elevated the relationship between the two countries to "Strategic Partnership". Since this upgradation, bilateral relationship has expanded beyond the traditional areas of cooperation in trade and investment to include security and defense cooperation. Our two countries are working closely bilaterally and in different regional and international fora to promote peace and security in the region and to secure sea lines of communications. The recent State Visit of President of India, Smt. Pratibha Devisingh Patil to Korea in July has given further momentum to our evolving strategic partnership.

The publication is a welcome addition to the scarce body of work on Korea-India bilateral relations, and I commend the ICRIER for this initiative. The papers included in this volume cover a wide variety of topics ranging from global economic crisis to G-20, while covering all aspects of Korea-India bilateral relationship. I express my heartfelt thanks to all those who have contributed papers for this volume. My sincere appreciation goes to Professor Choong Yong Ahn and Dr. Pravakar Sahoo for co-editing the publication. I do hope that this publication will create readers' interest in our bilateral relations and encourage more such works in the future.

Kim Joong Keun
Ambassador of the Republic of Korea to India

Preface

India and South Korea have almost equal GDPs and rank among the top 14 economies in the world, with highly commendable growth performance in the past two decades. At present, the two countries share common values on democracy, the market economic system, outward and global orientation, and an emphasis on higher learning, not to mention past colonial experiences. Both countries belong to the major economies of the G-20, which has become a major global economic cooperative entity after the global financial crisis in 2008. Despite these similarities, the two countries have almost opposite factor endowments in terms of land and population. Furthermore, until the late 1980s, the two countries pursued different paradigms of development; while India pursued an inward-looking development path, South Korea followed an outward-looking development strategy. As a result, the two countries show differences over time in their stages of industrial development, manpower development, and liberalization regimes. In light of the differences in the level of development and the diversity in both countries, in an increasingly globalizing world economy they are likely to benefit immensely from the comprehensive Economic Partnership Agreement, which became effective in 2010.

Immediately following the Korean War (1950-1953), South Korea was one of the poorest countries in the world with little natural resource deposits and suffering from a vicious circle of poverty. Since the early 1960s, South Korea has consistently pursued an outward-looking export-oriented development path to achieve "compressed rapid industrialization". Korea began experiencing rapid economic growth by developing labor-intensive products for export in the 1960s but shifted to government-led heavy and chemical industrialization with synergistic partnerships between government and business entrepreneurs beginning in the early 1970s in the field of iron and steel, shipbuilding, electronics, machinery, textiles, chemicals, and automobiles. While engulfed in the Asian financial crisis of 1997–98, South Korea successfully restructured its banking, corporate, public enterprises, and labor sectors under IMF reform mandates while seeking the then-largest amount of financial help from the IMF.

At present, South Korea has developed global brand names focusing on electronics, automobiles, ships, machinery, petrochemicals, and robotics. Korea joined the OECD in 1996 and is a founding member of APEC and the East Asia Summit. The country was the world's sixth-largest exporter and tenth-largest importer in 2010. South Korea is now searching for a new growth engine in knowledge-intensive industries in addition to a globally competitive industrial base. Korea, as an upper-middle income country, is addressing a variety of emerging issues, to join the advanced open-economy group.

In contrast to South Korea's outward-oriented path to development, India pursued an inward-looking import substitution policy until the late 1980s. India is home to the ancient Indus Valley civilization and a region of historic trade routes and vast empires. For much of its history, it has boasted commercial and cultural wealth and a multilingual/multiethnic society. However, since the introduction of market-based economic reforms in 1991 emphasising foreign trade and investment, India has become one of the fastest-growing major economies in the world as one of the four BRIC nations. It has adopted an open trade-oriented economic system to promote export activities and rapidly developed its IT sector.

With 467 million workers, India has the world's second largest labor force. The country's service sector makes up 54 per cent of the GDP, the agricultural sector 18 per cent, and industrial sector 28 per cent. India's industrial structure is in sharp contrast to that of South Korea. India's major industries include textiles, telecommunications, chemicals, food processing, steel, transport equipment, cement, mining, petroleum, machinery, and software. India was the world's fifth-largest importer in 2009 and the eighth-largest exporter. India ranks 16th in financial market sophistication, 24th in the banking sector, 27th in business sophistication, and 30th in innovation ahead of several advanced economies. With seven of the world's top technology outsourcing companies based in India, the country is viewed as the second most favored outsourcing destination after the United States.

In 1973, India and Korea established a diplomatic relationship with a variety of treaties including those for culture (1974), science and technology (1976), avoidance of double taxation (1985), investment guarantee (1996), industrial standardization and quality control (1989), aviation (1992), and investment promotion cooperation (2003), culminating in the historic Comprehensive Economic Partnership Agreement (2010). Since then, there have been numerous state visits by leaders to promote bilateral cooperation. This is significant for the two countries as the CEPA allows for freer flows of commodities, services, investment, etc.

There have been significant direct investments into India by major Korean multinational companies such as Hyundai, Samsung, LG, Doosan, and POSCO. Major export items include electronic communication devices, automobiles and auto parts, and iron and steel products, to name just a few. There have also been important direct investments into Korea by Indian companies such as the TATA group.

Given the outward-looking and liberalized economic orientation, economic diversity, and factor endowments inherent in India and Korea, the two countries are likely to benefit from each other by maximizing the potential benefit of the CEPA. It is fortunate and timely that the Indian Council for Research on International Economic Relations (ICRIER) and the Seoul Forum for International Affairs (SFIA) have conducted annual dialogues over a decade to deepen mutual cooperation and understanding between the two countries. As global economic gravity shifts to Asia, the mutual cooperation of these two like-minded countries will serve as an important step toward the Asian economic community.

Given the pending bilateral cooperation in the areas of trade, investment, R&D, energy, culture, and security between the two countries, especially after the CEPA, both ICRIER and SFIA agreed to compile all the papers presented at the 9th dialogue in a book so that it can be shared with the business, academic, and policy-making bodies of the two countries. We sincerely hope that this publication will be one among the symbolic works celebrating the year 2011 as the "Year of Korea" when viewed in India, and the "Year of India" when viewed in Korea, as agreed at the Summit Meeting in New Delhi between India and Korea in 2010. The co-editors would like to thank Dr. Rajiv Kumar, Director of ICRIER, and Dr. Kim Dalchoong,

President of SFIA, for their encouragement of the book's publication. We would also like to express our deep appreciation for those who contributed papers for this volume, the keynote speakers, discussants, and other participants of the 9th Korea-India Dialogue held in Seoul.

— Choong Yong Ahn and Pravakar Sahoo.

Introduction

PRAVAKAR SAHOO AND CHOONG YONG AHN

India and South Korea are the third and fourth largest economies in Asia. They have shared a close relationship since the establishment of formal diplomatic ties in 1973. The past three-and-a-half decades have seen high-level exchanges and the signing of several crucial agreements that have led to continued strengthening of bilateral economic relations. The economic relations between the two countries gained momentum after 1991 when the Indian economy launched its Economic Reform Program with a focus on liberalisation and globalization. The greater openness of the Indian economy has not only enhanced market access for Korean goods but has also provided investment opportunities for internationally competitive Korean companies. However, because of several tariff and non-tariff barriers in both economies, the current size of trade and investment is very low compared to the size and structural complementarities of the two economies. There is immense potential to enhance economic cooperation between the two sides. As a part of its "Look-East Policy", India has been making efforts to intensify its economic relations with East Asian economies. On the other hand, Korea is looking beyond its traditional trading partners like the US and China to sustain its trade and economic progress.

South Korea adopted outward-oriented economic policies with the inception of its first five-year economic development plan in 1962, which resulted in high growth and the integration of the Korean economy with the rest of the world. Subsequently, high and consistent economic growth made South Korea one of the high-income economies in Asia, and is still growing at a faster rate than other developed economies. India, on the other hand, adopted an import-substitution policy from its independence until the early 1990s. Since 1991, India has introduced wide-ranging economic policy reforms and is moving toward a market-driven economy. This has resulted in consistent high economic growth over the past one-and-a-half decades, making India the 10th largest economy in the world. At present, India is the second-fastest growing economy in the world. Both India and Korea have been getting integrated with the world economy, enhancing their role in the international economic order. The increasing scale of globalization is posing both opportunities and challenges to the two countries. There is potential not only for greater cooperation at various multilateral forums like the WTO and the IMF, but also immense scope at the regional level to strengthen bilateral ties given the deadlock and slow growth of negotiations on the Doha Round in the WTO. Realizing the need for greater economic cooperation, both countries agreed in 2005 to establish a Joint Study Group (JSG) to comprehensively evaluate their economic relations and the feasibility of an India-Korea Comprehensive Economic Partnership Agreement (CEPA). After several rounds of negotiations, the CEPA was finally signed on August 7, 2009. This is also India's first Free Trade Agreement (FTA) with an Organization for Economic Cooperation and Development (OECD) country.

Given the outward-looking and liberalized economic orientation, economic diversity, and factor endowments inherent in India and Korea, the two countries are likely to benefit from each other by maximizing the potential benefit of the CEPA. It is fortunate and timely that the Indian Council for Research on International Economic Relations (ICRIER) and Seoul Forum for International Affairs (SFIA) have conducted annual dialogues over a decade to deepen mutual cooperation and understanding between the two countries. As global economic gravity shifts to Asia, the mutual cooperation of two like-minded countries will serve as an important step toward the Asian economic community. Against this backdrop and given the fact that there is hardly any comprehensive study on India-Korea relations, the present volume is a compilation of papers presented in the Ninth India-Korea dialogue. The book covers a wide range of issues related to India and Korea and their role in changing the global financial architecture, which has been categorized into three sections. Section I includes issues related to the global economic crisis, the G-20 and the role of India and Korea; Section II discusses aspects of India-Korea bilateral economic cooperation and Section III analyses global security challenges and the role for India-Korea cooperation. The present chapter summarizes briefly the objectives and contribution of each paper.

Section I

Global Economic Crisis, G-20 and the Role of India and Korea

The paper, 'Crafting a New Economic Paradigm for the G-20 Era: Perspectives from Asia and Korea' by Choong Yong Ahn elaborates on how the global crisis of 2007-08 wreaked havoc in the world economy and the coordinated policy consensus among the members of the G-20 group which has been successfully implemented in various countries across the world. The financial crisis that stemmed from sub-prime mortgage-based derivatives in the US threatened the stability of the global financial system. However, the injection of stimulus funds coupled with easy monetary policies across G-20 economies made recovery from the crisis faster, in which the emerging market economies performed much better than the advanced nations. While the advanced economies collectively stepped up their growth rates by 2.3 per cent in 2010, emerging and developing countries experienced their output expanding by 6.3 per cent. In the Asian contribution to global recovery, the most notable performances have been from India and China. Due to financial and corporate sector reforms adopted by East Asian countries after the 1997 Asian financial crisis, they have been able to recover quickly from the financial crisis of 2007. The robustness of the financial sector and expansionary fiscal policies in order to increase the consumption demand have been the forces behind the recovery. There have also been reductions in interest rates in order to boost investment.

The author then explains why monetary, fiscal and financial policy makers will need to ensure a smooth transition of demand from the government to the private sector and from excessive trade deficit economies to excessive trade surplus economies. One consequence of expansionary policies is that they may create asset bubbles in excessive levels if their duration and strength exceed desired levels. An exit strategy has to be coordinated among all the countries of the world so as to expand the output of the world as a whole.

The crisis is a product of the Western world and spread to the Asian region through collapse in world trade; there was a sharp fall in exports and increased uncertainty due to volatility in world commodities markets. Overall in Asia, banks were well capitalized and the share of non-performing loans in total loans was low as a result of which the impact of the crisis was less. There is agreement among the G-20 nations on the need for a financial safety net and governance reform of international institutions. Beyond the IMF's lending capacity, it is highly relevant for Asian economies to strengthen their financial safety nets. The main policy issue under debate in the G-20 agenda is to raise funds to cover government bailouts and guard against another crisis.

The author also explains that global trade imbalances may not be tolerated indefinitely if the world is looking forward to sustainable and balanced growth. Since private consumption from the West declined drastically after the crisis, Asian countries must shift from excessive export reliance to internal domestic demand in order to regain their growth momentum. Protectionism is being applied by many countries, not in the form of tariffs for imported goods but in the form of subsidies for domestically produced goods. However, the view is held that protectionism should not be favored at this juncture. Financial globalization needs to be effectively managed so that capital flows do not become a source of instability. The Asian members of G-20 should design a new financial architecture that should have the most advanced financial practices.

The next paper by Joon-Kyung Kim on 'Economic Recovery and Challenges in the Post-Crisis Era: The Case of Korea' discusses the post-recovery scenario for Korea. He opines that since the US economy failed to bounce back to its original form after the crisis of 2007-08, countries like Korea, which rely heavily on exports for their growth, will have to find alternative strategies for the same. This may include shifting the demand to non-US markets and increasing domestic demand. Korea has relied mainly on manufacturing exports for the past four decades but it is time to improve the productivity of its services sector.

The global financial crisis has affected the Korean economy but to a lesser extent than the other economies. Though stock prices in Korea declined owing to large capital outflows and massive withdrawals, foreign capital has begun flowing into the economy again and stock prices and exchange rates have stabilized since March 2009. After the financial restructuring in Korea following the Asian financial crisis in 1997, large corporations managed to lower their debt leverage ratios. In spite of this, Korean exports fell by around USD 20 billion between 2008 and 2009, resulting in rise in unemployment. In response to the massive capital outflows, the Korean government set aside $55 billion for providing foreign currency liquidity and pumped 90 trillion won into the economy to boost aggregate demand in the economy.

One thing that Korea has learned from the current global crisis is that, to sustain growth it needs to diversify and re-focus on where it exports and what it exports and also that the services sector has to be globally competitive. Regulations in the form of entry barriers are one of the reasons for the poor performance of the service sector. Due to the restrictions on FDI in services, competition is weak and spillovers in technology from multinational companies are lacking. It is proposed that the credit guarantee schemes that guarantee existing SMEs indefinitely should be replaced with a policy that reduces guarantees. There has been extensive government assistance to SMEs but still their performance is not up to standard. Therefore it is an important area to improve productivity across sectors in Korea.

The paper titled 'Financial Sector in India: Challenges, Opportunities and Cooperation with Korea' by Tamal Bandyopadhyay discusses financial sector developments in India in recent years and opportunities for cooperation between the two countries in the financial sector. The CEPA consists of six agreements to open up trade in goods, services and the financial sector. Following this, Shinhan Bank, one of the oldest banks in Korea, has already opened its branches in India (Delhi and Mumbai) and Woori Bank, Hana Bank and Korea Exchange Bank are other banks that are planning to open up their branches soon. Under the agreement India has also allowed Korea to enter the insurance industry apart from several other industries like telecommunications, accounting, food processing, textiles, etc. The growth of the Indian economy will aid the banks from Korea to do good business.

Following the financial crisis of 2008, the Korean government too tried to protect its banking system by increasing the credit supply capacity of banks. It also established a corporate restructuring fund at Korea Asset Management Corporation to help in the restructuring of firms. In India,

The Reserve Bank of India (RBI) advised banks to set up a fund called Investment Fluctuation Reserve (IFR) to take care of fluctuations in the interest rates. Somewhat anticipating the real estate bubble, the RBI discouraged banks from aggressively disbursing real estate loans. The RBI is also in the process of introducing CDS or credit default swaps which are like instruments to insure creditors against the risk of borrower default.

It is suggested that the government should increase the limit of foreign ownership of public sector banks from 20 per cent to 25 per cent, thereby reducing its own stake, because it is held that government does not have the money to keep banks well-capitalized. Under a 1997 WTO agreement, the total assets of foreign banks in India should not exceed 15 per cent of the total banking system. It was in 1993 that India opened its banking system to private players. After freeing all loan rates, the RBI is expected to give banks the freedom to decide on the interest rates on savings accounts. The coverage of banks and other financial institutions is limited in India. Very few people in the low-income category have access to formal banking channels. Only 4 per cent of the population invests in mutual funds and have life insurance cover. Korea has proposed setting up a global financial safety net at the G-20 summit, which is fully supported by India.

The paper by Ajay Shankar titled 'The Recent Performance of the Indian Economy: Recovery and Challenge' discusses the performance of the Indian economy and future challenges. Compared to the East Asian economies, the growth of the Indian economy after its independence was pretty modest. India adopted its policies of being self-reliant and self-sufficient. Infant industries were given protection through barriers to imports and foreign investment, and the private sector was also denied entry into major industries in the country. With the opening of the economy to global competition in 1991, the past two decades have seen India's growth at good rates. The post-reforms period saw the service sector, especially the IT sector, perform much better than the manufacturing sector. This was because it took some time for the manufacturing sector to adjust to the reforms of 1991. However, after 2000, the manufacturing sector also turned competitive.

When the financial crisis began in 2007 it was thought that only the US and the UK would be affected by it because of their deregulated financial sector; however the crisis slowly became a global phenomenon and spread to almost all economies. Since the Indian financial sector was still regulated, it had zero holdings of the toxic assets that were causing havoc elsewhere. Indian banks were well-capitalized with only modest holdings of non-performing assets. However, the liquidity crisis hit India when Foreign Institutional Investors (FIIs) panicked after the collapse of Lehman Brothers and started withdrawing cash overnight. The sudden occurrence of this was the reason for the liquidity crunch that Indian banks experienced. The government had to provide banks and non-banking financial institutions with stimulus packages to increase their liquidity. These fiscal measures combined with other monetary measures were implemented by the central bank to stimulate demand. The key concerns for the economy that remain include the fight to curb inflation and manage fiscal deficit. Apart from high inflation and high fiscal deficits, the economy has been performing very decently. The government's debt as a percentage of GDP has been going down continuously. The enhanced capital inflows still pose a threat to the economy in the form of the creation of asset price bubbles. However, the existence of public sector government-controlled banks in India has helped in quicker decisions regarding rolling over of debt.

Section II

India-Korea Bilateral Economic Cooperation

The paper, 'India-Korea Trade and Investment Relations', by Pravakar Sahoo *et al.* elaborates in detail the bilateral economic relations between India and Korea. The authors explain economic relations between the two countries which have been strengthening over the years and argue that there is a lot of scope for further advancement. The current size of trade and investment between the two countries is low compared to the size and structural complementarities of the two economies. In this context, the present paper analyzes trade and investment relations and future areas of cooperation between India and Korea. The increase in merchandize trade between the two countries has been mainly because of the changing demand structures and comparative advantages of both economies in complementary sectors. While India's exports mainly constitute low value-added and industrial products, India's imports from Korea largely consist of relatively high value-added products. The analysis of revealed comparative advantage at both the aggregated and disaggregated levels shows that Korea has been specializing in a few products that are highly competitive as India's exports have been more diversified. Moreover, India shows a declining comparative advantage in cotton and textiles, rice and other primary products. The analysis at the disaggregated level shows that there are some industries where both countries have a comparative advantage in different products, pointing to opportunities for intra-industry trade. The intra-industry trade (IIT) analysis shows that the IIT is low in the top traded product groups and high in some products where trading is low. This offers huge opportunity for intra-industry trade if sector-specific barriers are removed along with general barriers. Further, the increasing trade complementarity index (TCI) shows that Indian and Korean trade has gradually become more compatible over the period under review as per the CEPA. The trade intensities between the two countries show that Korea is doing much better and there is scope for India to improve its export intensity with Korea.

Though foreign investment from Korea has increased over the years, the share in total FDI inflows to India has declined. Further, Korean investment is concentrated in a few sectors such as electrical equipment and metallurgical industries. There are opportunities for small and medium-sized Korean companies to synergize with Indian SMEs in the areas of semi-conductors, plastics, auto parts, agricultural instruments, textiles, multimedia, ceramic products, software, etc. Since development of infrastructure in India is a priority and requires both advanced technology and huge investment, there is tremendous scope for Korean companies to participate and collaborate in the infrastructure and construction sectors. Further, there is tremendous scope for improving trade in services between the two countries, particularly for India. There are areas such as information technology, science and technology, pharmaceuticals, broadcasting, tourism, healthcare, construction and related services and human resource development where collaborative relations can be further strengthened. The analysis also shows that there exist both tariff and non-tariff barriers and both countries need to remove sector-specific barriers to improve trade and investment relations.

The paper 'India-Korea CEPA: Likely Impact on Bilateral Economic Relations' by Pravakar Sahoo *et al.* also explores the impact of the CEPA signed by both countries. The overall conclusion is that CEPA is likely to benefit both nations immensely. There has been a reduction in the tariff and non-tariff barriers in a phased manner. Trade is expected to increase between both the countries in areas such as information technology, pharmaceutical industry, healthcare, human resource development, etc. Apart from this Korean FDI is also expected to flow into the Indian manufacturing industry. By entering into such an agreement, India can show its presence in the APEC region.

The main objectives of the CEPA are to liberalize and expand trade in goods and services and also expand investment. For India this is the first agreement with an OECD country and for Korea this is the first agreement with a BRIC country. CEPA came into effect in January 2010 and it is expected to increase trade by as much as $3 billion. Korea has agreed to reduce tariff on 93 per cent of its tariff lines. There are some industries like textiles, auto sector, agriculture, etc. where India has not reduced tariffs but it is likely to do so in the near future. Korea is relatively more competitive in some industries like automobiles, electricity, electronics, steel, etc. where it has offered concessions on tariff rates. There are also opportunities for collaboration between Korean small and medium-sized companies and Indian small and medium enterprises (SMEs).

Apart from goods, services form a very important component of CEPA. The service sector in India has been growing at a very fast pace as a result of which India has become a major exporter of services all over the world. Korea on the other hand is a services importer. There are some sectors like insurance, telecommunications, banking, etc. where India would like to provide services to Korea. Likewise there is a cap on foreign equity participation for Korea in sectors such as insurance and retail in India. CEPA contains mutual recognition agreements in professional services to facilitate the entry of Indian professionals. Further, there are no restrictions of any kind on investors of both countries. CEPA will encourage more investment in India's manufacturing and infrastructure sectors because Korea has already got a competitive advantage in those sectors. Although Indian investment in Korea is not very substantial, there is hope that Indian companies will establish themselves in Korea.

Various forms of cooperation have been proposed in several areas under the provisions in CEPA. Information and communications technology is one such area. Korea's strength lies in hardware manufacturing and India's strength lies in software, so it will be mutually beneficial to both countries to have cooperation in this sector. Energy is the second area where cooperation is sought, and science and technology is another area. India is endowed with well-educated scientists and Korea with financial resources, and so cooperation in this area will be of immense benefit to both. Other areas where cooperation may bring good results are SMEs, infrastructure, transportation, pharmaceuticals, tourism, healthcare, etc. The agreement, which proposes bilateral economic cooperation in 13 important areas, will strengthen economic cooperation and both countries will benefit immensely. Apart from an increase in trade and investment, outflows of professionals from India to Korea are expected in large numbers.

The paper 'India-Korea Strategic Dialogue in Technology and Climate Change' by Suresh Prabhu talks on the very important topic of bilateral cooperation in science and technology including climate change and clean and renewable energy. Climate change has occupied the minds and thoughts of all policy makers worldwide. It has become one of the most important policy issues to be dealt with in all countries. Not only the governments of various countries but many NGOs and civil society organizations have been working on this issue which occupies an important place in the list that contains major issues of the globe, because this has posed a serious threat to the very existence of mankind. The ill-effects of global warming have been realized and measures are being taken to keep a tab on activities that are causing the same. The concern for climate change is at an all-time high and people are trying to reduce greenhouse gas emissions that are known to be the causal factor for global warming. Brazil, South Africa, India and China have formed a group called BASIC to fight this cause. Europe's key instrument in tackling the problem of global warming is its emission-trading scheme (EU ETS), wherein businesses are encouraged to take up climate-friendly technologies. In 1992 the United Nations framework convention for climate change was set up which was succeeded by the establishment of the Kyoto Protocol in 1996. Since economic activities cannot be stopped, changing the technology to carry out the activities was something that was unanimously agreed upon. It is further said that developed countries should make such technologies and developing countries should get the same transferred from them. In this case though there crops up the issue of intellectual property rights.

There are some difficult choices to make to fight against global warming while selecting and deploying various strategies. Firstly, there are issues about the time frame to implement a given technology, hesitation from financial markets in supporting heavy and long-term investments in new infrastructure, and resistance from industries and countries against the introduction of new energy production and consumption patterns. Korea is one of the few countries that have shown tremendous growth in a matter of few years. It has more R&D centers than several developing countries put together. India being a hugely populated country can provide a good market to use such R&D for commercialization of such research.

The usage of energy determines greenhouse gas emissions. India's dependence on fossil fuels is greater than that on coal, which causes greater emissions. Nuclear power can be used as it is known not to cause any emission; however disposal of nuclear waste should be taken care of, as that is harmful from the radiation point of view. Storage of electricity can be another area where India and Korea can join hands and undertake research. Solar power can also be of tremendous help. Ocean waves and wind can be other sources from which electricity can be generated. Korea is one of the high energy-efficient countries of the world. India has a huge potential to save energy by cutting down on transmission and distribution losses.

The paper 'Cooperation between India and Korea in FDI and Services' by Chang-Ho Kwag is an important contribution in exploring the impact of CEPA on FDI flows between the two countries and trade in services. India and Korea were, in the past, not such close partners but now it seems that the CEPA will be able to not only bring them closer but also pave a new path for large-scale cooperation between the two countries. The success of the CEPA will largely depend on how sincerely both sides take it forward with win-win strategies.

This paper focuses on the structure of the Indian and Korean economies, which are complementary and have great potential to help each other in taking up challenges and utilizing opportunities for their economic development. India is a country that is eager to invite FDI in the manufacturing sector to create jobs and improve its trade balance. On the other hand, Korea is good at labor-intensive manufacturing and wants to enter a huge market in India. Thus, there are great opportunities for win-win strategies for both economies, particularly in bilateral investment and service trade if CEPA turns out to be a success.

Also, the performances of both countries in drawing FDI are far below the world average. Korea's low performance relative to the potential indicates that a couple of key factors among the determinants of FDI should be improved in order to attract more FDI. On the other hand, in India, despite overall improvement of performance and potential indexes, it still remains in the "Under Performer" category, meaning that India would need to improve the overall business climate. Among the "doing business indexes", Korea, China, and India ranked 19th, 89th and 133rd, respectively. In the case of India, the categories in which India ranks low are "starting a business", "dealing with licenses", "paying taxes", and "enforcing contracts". There are many procedures and it costs too much to get a license from the Indian government. It takes an average of around five years to resolve a business conflict through the courts, implying that India needs to reform its legal system to make it more business-friendly, i.e., setting-up costs are too high.

Finally, for an action plan to enhance mutual cooperation in bilateral investment and services trade, both economies need to exchange government persons who are in policy-making of FDI and service trade. By doing so, information can be shared, leading to increased understanding and can help more Korean manufacturing firms invest in India and more Indian professionals, particularly engineers, go to Korea, resulting in greater mutual benefits.

The paper, 'Trade Promotion after Korea-India CEPA' by Choongjae Cho explains the post-CEPA trade scenario between the two countries. The main content of CEPA is that about 85 per cent of the tariffs that Korea imposes on trading items will be eliminated or decreased in 10 years. India in turn will eliminate 74.5 per cent of tariffs. Korea's exports to India comprises mainly machinery, steel and automobiles. Both Korea and India agreed on liberalization on service items, which means Korea gets a share in the Indian market for telecommunications, energy distribution, transport services, construction, etc. The movement of independent professionals between the two countries has been introduced. Both India and Korea accepted that economic cooperation would take place in various sectors. Industry-wise, the impact of CEPA will be greater in the services sector than in the manufacturing sector, the reason being that Korea's service sector is bigger than its manufacturing sector. The automobile and machinery industries are expected to be the highest trading sectors. The others include chemicals, textiles, electrical and electronics, and telecommunication. India will export IT professionals to Korean companies.

The increase in the volume of trade has been tremendous especially after the year 2000. It has increased from $2.6 billion to over $10 billion in 2007. Trade imbalance has been the major feature and a challenge for the two countries. Korea has recorded only surpluses in its trade with India but as the trade volume goes up imbalances would tend to grow. The second feature and challenge has been that the trade structure between the two countries is not competitive but is more likely to be fixed. The trade structure, though not competitive, cannot be called complementary either because both countries are insufficient in terms of intra-industry specialization. The biggest challenge of trade imbalance is concentrated in the commodity sector, which means that there are differences in the competitiveness in both manufacturing sectors. More active trade in services can be offered as a solution. Korea's industries concentrate on hardware while India focuses on software, so these can be complementary industries. There is vast scope for expanding investment too. Korea and India will have to work together to realize an FTA with South Asia.

Section III

Global Security Challenges: Role for India-Korea Cooperation

The paper, 'Strategic Challenges and Risks in a Globalizing World: An Indian Perspective' by N. Sisodia discusses security issues and cooperation between these two countries which are facing similar challenges. The world seems to be facing new challenges in the era of globalization and progress. With two of the largest growing economies—China and India—Asia has gained power in the current century. This is particularly so after China and India escaped relatively unscathed from the global financial crisis of 2007-08. China not only is a highly growing economy but also has great military power. The world seems to be shifting from a uni-polar one to a multi-polar one, owing to the rapid development of economies such as India, Singapore, Korea, Taiwan, etc. The rise of China as a great power is a source of concern for many countries. The fact that China is extending its support to Pakistan on a continuous basis is somewhat disturbing to India, and the fact that China is asserting its position in Asia is somewhat disturbing to the Japanese economy as well. Chinese growth in the past three decades has primarily been export-driven. However there are other social problems that China has to deal with like pollution, social ills, etc.

There is growing mistrust and apprehension among the major powers. The global defense expenditure has grown from $1,053 billion to $1,572 billion between 2000 and 2009. The Afghanistan-Pakistan region is recognized as the epicenter of global terrorism. Despite this, India is committed to helping build a stable Afghanistan; India invested around $1.2 billion in development assistance to Afghanistan. India is surrounded by states affected by instability and intra-state violence in the recent past, like the Maoists in Nepal and Bangladesh, the LTTE in Sri Lanka, etc. The growth of production of weapons of mass destruction is a source of concern.

Apart from the challenges above, there are other systemic risks that may become vital in the coming years. Maritime security is important given the large magnitude of activities taking place via waterways. Energy security is another concern given the limited hydrocarbon resources. Climate change has been a major concern in recent years. With the melting of glaciers due to global warming and inefficient use of resources, there is fear of conflicts arising between countries. Cyber-risk is another area. Several systems like transportation, banking and finance, telecommunications, etc. are vulnerable to cyber attacks given their haevy dependence on information and communications technology.

Three important pillars in India-Korea bilateral relations that can be developed are: (a) economic ties through CEPA; (b) bilateral security relationship and (c) energy security and civil nuclear cooperation. In 2010 an agreement for cooperation in civil nuclear technology was announced. This will give a big opportunity to South Korea's large nuclear industry to participate in India's nuclear power sector. Cooperation among nations is needed to fight transnational terrorism, crisis, climate change, non-proliferation of weapons of mass destruction, etc. The challenge of depleting resources also calls for greater cooperation between the two countries.

The paper, 'The Korea-India Strategic Partnership for the 21st Century: Visions for Security and Military Cooperation', by Changsu Kim talks about the simplified "gradual global redistribution of economic power from the West to 'the Rest'" and the "rise of the new Asian hemisphere" proclaiming an Asian Century. But regional security as a whole, on the other hand, will almost certainly be the major source of regional security conflict and cooperation in East Asia and beyond. Also, rapidly changing security environments are bound to entail multiple sets of security arrangements and mechanisms in the beginning decades of the 21st century in order to enable effective responses and the promotion of the common interests of all the countries involved. A "strategic partnership" was proclaimed by South Korean President Lee Myung-bak and Indian Prime Minister Manmohan Singh at their summit on January 25, 2010.

They agreed to expand their countries' cooperation to cover diplomacy, security, global issues, and culture, based on their existing economic ties, and agreed to the need for a pact on the civilian use of nuclear energy, a prerequisite for South Korea's participation in India's atomic power plant construction. Thus, the overall Korea-India relationship started primarily from trade and investment and has moved toward a more comprehensive economic partnership.

In response to this, the Joint Vision Statement (JVS) envisions an "alliance to ensure a peaceful, secure and prosperous future for the Korean Peninsula, the Asia-Pacific region and the world; a comprehensive strategic alliance of bilateral, regional and global scope, based on common values and mutual trust; a better future for all people on the Korean Peninsula, establishing a durable peace on the Peninsula and leading to peaceful reunification on the principles of free democracy and a market economy.' Also, India has rekindled its interest in forming a security policy that can guarantee a uniquely stronger and more influential India. Its engagement with the US, China, Japan, Russia, Australia, and other major powers in addressing new security challenges deserves renewed interest in South Korea.

As a matter of fact, India has "initiated a series of initiatives to cater to the Chinese challenge," and "the Indian navy has stepped up its deployments throughout the Asia-Pacific and been regularly participating in bilateral and multilateral exercises." South Korea also needs to take into consideration these new developments in a broader security context.

Notably, today's changing security environments are characterized by terrorism, proliferation of weapons of mass destruction and ballistic missiles, and newly emerging and growing transnational security threats. This new form of regional cooperation has been viewed as functional cooperation for common concerns and Tokyo's counterparts were found in Canberra and New Delhi. The recent formation of an official US-Japan-Australia trilateral security cooperation mechanism and those of the proposed US-Japan-Australia-India security cooperation is a case in point.

Looking back, our security cooperation in the early part of the 21st century should not be focused on countering a single security challenge. Instead, security cooperation should be implemented in such a way so as to maximize the respective capacities and contributions to preserving regional stability. If our security cooperation and coordination is organized in such a way so as to maximize capacity and to respond to multiple threats and is embedded in a broader politically-based partnership designed to respond to various security needs in East Asia and beyond, it will be harder for our neighbors to object to such efforts.

In conclusion, India and South Korea have gained prominence on the international stage in recent years and they have sufficient potential to continue to do so in the foreseeable future. The two nations have valuable pools of strategic partnerships with many major powers in the region and elsewhere on the globe. Their relations with the US, China, Japan, Russia, Australia, and the EU, for example, continue to prove that they have more common security interests than differences. In the above context, this paper has focused on laying out visions for future security, defense, and military cooperation and puts forth some ways and means to implement them. It also has appreciated India's potential for deterring and defeating many non-traditional, transnational threats primarily through naval cooperation, other training and exercises, anti-piracy operations and PKOs, etc. Finally, in an era of globalization and networking, we can and should utilize the existing and emerging multilateral security dialogues and cooperative activities among major regional powers in the Asia-Pacific, including the US, Japan, Korea, China, India, and Australia to secure a peaceful and vibrant Asia.

Section I

Global Economic Crisis, G-20 and the Role of India and Korea

1

Crafting a New Global Economic Paradigm for the G-20 Era

Perspectives from Asia and Korea

CHOONG YONG AHN

Introduction

The worst global economic crisis since the Great Depression began to wreak havoc with the world's markets from mid-2008. If there is any silver lining to this dark cloud, which left few if any nations unaffected, the formation of the G-20 (Group of Twenty) leaders can be said to be one. The series of G-20 meetings, beginning with the first one in Washington in November 2008 and followed by those in London and Pittsburgh in April and November 2009, respectively, have contributed a great deal to the global economy recovering far quicker than originally expected, recovery which has come about due to well-coordinated policy consensus and action programs implemented on a global scale.

As was not the case of the largest economies in the Great Depression Era of the early 20th century, the G-20 economies[1] of today, which constitute 80 percent of global GDP and 65 percent of the global population, have been able to react effectively against the global economic turmoil with significant

1. The G-20 was originally created as a network of finance ministers and central bank governors in the wake of the 1997-98 Asian financial crisis to provide forward-looking, high-level consultation and information exchange among systemically important countries. There are no formal criteria for G-20 membership. The membership does not reflect exactly the world's top 20 largest economies in any given year. Instead, countries and regions of systemic significance to the international financial system were considered. Both geographical balance and population representation also played a major part.

collective and well-synchronized actions including the application of stimulus packages in unison and standstill measures taken to counter potential trade protectionism. Indeed, the global crisis created an urgent need for policies that warrant innovation in international institutions, mechanisms, and public policies that encourage more cohesive cooperation across the G-20 countries with somewhat varying degrees. At the Pittsburgh meeting, G-20 leaders agreed to meet annually to craft new economic architecture to address needed collective actions that could facilitate immediate economic recovery, a new global financial system, as well as sustainable and balanced growth in the post-G-20 era. With the Group of Twenty growing in stature since the 2008 Washington summit, G-20 leaders at the Pittsburgh meeting announced on September 25, 2009 that the G-20 would replace the G-8 as the premier forum at which to address not only urgent global issues but also long-term sustainable and balanced growth of the world economy. With emerging nations playing an increasingly more significant role in the global economy, the G-8 had proven to be ineffective to deal with global issues considered catastrophic in scale.

Given the historic role of the G-20 process, it is also highly significant for Korea to host the 5th G-20 summit on November 11-12, 2010. Following the 4th meeting in Canada held in June 2010, as the present chair of the troika economies, it is tremendously meaningful for Korea to play host to the G-20 summit, a first for a non-Western economy.

At the outset, the recent financial meltdown could be blamed on problems stemming from sub-prime mortgage-based financial derivatives in the US and the collapse of Lehman Brothers in September 2008. The crisis has been notable for its depth and severity and the degree to which it threatened the very stability of the global financial system. But what was equally notable from an Asian perspective was how countries in Asia, especially emerging Asian economies including China and India together with semi-advanced Korea, weathered the storm comparatively better than the United States and Europe.

The basic purpose of this paper is to reflect Asian and Korean perspectives in crafting a new global economic architecture to achieve the following objectives: a) to prevent a crisis similar to the Wall Street-originated world-wide financial crisis in 2008 from occurring again, b) to ensure a speedy recovery and smooth withdrawal from the extraordinary fiscal and monetary measures implemented during the crisis, and c) to search for sustainable, balanced, and robust global economic growth in the post-crisis era. In Section II, the paper attempts to reflect Asian responses and strategies to address some key on-going issues under the G-20 process. Section III discusses what collective actions are needed in the macro-economic framework to coordinate current on-going economic recovery efforts among the G-20 countries and then exit from the controls of the stimulus packages and eased monetary policies. Section IV discusses what factors need to be considered in designing a new global financial architecture to prevent a similar global financial crisis from occurring again and to improve the financial health of banks and security firms. Section V discusses how to enhance long-term growth potential to ensure sustainable and balanced growth in the G-20 era. Section VI concludes with policy implications for India and Korea and what role Korea can play as the chair economy and host of the forthcoming 5th G-20 leaders meeting to produce significant deliverables by effectively coordinating diverse interests and varying objectives among the G-20 economies.

Asian Response and Exit Strategy with Macroeconomic Coordination[2]

Thanks to the immediate success of mass injections of stimulus funds coupled with the eased monetary policies across the G-20 economies, the global economic recovery has evolved better than was expected at its onset in late 2007. However, the strength of the rebound has been uneven. Global activity is recovering at varying speeds—tepidly in many advanced economies, but solidly in most emerging and developing economies. Emerging Asia has weathered most successfully the global financial storm.

Shift of Global Economic Gravity to Asia

Surprisingly, the United States is off to a somewhat later but better start than Europe and Japan in their respective recovery paths. Both emerging and developing Asia have provided the most significant contribution to global economic recovery. As shown in Table 1.1, the International Monetary Fund

2. Some parts of this section draw heavily from Ahn (2010).

(IMF) revised its prediction for world output growth to 4.25 percent in 2010, up from a dismal –0.6 percent growth in 2009.

Table 1.1

GDP Growth Rate by Country and Region

(Unit %)

	2006	2007	2008	2009	2010(P)	2011(P)
United States	2.7	2.1	0.4	-2.4	3.1	2.6
European Union (EU-27)	3.4	3.1	0.9	-4.1	1.0	1.8
Japan	2.0	2.4	-1.2	-5.2	1.9	2.0
Developing Asia	9.8	10.6	7.9	6.6	8.7	8.7
East Asia	9.1	10.1	6.9	5.4	8.3	8.2
China	11.6	13.0	9.6	8.7	10.0	9.9
Hong Kong	7.0	6.4	2.1	-2.7	5.0	4.4
Korea	5.2	5.1	2.0	0.2	4.5	5.0
Chinese Taipei	5.4	6.0	0.7	-1.9	6.5	4.8
ASEAN 10	6.2	6.6	4.4	1.3	3.0	3.5
India	9.8	9.4	7.3	5.7	8.8	8.4
Australia	2.6	4.7	2.4	1.3	3.0	3.5
New Zealand	1.0	2.8	-0.1	-1.6	2.9	3.2
Western Hemisphere	5.6	5.8	4.3	-1.8	4.0	4.0
Central &Eastern Europe	6.5	5.5	3.0	-3.7	2.8	3.4
Russia	7.7	8.5	5.6	-7.9	4.0	3.3
Middle East & North Africa	5.7	5.6	5.1	2.4	4.5	4.8
Sub-Saharan Africa	6.5	6.9	5.5	2.1	4.7	5.9
World	5.1	5.2	3.0	-0.6	4.2	4.3

Source: *IMF, World Economic Outlook*, April 2010.

While advanced economies are collectively expected to grow by 2.3 percent in 2010, emerging and developing economies should see output expand by 6.3 percent. Asia is now at the forefront of the recovery, with the developing economies of the region expected to grow by an astounding 8.7 percent in 2010. According to the IMF, for the first time the Asian contribution to a global recovery has surpassed that of other regions, largely on the back of strong domestic demand. In due process, the most notable performers are China and India, two countries that have provided emerging Asian economies with a great cushion to mitigate the negative impact of the global crisis.

In 1997–98, Asia was ground zero for a major financial crisis, and subsequently was the subject of much blame. The backward and shallow financial systems embedded in East Asia's high growth regimes caused serious financial distress despite the so-called "miracle" economic performance in the region during preceding decades. This time around, Asian economies, especially the export-oriented ones, have been seriously affected not by internal financial problems but by the external financial shocks from financially advanced economies. However, thanks to some commendable financial and corporate sector reforms adopted since the earlier crisis, many Asian economies this time showed signs of bottoming-out earlier than expected from the global downturn, shifting to a mild V-shaped recovery. Still, the economic fortunes of Asia remain inextricably tied to the developments in the advanced economies of Western Europe and the United States.

However, the negative impact of the crisis on Asian economies this time appears to be less serious than what was experienced a decade ago. In particular, the economies of China and India, although seriously affected albeit temporarily, quickly regained their high growth path, followed by many of their Asian neighbors including Indonesia, Vietnam, and Korea, thus putting the region on a solid recovery track.

In line with the global policy guidelines as suggested at the G-20 meetings, almost every large economy in developing Asia has implemented measures to a varying degree to stimulate aggregate demand through fiscal and monetary expansion. In turn, households were relatively quick to spend fiscal windfalls that came in the form of tax cuts and income support, driving consumption, which in turn began to boost GDP by the second quarter of 2009.

Developing Asia last faced a debilitating financial crisis and regional recession in 1997–98 but has emerged from the more recent downturn more rapidly as a result of favorable external economic conditions. Clearly, the region will have to generate new demand through sources other than exports while contributing to resolving global imbalance, given the prolonged recession being seen in advanced western economies and global trade imbalances.

The Asian Development Bank (2009b: 27) reports that fiscal stimuli in Asian developing economies averaged 7.1 percent of nominal 2008 GDP. The emphasis on governments' efforts to boost demand through discretionary fiscal measures differed, although the boost from the stimulus was strong enough to arrest the decline in GDP growth despite the reality that automatic stabilizers remain fairly weak across most countries in the region. For example, almost all of China's CNY4 trillion package was invested in infrastructure projects or other types of construction activities. In contrast, authorities in Hong Kong, China emphasised tax cuts, public housing rent reductions, and other forms of household income support. Korea opted for a mix of tax cuts and expenditure measures.

On the monetary side, most Asian economies have reduced interest rates to nearly zero to provide liquidity so as to boost investment and expenditure on durable goods that are sensitive to interest rates. A general softening of inflation-related pressures and lower commodity prices helped Asian monetary authorities adopt monetary easing policies.

Developing Asia's Economic Prospects

Recently, the Asian Development Bank (ADB) raised its forecasts for GDP growth for developing Asia as whole from those of early 2009. The region is now projected to grow by 3.9 percent in 2009 and 6.4 percent in 2010, up from the respective 3.4 percent and 6.0 percent forecasts earlier. In short, however, the 2010 outlook for the region as a whole is that it will come back strongly relative to 2009, giving a mild V-shape trajectory to developing Asia's recovery from the world recession.

According to the latest IMF forecast from late October in 2009, the Asian economic growth rate more than doubled the Fund's forecast from earlier in the year and was projected even higher for 2010, reflecting a sharp improvement in the region's prospects over the past six months. The IMF points out that the primary driver of Asia's recovery has been a progressive return toward normality following the abrupt collapse in global trade and finance at the end of 2008.

One reason that developing Asia has recovered faster than the rest of the world is the relative robustness of its financial sector, which provided a buffer against the global financial turmoil. The strong fiscal position of most large economies in developing Asia also enabled them to pursue expansionary fiscal policies. Existing high saving rates and low levels of household debt made consumers in developing Asia more amenable to spending the additions to income from the fiscal stimulus (ADB, 2009b).

Fortunately, the resumption of growth has taken place against a backdrop of low or even mild deflation. The region as a whole has benefited from the steep slide in oil prices and from improved supply of food and raw materials. Despite the sharp fall in short-term interest rates engineered by central banks and the pumping of liquidity into financial markets, the threat of inflation remains muted.

More recently, there has been apparent recovery of portfolio capital flowing into the region as equities markets have rallied. Less foreign direct investment is flowing into the region but there are early signs that multinational enterprises have sharply reduced unwanted inventories and are now in a position to increase production. Once the impetus from fiscal stimulus packages wears off, it will be essential that domestic consumption and private investment take over the drivers of growth as a result of the painful restructuring of the corporate and financial sectors.

Rebalancing Asian growth through increasing domestic investment and consumption expenditures relative to income will help keep momentum behind the global recovery. In some instances, structural reforms in the corporate and banking sectors and industrial restructuring toward labor-absorptive service sectors need to be stepped up to rekindle growth. Fortunately though, most developing Asian economies have relatively low debt-to-GDP ratios and are on a sound fiscal footing.

Coordination of an Exit Strategy

Given quicker than expected recovery in the world economy, the question arises: when is the appropriate time for an exit from expansionary policies? As long as the recovery remains fragile and subject to serious downside risks, the implementation of an exit strategy should be very cautious and must be coordinated with major economies of the world. Global trade prospects should be carefully assessed even though the trough in world trade volume may have been reached in the first quarter of 2009. Both imports and exports remain well below levels attained two years earlier. Hence, continuing the expansionary stance is warranted until global markets and demand are on a firm recovery path.

Monetary, fiscal, and financial policy makers will need to ensure a smooth transition of demand from the government to the private sector and from excessive trade deficit economies to excessive trade surplus economies. One consequence of expansionary monetary policies is that they may create asset bubbles in excessive levels if their duration and strength exceed desired levels. Asian equity markets, along with those around the world, have rallied in hopeful anticipation of a global economic recovery and regional recovery faster than elsewhere in the world.

However, the region's asset price rally is also being fuelled by excess liquidity from the expansionary monetary policies. This overhang is finding its way into equity and property markets, causing asset price inflation that may pose a threat to the soundness of the region's financial systems. In light of this circumstance, a failure to tighten monetary policy at some point will create conditions that are conducive to the formation of bubbles in the future. A downward correction in asset prices is warranted despite some painful consequences for the financial system and the economy, as illustrated by the bursting of East Asia's asset bubbles in 1997-98 and the recent US housing bubble.

As generally agreed, the current financial crisis has originated from the United States in an asset price bubble that interacted with slick repackaging of "innovative financial derivatives," which were described as the "Yankees' unique innovation" (Litan and Rauch, 1997). While the financial crisis kept unfolding, so-called "financial innovation" practised on Wall Street proved to mask a variety of inherent risks involving companies that failed to follow their own risk management, and regulators and supervisors that failed to foresee the consequences of excessive securitization of sub-prime mortgage loans. Many Asian countries were dismayed and appalled at the serious hidden caveats of what was coined "greedy Wall Street capitalism."

In economies where growth is still highly dependent on policy support and consistent with sustainable public finances, it is desirable that the recovery is firmly driven by the private sector and becomes more entrenched. However, some early risers from the economic meltdown such as India, Australia, and Brazil have already raised interest rates. To the extent that both a double dip and spillover effects are avoided, each country would be advised to take flexible actions to raise interest rates to adjust to country-specific macroeconomic conditions. An exit strategy must be firmly based on this principle to minimize any contagion effects due to PIGGS countries (Portugal, Ireland, Italy, and Spain) under the largest-ever bailout programs initiated by both the EU and the IMF.

Relative Robustness of Asian Economies

There are two major links acting as a channel between the current crisis from advanced economies to emerging Asia's economic performance. The first one is trade linkage between Western advanced economies and emerging Asia. The second channel is a "sudden stop" in net private capital inflows due to the sudden reversal of capital from Asia. Once beaten badly during the Asian financial crisis and having learned difficult lessons on restructuring its banking and corporate sectors,[3] emerging Asia has faced quite different circumstances this time around. To name several, first, the financial crisis originated in Western industrial economies and spread to Asia largely through a collapse in world trade. Second, while Asian financial systems have generally been robust, the collapse in external demand has hit the region hard as industrial production contracted sharply with a fall in exports. Third, extreme volatility in global commodity markets has created additional uncertainty.

Fortunately, the economies of developing Asia had rather limited direct exposure to the toxic assets that originated in US banks, mortgage lenders, hedge funds, and other financial companies. Various financial indicators and banking sector data suggest that Asia's financial systems were rather well prepared for this crisis as is evident in Table 1.2. It is clear by the fact that risk-weighted capital adequacy ratios at above 10 percent in the region's banks have provided a strong capital cushion in the middle of severe depression of the real sector as well as the substantial pull-out of

3. For example, South Korea had carried out comprehensive four-sector reforms under the IMF conditionality when it received the largest-ever financial bailout package during the Asian financial crisis. The most notable achievement emerging from the said reforms can be witnessed by the fact that Korea's conglomerates reduced their debt-to-equity ratio from above 400 percent to less than 100 percent. For details, see Ahn (2001).

western portfolio investment from Asia. Since the Asian financial crisis in 1997–98, most of the crisis-hit Asian economies have adopted the BIS capital adequacy rule under Basel II as the most important criteria for a robust banking system.

Table 1.2

Risk-Weighted Capital Adequacy Ratios as Percentage of Risk-Weighted Assets

(Unit %)

Economy	*2000–2004 Annual Average*	*2008*	*2009*
People's Rep. of China	–2.3	8.2	–
Hong Kong, China	16.1	14.7	15.6
Indonesia	18.7	16.8	17.8
Republic of Korea	10.7	12.7	13.4
Malaysia	13.4	12.2	13.7
Philippines	17.0	15.7	–
Singapore	17.7	14.3	–
Chinese Taipei	10.5	10.8	–
Thailand	13.2	14.1	15.2

Source: Asian Development Bank (2009c). *Asia Economic Monitor*, July, p.22.

Overall, non-performing loans were also quite low as a share of total loans; banks were well capitalized and reliance on credit lines to Western banks was minimal. Table 1.3 shows that the ratios of non-performing loans as a percentage of commercial bank loans have decreased substantially from the high average ratios observed during 2000–2004 to the 1–5.5 percent level in 2008 and early 2009. China, Indonesia, Malaysia, the Philippines, and Thailand improved a great deal.

In addition to the downfall in export demand, both portfolio investment and foreign loans into 24 emerging Asian countries have continued to drop sharply since the present crisis started to show its early symptoms in mid-2007 as shown in Figure 1.1. One year later, foreign direct investment inflows from the major industrial economies tumbled in the midst of the global financial panic after September/October 2008. Some argue this phenomenon is "financial protectionism".

Table 1.3

Non-Performing Loans as Percentage of Commercial Bank Loans

Economy	*2000–2004 Annual Average*	*2008*	*2009*
People's Rep. of China	21.0	2.5	2.0
Hong Kong, China	4.0	1.2	1.5
Indonesia	10.2	3.2	3.6
Republic of Korea	3.1	1.2	1.5
Malaysia	8.9	2.2	2.2
Philippines	14.8	3.5	3.7
Singapore	5.3	1.4	–
Chinese Taipei	5.2	1.5	–
Thailand	13.5	5.3	5.5

Source: Asian Development Bank (2009c). *Asia Economic Monitor*, July, p.24.

Figure 1.1

Capital Flow to Emerging Economies, 1999–2009

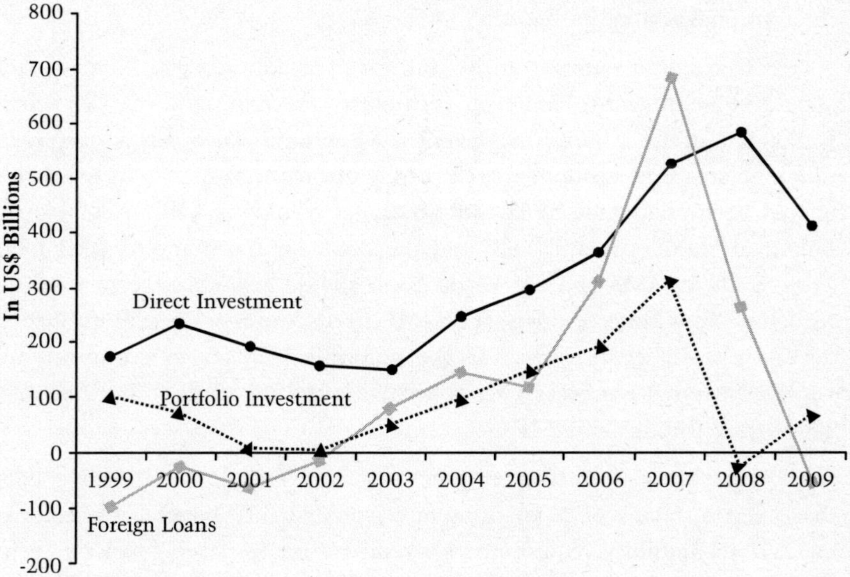

Source: Tong and Wei (2009). *IMF's World Economic Outlook* database. The sample includes 24 emerging economies.

Directions for New Global Financial Architecture

As financial contagion shocks strongly reverberated around the world in late 2008, Asian equity and bond markets could not escape the asset-price implosion and contraction in trade credit. Following the failure of Lehman Brothers in September 2008, frightened depositors were even tempted to withdraw funds on any rumor that a particular bank was exposed to losses. Due to the significant shares of foreign investors in Asia's portfolio market, stock prices in Asia were closely linked to global markets and thus suffered badly from 2008 through to the second quarter of 2009, although emerging Asia at this time faced a sudden stop of net capital inflow amounting to 2 percent of GDP, which is considerably smaller than that experienced during the Asian financial crisis and also far smaller than Europe's 11 percent of GDP.

The original motivation for the G-20 process to face the unprecedented global financial meltdown and subsequent economic recession was to come up with a synchronized collective action to inject immediate stimulus measures and then to address a post-crisis financial architecture. Obviously, the immediate test for the G-20 relates to international regulatory reforms.

Perhaps, most importantly, one form of countercyclical regulation should be addressed to come up with clear and automatic rules by which banks can adjust a buffer to prevent a weakening of regulators' resolve at different stages of economic cycles. Macroprudential modes of regulation should be strengthened by key international regulatory bodies, notably the Financial Stability Board (FSB) and the Bank for International settlement (BIS). Both the IMF and the World Bank should also enhance their ability to deliver in a time of crisis. The IMF needs to embrace a more flexible governance structure reflecting the dynamic changes in economic and social system. The spirit of reform embodied in the G-20 should reverberate through the IMF.

Many issues relating to a new financial architecture have been discussed in terms of regulations and oversight of financial institutions, capital and liquidity requirements, credit rating agencies, financial sector compensations, and credit default swaps, and regulation on short selling. We can see some critical differences between advanced and emerging economies within the G-20 as to the directional guidelines to design new financial architecture for the post-crisis period.

Asia's emerging economies in the G-20 need to voice their own positions on reform of financial regulation toward a more resilient global financial system. Excessive regulations which might be deemed appropriate for financially advanced economies might not necessarily be applicable to emerging G-20 members because their financial systems are still backward and, moreover, they have never played an active role in the global market. Furthermore, they need to be developed to equip themselves with new financial techniques including derivatives and risk management so that they can play competitively on an international stage. Consequently, whatever regulations are introduced should not discourage Asia's financial sector development itself.

Given Asia's relative robustness and effectiveness in the real and financial sectors as proven during the present crisis, the region is well poised to register its views on designing a new financial architecture. Thanks to Asia's strong representation in the G-20, it should utilize effectively a solid platform from which to make valuable contributions to redesigning the global financial architecture.

Rather than remain complacent about Asian recovery, Asia should pay full attention to the fact that a second round of financial crisis around the world is not out of the question. Roubini (2010) points out in his "Crises Economics" that governments which bailed out private firms are now in need of bailouts themselves as seen in Greece and some PIGGS countries. The socialization of private losses and fiscal laxity aimed at stimulating economies experiencing a slump has led to a dangerous build-up of public debt. In this light, "crisis economics" is likely to linger. Our global debt mechanics are looking increasingly like a Ponzi scheme. Thus, the new paradigm should rest on the principle that fiscal discipline and austerity must be implemented together with a transparent and efficiently functioning oversight and supervision system in the financial sector.

Pros and Cons of the Volker Rule and Advocating a Financial Safety Net and Regulation on Hedge Funds

Following recognition of the fraudulent activities by Goldman Sachs, the Obama Administration is determined to tighten financial regulations, including derivatives, a move to which the Republican Party is opposed. The financial industry wants to avoid serious regulation and wishes to be left free to engage in the same behavior that led to the most recent crisis. The appeal of the Volker Rule[4] to separate the banking industry from investment banks has been a focal point of financial sector reform. Both the US Senate and the House of Representatives passed their respective financial overhaul bills on May 21 to restrict banks from using their own money to make bets in the market, and dealing with failing institutions that threaten the financial system.[5] The two bills are very close to each other but differ on the extent to which the new agency's rules would override consumer standards promulgated by states, known as pre-emption. Most banks prefer the Senate bills, which would allow greater pre-emption in certain instances.

To implement the needed regulations on the financial sector to prevent another similar crisis from occurring again, G-20 leaders have yet to come up with a consensus on financial regulations, and remain focused more on the pros and cons, which could result from the scope and severity of the introduction of these regulations. The US government is strongly requesting the global adoption of the rules because they are introduced only in the United States; such a move could weaken the competitiveness of US financial businesses.

The Volker Rule has some variations, one of which dictates that financial businesses that account for more than 10 percent of the market share in terms of liability cannot engage in mergers and acquisition (M&A) or acquire stakes in other companies. If this rule is implemented in financially developing countries including Korea and India, it will have a serious impact on emerging economies' globally competitive "mega bank" drive. It is fair to say that there should not be a "one size fits all" direction in applying the variants of the Volker Rule to emerging economies.

There is also more or less an agreement on the need for a financial safety net and governance reform of international institutions. The establishment of a "Global Financial Safety Net" should be considered in

4. The Volker Rule refers to a ban on banks making market bets with their own money, as opposed to trading on behalf of their clients in order to block moral hazards at huge financial businesses and restrict risky investment in hedge or private equity funds.

5. New York Times (2010). "Reconciliation for Two Financial Overhaul Bills", May 21.

order to put into effect a global mechanism for addressing the sudden reversal of international capital flows on emerging and developing economies. In this regard, the G-20 has helped the IMF, lending resources triple to USD 750 billion to provide critical financing to a broad spectrum of economies hit by the crisis. The IMF has also introduced a flexible credit line through which the Fund now offers a pre-emptive insurance facility without conditionality.

Beyond the IMF's lending capacity, it is highly relevant for Asia's emerging and developing economies to strengthen their own individual and regional financial safety nets. The Chiang Mai Initiative, which was created as a self-help regional financial support program during the Asian financial crisis, should be an important regional safety net with USD 120 billion in pledged reserves from its ASEAN Plus Three members. After seeing the catastrophic shocks embedded in the cross-border flow of hedge funds, the G-20 favored increasing regulatory oversight over hedge funds/hedge fund managers. With Asia having been hit many times by volatile and irregular inflows and outflows of "hedge funds",[6] there exists a need to advocate the proposal made by the Technical Committee of the International Organization of Security Commissions (IOSCO). Some key points deserve to be elaborated upon for recommendation:

- Hedge funds and/or managers/advisors should be subject to mandatory registration and also to on-going regulatory requirements relating to operational as well as disclosure standards to investors.

---

6. The IOSCO Technical Committee acknowledges that there is no consistent or agreed-upon definition of the term hedge fund. Normally, the IOSCO considers as "hedge funds" all those investment schemes displaying of some of the following combinations:

   1) Borrowing and leverage restrictions are not applied.
   2) Significant performance fees are paid to the managers in addition to annual management fee.
   3) Investors are typically permitted to redeem their interests periodically.
   4) Often significant 'own' funds are invested by the manager.
   5) Derivatives are used, often for speculative purposes, and there is an ability to short sell securities.
   6) More diverse risks or complex underlying products are involved.

   For details, see OICU-IOSCO (2009). *Hedge Funds Oversight* (final report).

- Regulators should have the authority to cooperate and share information, where appropriate, with each other in order to facilitate efficient and effective oversight of globally active managers and to help indentify systematic risks. Although there could be some variations with a certain degree of freedom, the G-20 needs to work out global best practices in place of the Tobin Tax.

It is widely agreed that financial systems at the global as well as national level should be strengthened in terms of transparency, oversight, and supervision. A concerted global effort is needed to reform the regulatory and surveillance mechanisms at the international level.

Disagreement on Bank Tax

The recent crisis revealed the over-leveraged banking systems of the United States, the United Kingdom and elsewhere by taking excessive risks. Fueled by a compensation system based on short-term profits, that they outsourced due diligence to credit agencies hidden from regulators represented large risk concentrations and leverage.

Perhaps the most important policy issue under debate as part of the G-20 agenda is related to the global bank tax, which obliges banks and other institutes causing market chaos to pay for their prescriptions. The basic principle is to raise a fund to cover government bailouts and guard against other crises. The United States, the United Kingdom, and Germany, with the condition that the money to be set aside for a future crisis, favor taxing banks for risky assets as part of efforts to mobilize tax-payer's money spent bailing out troubled financial firms. The IMF's preliminary report recommends a global bank tax on compensation financial institutions received for bailouts and non-deposit liabilities or profits. However, Canada, Australia, India, and most developing economies remain opposed to the plan. We need to pay attention to how a "global" bank tax can be embraced by all nations, as developing countries' still–fledgling financial institutions are not culpable in the recent financial crisis and cannot afford such a tax.

Given the different views on the bank tax, a "menu of options" will be the most likely agreement on the issue. Each of the G-20 countries acts in ways that do the job but do not distort the international playing field. The moral hazard problem is also an argument against it. An extra layer of tax could bring a new round of risk-taking as banks are assured that governments have the bailout funds set aside to rescue them.

Based on the major characteristics of the present global financial crisis and the subsequent economic downturn in the Asian economy, emerging Asia was not able to "decouple" from the crisis in the advanced economies. However, emerging Asia's improved fundamentals resulted in a quicker-than-expected recovery relative to the rest of the world. Taking these two points into consideration, the bank tax cannot be applied to G-20 countries across the board in a uniform format.

Balanced and Sustainable Growth

It has been long recognized that the global trade imbalance could not be tolerated indefinitely if the world is in search of sustainable and balanced growth. As agreed at the Pittsburgh summit last year, the successful implementation of a "Framework for Strong, Sustainable, and Balanced Growth" is a critical test for the G-20 process to be sustainable as the premier forum. In this context, the chronic structural trade imbalance between the US and China has been a major focus of policy coordination and conflicts in a decade. Table 1.4 clearly shows that the trade imbalance between the United States and China has risen at an alarming rate in the past decade in favor of China. About one-third to one-half of the overall US trade deficit can be attributed to the trade deficit with China.

Revaluation Issue of Chinese Yuan

When China re-valued its currency in 2005, the shift failed to balance trade with the United States. A smaller Chinese trade surplus combined with a US deficit would be good for the global economy, easing protectionist pressures and reducing another boom-bust cycle driven by excess savings in China and debt-driven consumption in the US. The People's Bank of China announced a 2.1 percent devaluation of the yuan from 8.28 to the dollar on July 21, 2005, and subsequently allowed the currency to rise through July 2008, although the government virtually pegged it at 6.83 onward to protect Chinese exporters from the global recession.

Table 1.4

US Trade with China

(Unit: USD million)

Year	*US Exports to China*	*US Imports from China*	*US Trade Balance against China*	*US Total Trade Deficit with the World*
1997	12,805	62,552	–49,747	–182,615
1998	14,258	71,156	–56,898	–233,411
1999	13,118	81,786	–68,668	–331,945
2000	16,253	100,063	–83,810	–436,469
2001	19,235	102,280	–83,045	–410,933
2002	22,053	125,168	–103,115	–470,291
2003	28,418	152,379	–123,961	–535,652
2004	34,721	196,699	–161,978	–653,123
2005	41,837	243,462	–201,625	–766,561
2006	55,224	287,773	–232,549	–817,976
2007	65,238	321,508	–256,270	–790,991
2008	71,457	337,790	–266,333	–800,006
2009	69,576	296,402	–226,826	–500,944

Source: Korea International Trade Association.

In this light, China should revalue its currency. Furthermore, the country needs to shift to a more market-determined exchange rate regime, which will in turn benefit Chinese consumers. A stronger yuan would also boost consumer purchasing power thus allowing Chinese consumers to buy foreign goods at lower prices and serving to push up the cost of the country's own goods in international markets. According to one study, a 5 percent revaluation of the yuan would improve the US deficit by about one-fifth and narrow the US trade gap with China by USD 61 billion. Needless to say, a reevaluation of the yuan would be a lot healthier in the long run for the world economy, thanks to the more balanced trade and growth that would ensue.

Rebalancing Extra-Regional Exports and Intra-Regional Trade

The economic prospects for developing Asia this year as well as for next year are promising, although it is likely that growth performance will remain well below the average of pre-crisis years as many global institutions have forecast. Developing Asia will only be able to achieve a full-fledged high-growth path if the global economy succeeds in growing closer to its potential. A major challenge in this context is whether Asia can adjust to long-standing global trade imbalances by striking an optimal balance between export orientation and increased reliance on domestic demand-driven growth. Looking ahead to the next decade, it is likely that private demand from advanced economies and the US is not going to be as robust as it used to be. This implies that for Asia to regain its strong growth momentum, it needs to shift from excessive export reliance more into internal domestic demand within Asia.

Emerging Asia's rising prosperity in the past two decades or so has been closely associated with its outward orientation to foreign trade. Indeed, many other developing countries have attempted to emulate the success stories of the East Asian tiger economies. Similarly, both India and China are likely to enjoy the benefits of the trade-oriented development model.

Although trade orientation became the symbol of the Asian model, liberalization and openness to cross-border flows of capital and labor also played an important role in the region's success. Yet excessive openness is not without risks for the region, as experienced during two major crises in a decade. The 1997–98 Asian financial crisis had its roots in the sudden reversal of capital inflows in the region's financial institutions, which were overexposed to foreign borrowings to maintain stable exchange rate pegs. This time, a sudden stop of private capital inflows into emerging Asian markets coupled with a sudden pull-out from there caused extremely volatile exchange rates as witnessed in Korea.

More specifically, the region's heightened reliance on external demand for growth hindered consumption and catalyzed reserves accumulation, which was widely viewed as insurance against a repeat of the 1997–98 devastation. This heavy reliance left the region vulnerable to the synchronized collapse of the major industrial economies. Trade within Asia should be pursued by encouraging cross-border production networks and consuming completed goods within Asia.

One way of effectively creating a significant intra-regional demand in East Asia is to generate an East Asian free trade agreement (FTA) to benchmark the European Union integration process. The Asian financial crisis triggered a rising sense of East Asian identity and, as a result, in November 1999 the ASEAN+3 (China, Japan, Korea) Summit released the joint statement on East Asian Cooperation that outlines a wide range of possible areas for regional cooperation. Most notable developments in this context involve the ASEAN+3 Chiang Mai Initiative (CMI), which involves a regional currency swap to provide financial self-help and support mechanisms, and trade integration efforts through intra-regional FTAs. Given the three separate FTAs in effect with ASEAN by China, Japan, and Korea respectively, ASEAN+3 needs to consider seriously an ASEAN+3 FTA to realize potential benefits due to geographical proximity, complementary endowments of production factors, and growing economic ties after the Asian financial crisis. As time goes by, the intra-regional framework could be open to extra-East Asian economies like India, Australia, and New Zealand.

For merchandize trade, a broader customer base for final goods is needed. Strengthening intra-regional trade can help reduce developing Asia's overdependence on the major industrial economies and remedy unsustainable current account imbalances. For policy makers in Asia, the decision to accelerate economic growth and job creation through cross-border movements of goods and services, capital, and labor must be made within intra-regional markets in Asia.

Standstill of Protectionist Measures

While major economies employ economic stimulus packages to ensure a speedy recovery from the present economic setback, trade officials and export dependent economies are worried about creeping protectionism in the EU, the US, China, Russia, and elsewhere. Given rising unemployment and tremendous uncertainties on the financial market with toxic assets of large-scale financial institutions and a likely prolonged recession in most advanced economies, the majority of economic recovery measures adopted by major economies come with a high risk of protectionism.

A newly employed protectionism appears not of the traditional sort in the form of higher tariffs, but the more subtle type like subsidies tied to local purchase and buy-local products that favor domestic industries at the expense of competitors in other countries. Such actions could well do more harm than good by choking off international trade and provoking a down spiral of tit-for-tat actions worldwide. If this happens, negotiated tariff reductions would be meaningless if countries could simply use taxes or subsidies to discriminate in favor of local products. The prospect of countries pursuing such policies underpins the rising concerns about protectionism and economic nationalism in economic recovery efforts.

Given these protectionist symptoms, the G-20 leaders, however, have agreed on standstill of the trade protectionist measures and declaring the critical importance of rejecting protectionism and refraining from raising new barriers to investment or trade in goods and services, which have been already accepted and practised and rollback to strong political commitments to recharge a framework for the WTO Doha Round. Protectionism at this critical point of the global economic downturn is likely to harm the spirit of cooperation that is needed for global economic recovery. The G-20 should go further and make affirmative trade-creating and trade-liberalizing actions.

To ensure a robust revival of world trade in the coming years, large Asian economies could take up the mantle of the Doha Round. An example is India's hosting of the meeting of trade ministers in New Delhi in September this year, aiding the G-20's goal of reaching agreement on the Doha Round by the end of 2010. Efforts to head off protectionist tendencies are still important as governments continue to implement stimulus packages that involve procurement of tradable goods and services. The G-20 consultations provide an excellent opportunity for developing Asia to push the trade talks forward. There are opportunities for successful agricultural negotiations as the G3 economies have proposed to step up assistance for agricultural development.

It is very important to address the global warming issue but we need to avoid the undermining of a half-century of expanding world trade. The US passed a climate bill that would impose trade penalties on countries that do not accept limits on carbon emissions. The EU has already approved the idea of an "equalization" levy on imports from countries that have not agreed to cut emissions. It should be noted that unilateral sanctions are unlikely to work and more than likely to provoke a dangerous protectionist trade war. The main reason that trade and climate change are linked is that the damage inflicted by greenhouse gases is not local but regional. If large-scale emitters do not cut back, atmospheric concentrations of greenhouse gases will continue to rise dangerously no matter what the rest of the world does. There are precedents for using trade measures for environmental goals. The World Trade Organization (WTO) has suggested that levying taxes at the border on the carbon contents of imports would be acceptable if they are devised properly. Such tariff must be part of an international agreement on climate change.

An international accord that includes trade-related enforcement must also include commitments on emission reductions all around, as well as financial aid for poor countries to meet the caps without sacrificing economic growth. How can we set up clear guideline on how to identify and quantify transgressions and establish appropriate countermeasures? However this is done, it must not open a back door for protectionism. The green growth model needs to be addressed as an important topic at future G-20 summits.

Knowledge-Sharing Program

In order to draw the full support of non-G-20 members, we should emphasize that the fruits of strong and sustainable growth are shared evenly among all nations including the poorest. The G-20 needs to be mindful of the side effects of globalization that generate greater antipathy toward greater global integration. To this end, the G-20 member countries need to look beyond themselves and take on the responsibility of considering a larger constituency of countries by reaching out to partners outside the G-20.

In this context, Korea can play an effective role by sharing its experiences accumulated as a latecomer to achieving such rapid industrialization in the past half-century while pushing through an open trade regime. A number of developing economies have expressed their keen interest to share Korea's experiences as a model of a successful industrializing nation. The G-20 countries can offer a variety of programs to less developed economies among non-G20 countries.

Policy Implications and the Role of Korea

We examined how the unprecedented global economic downturn after the Great Depression in the 1930s affected Asia. After painful restructuring of its economic system after the Asian financial crisis in 1997–98, the Asian economies this time appear prepared to successfully weather the global downturn. Financial globalization needs to be effectively managed so that capital flows do not become a source of instability. This requires policy changes and domestic financial market development to create an environment that both foster Asian intermediation for the region's savings and huge foreign exchange reserves that serve to attract long-term foreign investment.

Excessive opening of domestic capital markets without clear monitoring on hedge fund flows and appropriate corrective mechanisms have contributed to exacerbating the current crisis in Asia. Under the G-20 Process, major Asian members of the G-20 represented by Japan, China, India, Indonesia, and Korea should play an important role to design a new global financial architecture. Emerging Asian economies still contain many caveats in their financial system, especially in risk management. As learned during the Asian financial crisis and during the present crisis, as well, emerging Asia should continue to update its financial systems by adopting the most advanced best practices.

The emerging Asian economy should be one in which more efficiently functioning financial development is promoted along with manufacturing efficiency. On the eve of the birth of the "United States of Europe" and the existing NAFTA treaty, emerging Asia should continue to accelerate on-going East Asian regional integration in the form of ASEAN+3 FTA and gradual expansion of membership toward an "East Asian Community" which would help enhance intra-regional financial and trade cooperation.

The role of Korea as the chair of the G-20 this year is truly important. Korea's capability to derive some tangible deliverables can have an important bearing on setting the G-20 process on the path to becoming a formidable and trustworthy institution. Both Korea and India can work together to ensure the G-20 process as the premier forum in the years to come. Korea's chairing of the G-20 this November was supported by the fact that it was exemplary in its recovery from the crisis and from its firm commitment to an open and transparent economy as evident in the leadership for arguing against protectionist measures and the rollback to the pre-crisis free trade regime displayed during earlier G-20 summits.

The G-20 represents an important step toward restructuring the world economic leadership. Taking maximum advantage of the equal status given to advanced and emerging economies, both India and Korea, for that matter all of the Asian G-20 members, should adapt global institutions to the shifting global economic power. Korea's rise to becoming host of the G-20 summit is a reflection of international expectations that the country is well positioned to play a bridging role between advanced and emerging economies. Most importantly, Korea should do its best to make sure that any further slippage between the G-20's declarations made so far and their actual implementation could be minimized. Korea's leadership in putting current global issues on the agenda, balancing many conflicts of interest, and proposing alternatives is critical to making the G-20 the premier formidable institution and a credible process in the years to come.

References

Ahn, Choong Yong (2001). "Financial and Corporate Sector Restructuring in South Korea:0Accomplishments and Unfinished Agenda", *The Japanese Economic Review* 52(4), December.

————. (2008). "South Korea: Wary of Another Financial Crisis", *Global Asia* 3(4), Winter.

————. (2010). "Weathering the Storm: The Impact of the Global Financial Crisis on Asia", *Global Asia* 5(1).

Ahn, Choong Yong and Inkyo Cheong (2007). "A Search for Closer Economic Relations in East Asia", *The Japanese Economic Review* 58(2), June.

Asian Development Bank (2009a), *Asian Development Outlook 2009: Rebalancing Asia's Growth*. pp.51–124.

————. (2009b). *Asian Development Outlook 2009.* Update: "Developing Asia's Response to the Turmoil". pp.26-–32.

————. (2009c). *Asia Economic Monitor.* July.

Baily, Martin Neil, Robert E. Litan and Matthew S. Johnson (2008). "The Origins of the Financial Crisis", *Initiative on Business and Public Policy.*

Bank for International Settlements (2009). *International Framework for Liquidity Risk Measurement, Standards and Monitoring*. December.

————. (2009) *Strengthening the Resilience of the Banking Sector.* December.

Beatrice, Weder di Mauro (2010). *Taxing Systemic Risk: Proposal for a Systemic Risk Charge and a systemic Risk Fund.* January.

Deutsche Bank Research (2010). *The Case for a Financial Sector Stabilization Fund.* April 6.

Eder, Gregor and Michaela Grimm (2009). "Asia and the Global Economic Crisis: Challenges and Opportunities", *Allianz*, June 3.

FSB (Financial Stability Board) (2010). *Progress since the St. Andrews Meeting in Implementing the G-20 Recommendations for Strengthening Financial Stability: Report on the Financial Stability Board to G-20 Finance Ministers and Governors*. April 19.

Glodstein, Morris and Daniel Xie (2009). "Impact of Financial Crisis on Emerging Asia", *Working Paper* 09-11, Peterson Institute for International Economics.

IMF (2010). *The World Economic: Rebalancing the Growth*. April.

Institute for Global Economics (2009). "G-20 Reform Initiatives: Implications for the Future of Financial Regulation," November 10.

Korea Institute for International Economic Policy (2009). "The World Economy with the G-20".

Korea Institute of Finance (2009). "The Korean G-20 Leadership: Assessing the Key Issues for 2010", December.

Litan, R.E and J. Raouch (1998). *American Finance for the 21st Century.* Brookings: Washington DC.

Roubini, Nouriel (2010). "Second Stage of Global Financial Crisis", *Korea Herald*, May 10.

Technical Committee of the International Organization of Securities Commissions (2009). *Hedge Funds Oversight: Final Report*. June.

———. (2009). *Regulation of Short Selling: Final Report.* June.

The Center for International Governance Innovation (2009). *Flashpoints for the Pittsburgh Summit.* September 24.

World Bank (2009). *Prospects for the Global Economy.* June.

World Trade Organization (WTO) (2009). "Global Crisis Requires Global Solutions", *2009 News Item Report on Recent Development*, July 13.

2 Economic Recovery and Challenges in the Post-Crisis Era

The Case of Korea

JOON-KYUNG KIM

Introduction

What will the world economy look like when it eventually emerges from the current global crisis? It will depend very much on what the leading economies of the world such as the US, the EU, China, Japan, and India do. It is difficult to tell what it will be like as we are yet to emerge from the recession and do not know how these economies will be restructured in the aftermath of the crisis.

One thing that seems to be certain, however, is that the US economy will become "de-leveraged" as its saving rate increases and, as a result, its status as the "demander of last resort" that has served as a final destination of exports from the rest of the world will diminish. If this truly happens it will have a profound effect on many economies in Asia that have relied on exports for their economic growth. In that event, these countries in Asia including Korea may not continue with export-oriented policies of the past; they will have to find new growth strategies and these may include relying more on domestic demand and expanding exports to non-US markets.

In this paper, we argue that in anticipation of contraction in the US demand for Asian manufacturing exports and for reasons relating to its own internal economic conditions, Korea will have to radically restructure its economy to improve productivity in lagging sectors in the economy. Specifically, it will need to improve the productivity of service industries where small and medium-sized enterprises (SMEs) dominate and turn them into a new export sector. For economic growth in the past four decades Korea has relied mainly on manufacturing exports to advanced industrialized countries. Its service exports have been minimal although in the 70s Korea thrived on the export of construction services to the Middle East and, in recent years, exports relating to "hanryu" (wave of the Korean culture)—Korean movies and TV programs—have seen some popularity in Asian countries. The service sector in general, however, suffers from low productivity and has been a drag on the Korean economy.

Given what we expect to happen in the US economy as it emerges from the current crisis, the Korean economy will have to become more domestic demand-oriented and to expand manufacturing exports to non-US markets. In addition, its service industries with their many SMEs will have to become more productive and competitive, becoming part of Korea's more diversified export sector.

The rest of the paper is organized as follows. Section II discusses the impact of the current crisis on Korea's financial and real sectors, as well as the impact of some of the government measures that have been adopted in response to the crisis. Section III examines various features of Korea's service sector, comparing it with the manufacturing sector, and takes a critical look into troubled firms in service industries. In Section IV, we discuss the reasons for low productivity in service industries. Section V offers some concluding remarks.

Impact of the Global Crisis on the Korean Economy and the Government Response[1]

Impact on the Korean Economy

Although the current global crisis that has emanated from the United States has had an adverse impact on the Korean economy, other major countries have been more severely affected. In fact, Korean stock market (KOSPI index) performed better, in relative terms, than Standard and Poor Index in United States, Nikkei in Japan, Shanghai in China and BSE in India. Its stock prices certainly declined, with the Korea Composite Stock Price Index (KOSPI) falling by 44 percent from year end of 2007 to the end of February 2009. The decline was due to a surge in capital outflow, largely

1. This section draws on Kim and Lee (2009a) with updated data.

driven by the massive withdrawal of foreign debts by financial institutions.[2] The won/dollar exchange rate consequently fell, the won depreciating by 40 percent between October 2007 and February 2009 to 1,516 by the end of the period. Since March 2009, a large foreign capital began to flow into Korea again and stock prices and foreign exchange rates have rapidly stabilized, thanks to the increased current account surplus as well as to the expansionary policy by central banks under the global policy coordination. The KOSPI increased by 64 percent between the end of February 2009 and the end of April 2010, and the won appreciated by 26 percent over the same period.

Korea's comparatively good performance may be due in part to the institutional reforms taken by the country in the aftermath of the 1997 crisis that led to changes in the financial structure of its corporations and in risk management of its banks. Large corporations managed to actually reduce their debt leverage ratios and improve their debt service capacity. It is not surprising then that the Korean economy has been able to withstand the current global crisis better than other major economies.

Korea did not have as large a housing bubble as the United States. In fact, in 2001–2007 the housing prices rose by 6.7 percent on a year-on-year basis and in 2008 they registered an increase of 3.1 percent in Korea. Two factors accounted for this moderate increase in Korea: one was the deflationary effect of economic restructuring after the 1997 crisis (over the period of 1996–2000), and the other was the restrictive mortgage-loan regulations that the government introduced a few years before the current crisis.[3] These mortgage loan regulations contributed greatly to such low

---

2. After the 1997 financial crisis, the Korean government fully opened the capital market. Foreign portfolio investments in the stock and bond as well as the short-term money markets were completely liberalized. The removal of restrictions on capital inflow was accompanied by the liberalization of foreign exchange transactions. In particular, the Foreign Exchange Management Law was abolished in 1999 and replaced with the Foreign Exchange Transaction Law. The old law constituted a positive list system in capital account transactions, which prohibited all capital account transactions that were not on the list. The new law introduced a negative list system that allows all capital account transactions except those on the list.
3. In 2002, the government began to tighten the loan-to-value (LTV) regulation on apartments in "speculative areas" with ratios ranging from 40 percent to 70 percent. In August 2005, the regulation on DTI (debt-to-income ratio, which is the principle and interest payments on total loan to income) was also introduced to reduce the default risk on housing loans. 40 percent DTI ratio has begun to be applied to "speculative areas".

delinquency ratio of mortgage loans in Korea as 0.44 percent in July 2009.

In spite of this relative stability in the financial market, Korea's real economy has suffered much from the current global recession, which had brought about a severe contraction in its exports. As a matter of fact, monthly exports recorded an unprecedented decline from $41 billion in July 2008 to $21.1 billion in January 2009 (Figure 2.1). This decline in exports had a direct negative impact on Korea's manufacturing sector: the manufacturing production index fell significantly from November 2008 and its growth rate recorded a 22.5 percent decrease only during October 2008 and February 2009. The severity of the impact of the current crisis on manufacturing can also be seen in the sharp decline in the capacity utilization index to 79 for January 2009, which is even lower than during the 1997 crisis (Figure 2.4). The contraction in manufacturing has caused the unemployment rate to rise from 3.0 percent in January 2008 to 3.9 percent in February 2009.

Figure 2.1

Korea's Total Exports ($ billion)

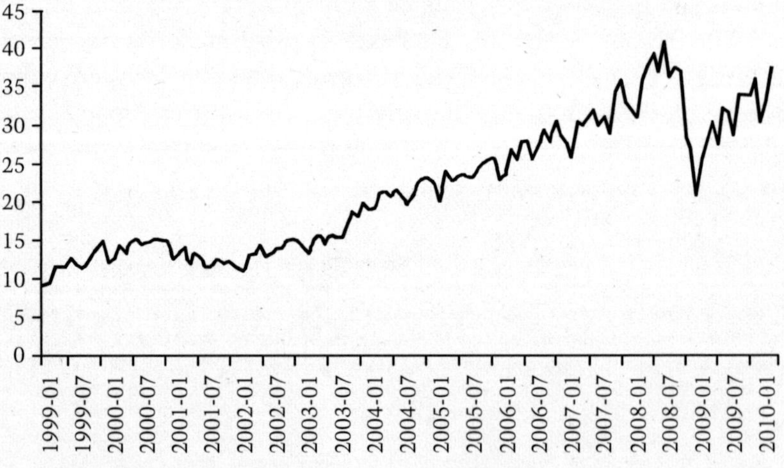

Source: Korea International Trade Association.

Beginning in March 2009, however, exports rebounded thanks to the rapid recovery of exports to China, though exports to the US and the EU

Figure 2.2

Korea's Export Growth to the US, EU and China (%)

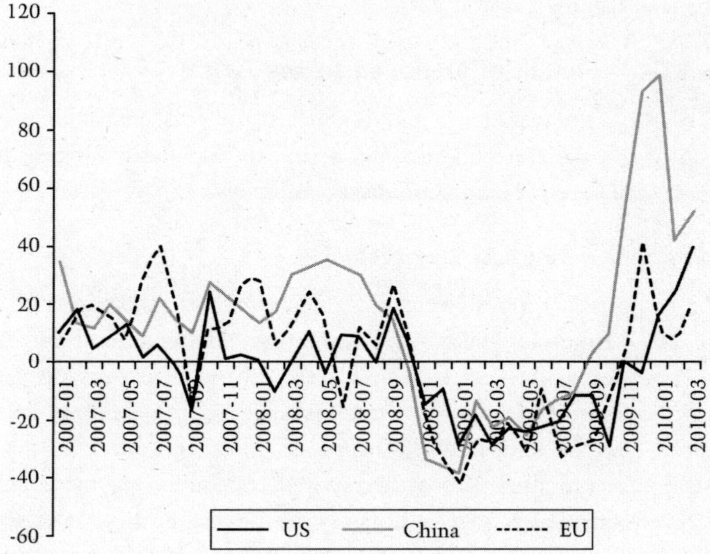

Source: Korea International Trade Association.

Figure 2.3

Manufacturing and Services Production

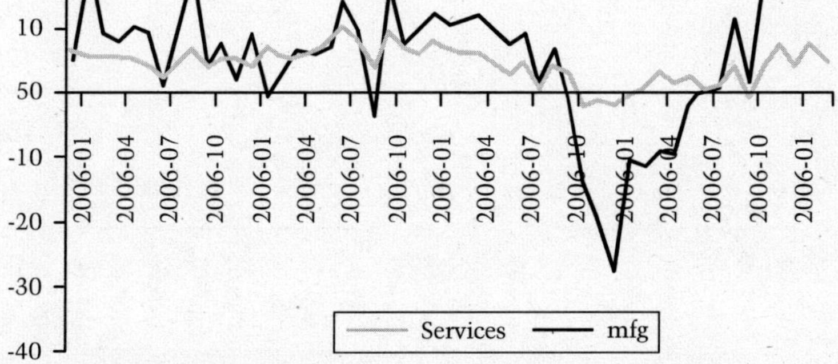

Source: Korea International Trade Association.

has been relatively weak (Figure 2.2). Manufacturing production as well as capacity utilization indices have seen a rapid improvement during the same time period (Figures 2.3 and 2.4).

Korean Government's Response to the Crisis

The Korean government has taken a number of comprehensive and pre-emptive measures to address the actual or potentially adverse impacts of the crisis. These measures are discussed below.

(a) Foreign Currency Liquidity Provision

In response to massive outflows of capital—a sum larger than that during 1997 financial crisis—the Korean government and the Bank of Korea have set aside $55 billion for the purpose of providing foreign currency liquidity ($21 billion for trade finance and $34 billion for liquidity provision) during October 2008–February 2009. In addition, in October 2008 the government set up a three-year $100 billion payment guarantee for foreign currency borrowings by domestic banks. It also made agreements with the United States (November 2008), Japan and China (December 2008) to establish currency swap lines ($30 billion each and $90 billion total).

Figure 2.4

Manufacturing Capacity Utilization Index (2005=100)

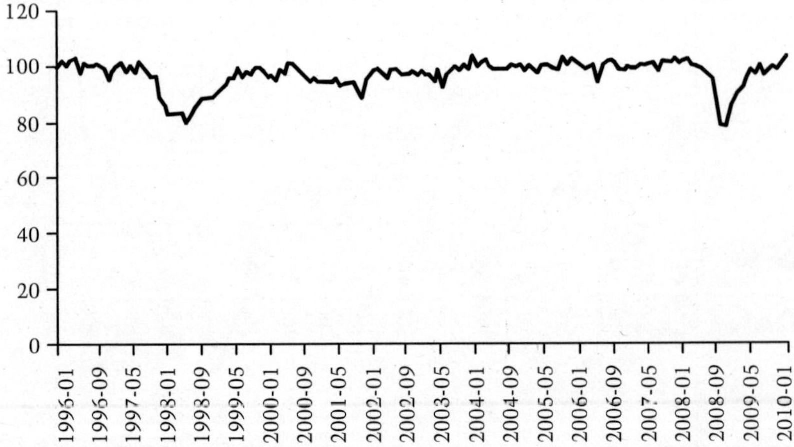

Source: Korea National Statistical Office.

These measures have significantly alleviated the credit squeeze in the financial market. The term-loan rollover ratio increased to around 90 percent by January 2009 from 50–60 percent in October 2008. In March 2009 the rollover ratio further increased to 106 percent, mainly due to the current account surplus, which rebounded to $3.7 billion from a deficit of $1.6 billion in the previous month. The banks have secured enough funding to pay off maturing loans, while obtaining long-term funds by issuing bonds.

(b) Policy Interest Rate Cut and Liquidity Provision

To prevent a credit crunch upon the post-Lehman fallout (September 2008) the Bank of Korea reduced the policy interest rate by 325 base points—from 5.25 percent to 2.0 percent. To assure liquidity it also pumped 23.3 trillion won into the banking system through the purchase of RP (Repurchase Agreement, 16.8 trillion won) and treasury bonds (1.7 trillion won) and the buyback of the Monetary Stabilization Bond (0.7 trillion won).

(c) Large-scale Fiscal Stimulus Package

In response to the fall in aggregate demand the Korean government has adopted expansionary fiscal measures. Specifically, for the period of 2008–2012, it has earmarked 67.1 trillion won (6.9% of GDP) for a stimulus package, which includes investment in infrastructure, provision for job creation and social safety net (33.2 trillion won), and a reduction in corporate and personal income tax rates (33.9 trillion won).

These expansionary fiscal measures may lead to a deterioration of the fiscal balance and an increase in the national debt. The Korean economy is, however, unlikely to suffer much from these consequences of expansionary fiscal measures. The government has been running surpluses in the budget for the past several years, and the national debt is well below the average for the OECD countries.

(d) Enhanced Support for SMEs

Government credit guarantees to SMEs increased to 63 trillion won at year-end 2009 from 49 trillion won at year-end 2008. Credit guarantees maturing in 2009, which amount to 33 trillion won, received an extension. The criteria for credit guarantee screening has been eased and, moreover, the guarantees that have an upper limit of one-fourth or one-third of the sales revenue of a firm have been raised to one-half. In particular, exporting firms, "green-growth" firms, high-tech firms, and start-up companies has received full guarantee coverage, up from the current 85 percent coverage. In addition, other SME loans maturing in 2009 and up to now have been rolled over. Thanks to these measures, SME loans by banks that experienced a precipitous drop immediately after the onset of the global crisis could be expanded by the banks. However, as will be seen in Section III, these measures may pronounce the effect of keeping unviable "zombie" firms alive, imposing a drag on rapid sustainable economic recovery.

(e) Enhancing the Soundness of the Banking System

The government has implemented various policy measures, including the Bank Recapitalization Fund to expand the credit supply capacity of banks. The government announced it would mobilize 20 trillion won and has used the Fund to buy subordinated bonds, hybrid loans and redeemable preferred stock upon banks' request. The government also announced that it would establish the Corporate Restructuring Fund of 40 trillion won at Korea Asset Management Corporation (KAMCO) to purchase bad debts and support restructuring. This fund was expected to conduct a role similar to the Non-Performing Loan Resolution Fund, which was created during the 1997 financial crisis. Key soundness indicators of Korean banks, including the BIS ratio (14.4% as at end-December 2009) and the NPL ratio (1.45% as at end-March 2010), are all in good standing.

(f) Support for Household Loan/Mortgage Lenders

The Korean government has put in place various measures aimed at easing household burdens, including: 1) guarantee of collateral supplementation for depreciated value of housing (maximum guarantee of 100 million won), 2) extension of maturity and grace period of mortgage loans, and 3) exemption of early repayment fees on the transfer from floating to fixed rate.

(g) Job Sharing

In order to create new jobs and retain employment the government launched the Green New Deal Project, which plans to invest 50 trillion won for the purpose of securing future economic growth and employment. Youth unemployment is a serious problem in Korea and has spurred the government to initiate the Youth Internship Program in order to train unemployed youth for employment in an economy that is becoming more technologically sophisticated. The government also plans to revise labor laws and institutions to make the labor market more flexible and to promote job creation. Specifically, the government has offered tax credits and financial incentives to companies that are devising ways to bring about cooperation between labor and management for job-sharing and improved industrial relations. Also, to address the inequities between regular and non-regular workers, the government has revised the relevant labor laws and institutions—for example, by extending the employment of non-regular workers.

Current State of Service Industries and Troubled Firms in Service Industries[4]

Current State of Service Industries in Korea

Since the 1997 financial crisis, the share of services in GDP (value-added) has exhibited a declining trend as can be seen in Figure 2.5. In contrast, the share of manufacturing has increased due to growth in exports resulting from a rapid depreciation of the won, extensive corporate restructuring, and technological advancement (Kim and Tcha, 2007).

The share of employment in services had increased steadily since the early 90s (Figure 2.6). It has continued to increase in the aftermath of the 1997 crisis due to a large influx of laid-off workers from the manufacturing sector and the hiring of new employees coming on the market. Employment in manufacturing decreased considerably during the crisis but, unlike in services, it did not rebound to the pre-crisis level. This is mainly due to the fact that the manufacturing sector faces vigorous international competition and is continually subject to the restructuring pressure. In contrast, the service sector, which is little exposed to external competition, has accommodated unemployed workers from manufacturing, thus playing the role of a buffer to the crisis-driven unemployment shock.

4. Sections III, IV and V draw heavily on Kim and Lee (2009b).

Figure 2.5

Shares of Services and Manufacturing in GDP (in Real Price, %)

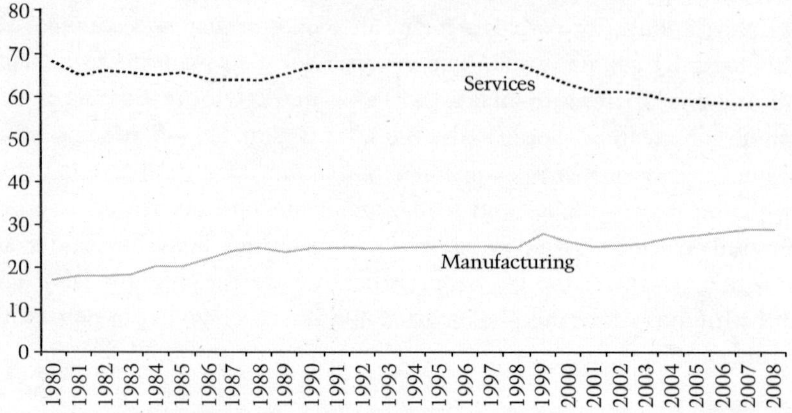

Source: Bank of Korea, National Accounts. Quoted from Kim and Lee (2009).

Figure 2.6

Share of Employment in Services and Manufacturing (%)

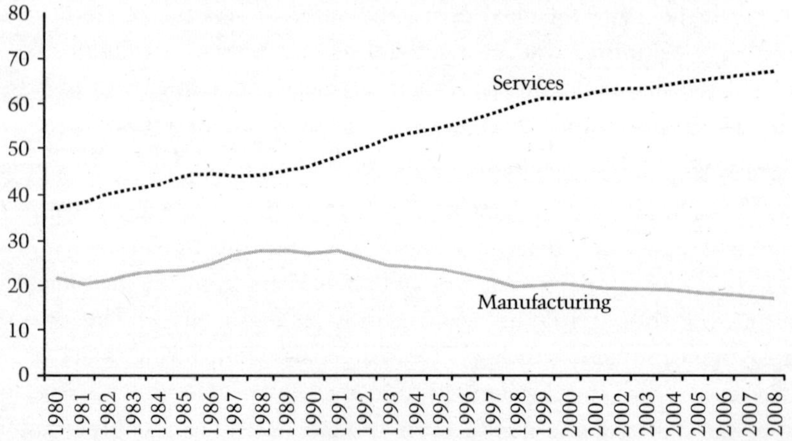

Source: Statistics Korea, KOSIS. Quoted from Kim and Lee (2009).

A result of sluggish growth in value-added and a large inflow of workers into the service sector was a lowering of productivity in services. As can be seen in Figure 2.7, the overall labor productivity growth in manufacturing improved during 1980-2007, while that of services dropped from 2.6 percent (annual average) during 1980–1990 to 1.5 percent during 1990–1997 and further to 1.2 percent during 1997–2007, hence contributing to lowering the total productivity in Korea.

The service account of Korea has continued to experience a deficit since 1990, the deficit growing bigger since the 1997 crisis (Figure 2.8). The reason for this chronic and growing deficit is the weak competitiveness of service industries as well as the post-crisis liberalization of foreign exchange transactions that have allowed greater freedom to import foreign services. In 2008 the service account deficit amounted to $16.7 billion, 1.8 percent of GDP.

Figure 2.7

Labor Productivity Growth in Services and Manufacturing: Annual Growth Rate of Value Added per Employee (%)

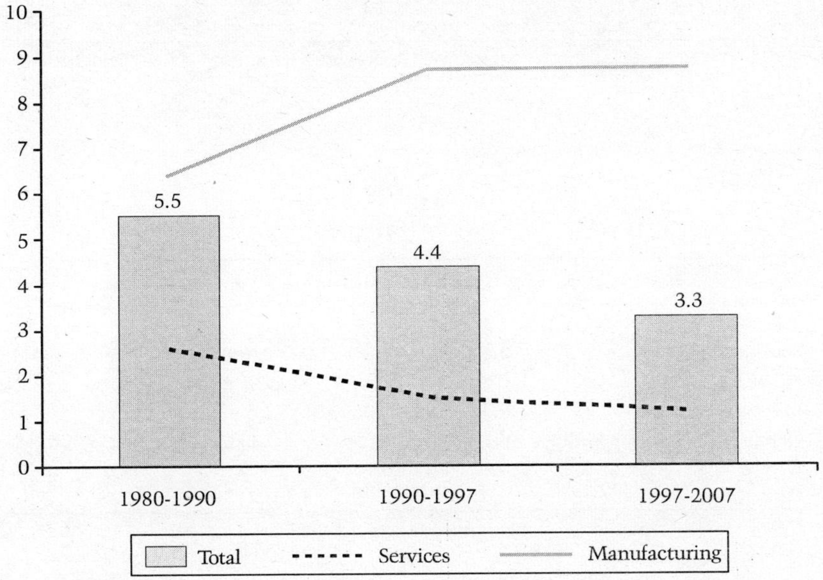

Source: Quoted from OECD (2008).

Estimates of the revealed comparative advantage (RCA) of Korea's service industries show that Korea has a comparative advantage only in transportation and does poorly in all other industries. This compares poorly with the US and other advanced countries, which have a comparative advantage in other service industries as well (Table 2.1).

Figure 2.8

Exports and Imports of Services (% of GDP)

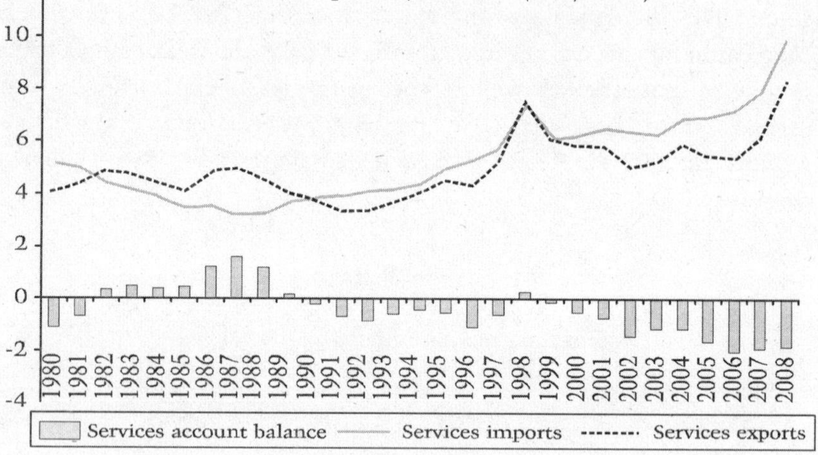

Source: Bank of Korea, *http://ecos.bok.or.kr*

Table 2.1

RCAs of Service Exports in Major Countries as of 2007

	Korea	*US*	*EU (27)*	*Japan*	*China*
Transportation	2.4	0.7	1.0	1.4	1.1
Tourism	0.4	1.0	0.9	0.3	1.2
Finance	0.8	1.4	1.2	0.6	NA
Insurance	0.3	1.0	1.1	0.5	0.3
Computers & information	0.1	0.6	1.2	0.2	0.8
Royalty & Licenses	0.5	3.1	0.7	3.2	0.0
Other business services	0.9	0.7	1.1	1.0	1.3

Source: WTO, *International Trade Statistics*. Quoted from Kim and Lee (2009).

In addition, the share of Korean service exports in the world market has stagnated at about 2 percent during the past two decades or so. This level is far below that of the US (14.0%), Germany (6.3%), and Japan (3.8%). It is noteworthy that the world market share of China, which was less than that of Korea until 2000, has increased steadily, reaching (3.7%), which is twice that of Korea's in 2008 (Figure 2.9).

Troubled Firms in Service Industries

Here, we report on troubled firms in service industries using the financial data for more than 18,000 externally audited firms. To measure the debt service capacity of these firms we use the interest payment coverage ratio (IPCR)—the ratio of operating profits to interest expenses. This definition implies that the firms with IPCR less than 1 are unable to even cover the interest payments, let alone the principal, with their current earnings.

Figure 2.10 shows that the manufacturing sector has been improving its IPCR, albeit with some fluctuations, since the 1997 crisis whereas the service sector has been doing less well. Between 1997 and 2008, IPCR in manufacturing rose from 1.3 to 4.9, more than a three-fold increase while that of services rose from 1.1 to 1.9.

Figure 2.9

Service Export Share of Select Countries in World Markets

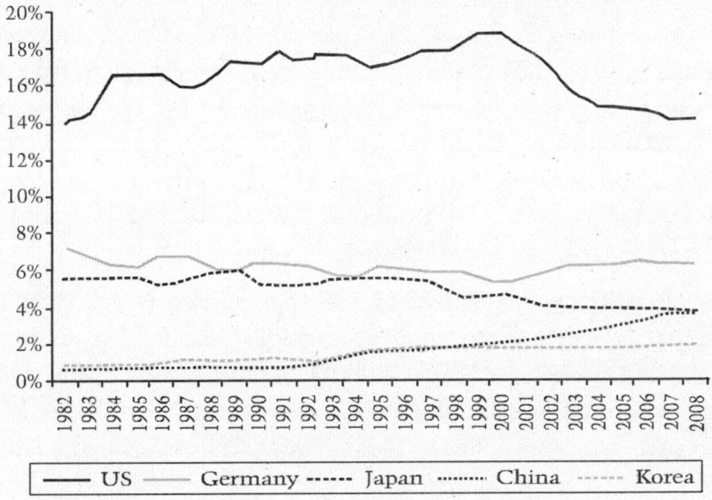

Source: WTO, International Trade Statistics. Quoted from Kim and Lee (2009).

Figure 2.10

Interest Payment Coverage Ratio (IPCR) in Manufacturing and Services

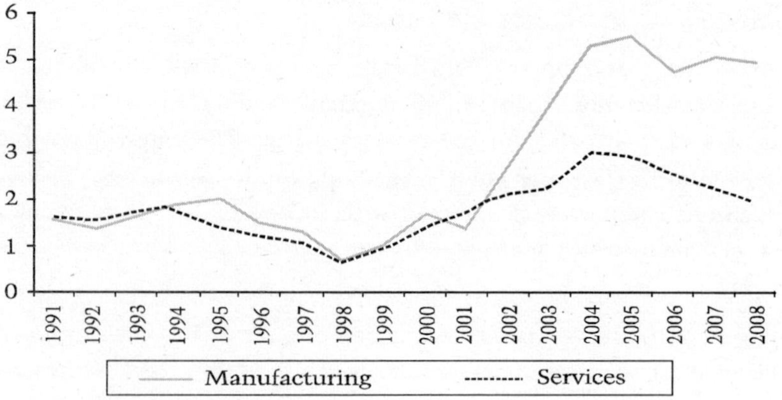

Note: The ratios are a weighted average across firms.

Source: Korea Investors Service, Inc., data. Quoted from Kim and Lee (2009).

There are at least two reasons for the service sector's weak debt service capacity: one is their stagnant profitability (Figure 2.11) and the other their higher debt leverages than in manufacturing (Figure 2.12). In particular, there was little improvement in the operating profitability of services compared to their pre-crisis performance. Manufacturing industries were able to reduce the debt leverage at a more rapid rate than service industries: the ratio of total borrowings to total assets for manufacturing dropped from 52.3 percent in 1997 to 23.1 percent in 2008. Although it initially decreased after 1997 the service sector began to raise its debt leverage in 2006, reaching 35.5 percent in 2008, almost the same as before the crisis.

Following the approach used by Eichengreen and Gupta (2009) we now separate services into two groups, traditional and modern. Using the EU KLEMS data, Eichengreen and Gupta (2009) distinguished three groups of services according to their shares of GDP whether it has fallen, risen slowly, or risen rapidly over time: 1) traditional services include retail and wholesale trade, transport and storage, public administration and defense; 2) hybrid services (traditional plus modern) consumed mainly by households include education, health and social work, hotels and restaurants, and other community, social and personal service; and 3) modern services consumed by both the household and corporate sectors include financial intermediation, computer services, business services, communication and legal, and technical services. However, in our study, traditional services include both traditional and hybrid.[5]

Figure 2.11

Ratio of Operating Profits to Total Assets: Manufacturing vs. Services (%)

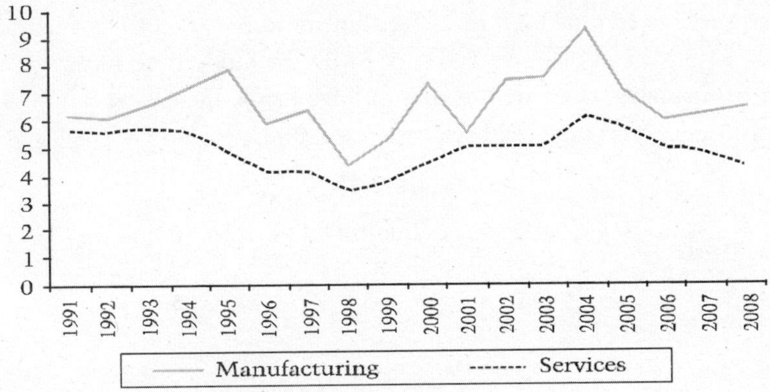

Note: The ratios are a weighted average across firms.

Source: Korea Investors Service, Inc., data. Quoted from Kim and Lee (2009).

Figure 2.12

Ratio of Total Borrowings to Total Assets: Manufacturing vs. Services (%)

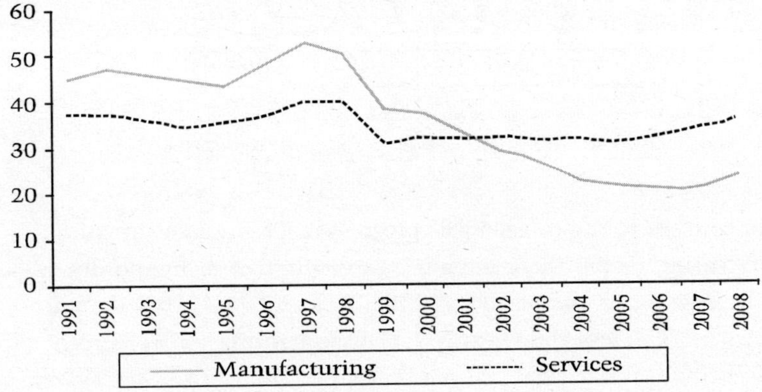

Note: The ratios are a weighted average across firms.

Source: Korea Investors Service, Inc., data. Quoted from Kim and Lee (2009).

5. In our traditional services, arts, sports and recreational services were added.

Figure 2.13 shows that the IPCR of modern services had been improving since the crisis until 2007 but fell rapidly in 2008, while that of traditional services has been improving slowly during the same period. In Figure 2.14, the IPCR of traditional services are separated by firm size: both IPCRs of large firms and SMEs show some improvements, but large firms show a higher degree of improvement. Figure 2.15 shows the IPCR of large firms and SMEs in modern services. The IPCR of large firms in modern services recorded 2.0 in 1997, shot up to 6.8 in 2007 but fell back slightly to 5.3 in 2008. The IPCR of SMEs in modern services showed poorer performance compared to that of large firms, increasing from 0.9 in 1997 to 3.1 in 2005, and fell back to 1.5 in 2008.

Figure 2.13

IPCR in Services: Traditional vs. Modern

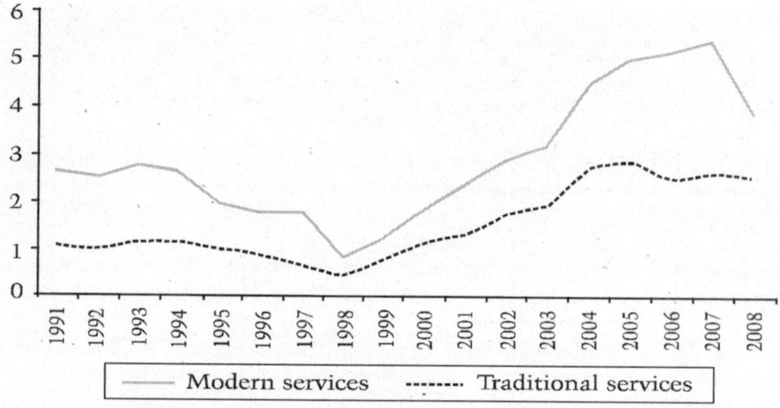

Note: The ratios are a weighted average across firms.

Source: Korea Investors Service, Inc., data. Quoted from Kim and Lee (2009).

In contrast to the considerable progress made in the restructuring of the manufacturing sector, there remain a large number of financially unviable firms in services, as measured in IPCR (Table 2.2). In 2008, the number of firms with IPCR less than 1 was 7,470, accounting for 42 percent of the sample firms. In particular, the proportion of such firms was significantly higher in services than in manufacturing. Among the total number of troubled firms, 3,941 were in services (excluding construction), accounting for 49 percent of total services, while there were 2,763 troubled firms in

Figure 2.14

IPCR in Traditional Services: Large Firms vs. SMEs

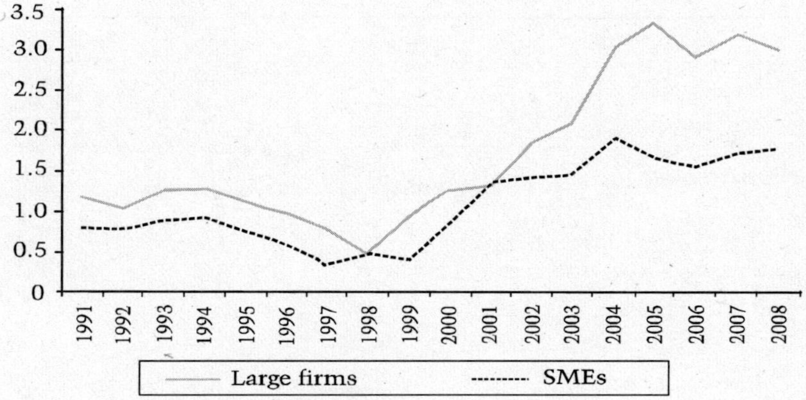

Note: The ratios are a weighted average across firms.

Source: Korea Investors Service, Inc., data. Quoted from Kim and Lee (2009).

Figure 2.15

IPCR in Modern Services: Large Firms vs. SMEs

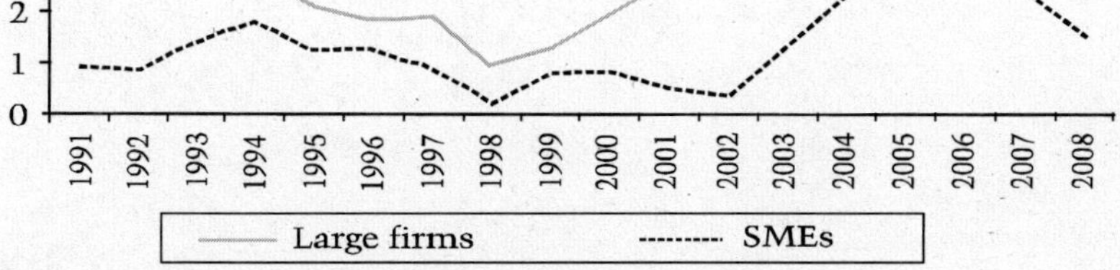

Note: The ratios are a weighted average across firms.

Source: Korea Investors Service, Inc., data. Quoted from Kim and Lee (2009).

manufacturing, 34 percent of the group. While an IPCR of less than 1 for a single year may reflect only a short-term liquidity problem; the same lasting longer, say, three consecutive years, may point to severe credit risks, a sign of

Table 2.2(a)

Share of Firms with IPCR Less than 1

(Number of firms, trillion won)

		IPCR < 1		
		2008	Two Consecutive Years (2007, 2008)	Three Consecutive Years (2006, 2007, 2008)
Manufacturing	No. of firms (8,182)	2,763 [34%]	1,435 [18%]	850 [10%]
	Borrowings (230 trillion won)	71 [31%]	38 [17%]	29 [13%]
Construction	No. of firms (1,809)	766 [42%]	443 [25%]	207 [11%]
	Borrowings (69 trillion won)	31 [45%]	20 [29%]	11 [17%]
Services	No. of firms (8,029)	3,941 [49%]	2,707 [34%]	1,605 [21%]
	Borrowings (286 trillion won)	162 [57%]	117 [41%]	61 [21%]
Traditional services	No. of firms (3,571)	1,450 [41%]	939 [26%]	607 [17%]
	Borrowings (102 trillion won)	46 [45%]	28 [27%]	21 [20%]
(large)	No. of firms (479)	154 [32%]	101 [21%]	69 [14%]
	Borrowings (62 trillion won)	23 [37%]	11 [17%]	9 [14%]
(SMEs)	No. of firms (3,092)	1,296 [42%]	838 [27%]	538 [17%]
	Borrowings (40 trillion won)	23 [57%]	17 [42%]	12 [30%]
Modern services	No. of firms (1,712)	721 [42%]	437 [26%]	250 [15%]
	Borrowings (44 trillion won)	16 [36%]	10 [23%]	4 [10%]
(large)	No. of firms (350)	96 [27%]	55 [16%]	36 [10%]
	Borrowings (29 trillion won)	6 [21%]	2 [8%]	2 [5%]
(SMEs)	No. of firms (1,362)	625 [46%]	382 [28%]	214 [16%]
	Borrowings (15 trillion won)	10 [66%]	8 [50%]	3[18%]
Total	No. of firms (18,024)	7,470 [42%]	4,585 [25%]	2,662 [15%]
	Borrowings (586 trillion won)	264 [45%]	175 [30%]	101 [17%]

Note: Figures in parentheses indicate the share of firms and the share of total borrowings in each group.
Source: Quoted from Kim and Lee (2009).

Table 2.2(b)

Share of Firms with IPCR < 1 in Traditional Services

(Number of firms, trillion won)

		IPCR<1		
		2008	Two Consecutive Years (2007, 2008)	Three Consecutive Years (2006, 2007, 2008)
Retail & wholesale trade	No. of firms (2,018)	611 [30 %]	336 [17%]	203 [10%]
	Borrowings (42 trillion won)	12 [28%]	7 [17%]	4 [10%]
Transportation	No.of firms (688)	305 [44%]	185 [27%]	111 [16%]
	Borrowings (41 trillion won)	22 [53%]	10 [24%]	9 [21%]
Restaurants and Hotels	No. of firms (287)	183 [64%]	143 [50%]	107 [37%]
	Borrowings (7 trillion won)	4 [59%]	4 [48%]	3 [37%]
Education	No. of firms (64)	29 [45%]	12 [19%]	6 [9%]
	Borrowings (0.4 trillion won)	0.2 [40%]	0.1 [26%]	0.04 [10%]
Healthcare and Social works	No. of firms (10)	8 [80%]	4 [40%]	2 [20%]
	Borrowings (0.1 trillion won)	0.1 [81%]	0.003 [3%]	0.00 [0%]
Other community, social & personal service	No. of firms (85)	46 [54%]	31 [36%]	17 [20%]
	Borrowings (0.7 trillion won)	0.4 [60%]	0.3 [42%]	0.2 [28%]
Arts, sports and leisure	No. of firms (417)	266 [64%]	227 [54%]	160 [38%]
	Borrowings (10 trillion won)	7 [73%]	7 [65%]	5 [49%]

Note: Figures in parentheses indicate the share of firms and the share of total borrowings in each group.

Source: Quoted from Kim and Lee (2009).

a "distressed firm."[6] In 2006–2008, 2,662 firms recorded IPCR of less than 1 for three consecutive years, accounting for 15 percent of the total sample firms. The share of "distressed firms" was significantly higher for services (21%) than manufacturing (10%).

The above figures imply that a sizable number of SMEs have been facing insolvency risks in traditional services, even in modern services. These numbers clearly indicate that further restructuring is critically necessary, especially centering on SMEs.

Table 2.2(c)

Share of Firms with IPCR Less than 1 in Modern Services

		IPCR < 1		
		2008	*Two Consecutive Years (2007, 2008)*	*Three Consecutive Years (2006, 2007, 2008)*
Communication & Information	No. of firms (1,006)	425 [42 %]	277 [28%]	173 [17%]
	Borrowings (28 trillion won)	7 [25%]	4 [16%]	3 [11%]
Professional, Science and Technical	No. of firms (457)	206 [45%]	110 [24%]	56 [12%]
	Borrowings (10 trillion won)	4 [44%]	3 [28%]	1 [8%]
Business services	No. of firms (172)	53 [31%]	30 [17%]	12 [7%]
	Borrowings (3 trillion won)	2 [67%]	0.3 [14%]	0.1 [5%]

Note: Figures in parentheses indicate the share of firms and the share of total borrowings in each group.
Source: Quoted from Kim and Lee (2009).

Why is there Low Productivity in Service Industries?

There are a number of sector-specific reasons for the poor performance of Korea's service industries, but here we concentrate on five reasons that we consider to be of major importance.

First, there are numerous regulations that in effect act as entry barriers and thus restrain productivity growth. Among 543 service

6. According to an empirical study (Hahn *et al.*, 2000), having IPCRs of less than 1 for three consecutive years was found to be a good predictor of business failures.

industries in Korea, 32 percent of them have entry barriers (OECD, 2008). Entry regulations such as a certification system breed rent-seeking activities. For example, Korea's population per lawyer is the largest among OECD nations, being four times higher than the OECD average. Moreover, according to *Doing Business 2009*, start-ups in Korea experience difficulties such as time consumption and costs, making it the 126th out of 178 economies in the world. Such regulations hinder competition, entry, and innovation and encourage at the same time rent-seeking behavior and low productivity.

Second, Korea's service sector is composed mostly of small firms. In 2006, 89.3 percent of the firms in service industries had fewer than five employees, which is far greater than Japan with 62.6 percent, although both countries have a similar industrial structure (SERI, 2009). Particularly, in transportation (95.4%), wholesale & retail (90.3%), and restaurant and hotels (90.6%) small firms with fewer than five employees were most typical.

Third, equity is emphasized in social services such as medical and education, thereby further making it difficult to alleviate regulations to develop into a separate industry.

Fourth, due to restrictions on inbound FDI in services, competition is weak and spillovers in technology from multinational companies are lacking. The share of inbound FDI in services is 49 percent, which is 27th among 30 OECD countries. Foreign companies in Korea's services industries account for only 8 percent of Korea's total revenue and 4 percent of total employment, while OECD averages are 19 percent and 10 percent, respectively.

Fifth, the most important factor behind the low productivity in services is the prolonged extensive government protection of SMEs, which has restricted competition and thus delayed necessary restructuring. An unintended consequence of such protective policy has been the loss of their competitiveness in the industries that are dominated by SMEs. (As of 2005, SMEs accounted for 88 percent of total employment and 82 percent of total value added[7] in the service sector.)

---

7. In contrast, in manufacturing, SMEs account for almost 50 percent in manufacturing production and sales (Korea Federation of Small and Medium Business, 2009).

SME Policies and their Effect on Service Industries

Korea conducted industrial policy in the 1960s and 1970s with government support going mostly to manufacturing at first to spur exports and then to support the drive toward expanding heavy and chemical industries (HCIs). In 1970 and 1980, for instance, the manufacturing sector received 46 percent and 54 percent of total bank loans, while the service sector received 29 percent and 24 percent, respectively, in those two years (Cho and Kim, 1995).

Starting in the 1980s, as the country was well into establishing HCIs and as political democratization increased the demand for social equity, an equitable distribution of income, and more balanced growth, SMEs were placed high on the list for government support.[8] Such government policy changes toward social equity and SMEs were brought about by changes in the administration. In 1980, after the fall of the Park Chung-Hee administration, the Constitution was revised to include: "the government must protect and nurture SMEs and their business activities" (Article 124 Clause 2).[9] The government protection of SMEs has been strengthened by the democratization pledge of June 29, 1987. The most crucial element underlying political democratization is in Article 119, Clause 2 of the Korean Constitution, which states:

> "[T]he state may regulate and coordinate economic affairs in order to maintain the balanced growth and stability of the national economy, to ensure proper distribution of income, to prevent the domination of the market and the abuse of economic power and to democratize the economy through harmony among the economic agents."
>
> (Quoted from Jwa and Yoon, 2004)

---

8. Directed credit programs to support SMEs were available even in the 60s and 70s. First, the state-owned Industrial Bank of Korea (established in 1961) specialized in SME-lending with funds mobilized from government borrowing, deposits, and debentures. Second, the Korea Credit Guarantee Fund (KODIT) was established in 1976 with capital funds contributed by the government and financial institutions. However, the share of SME loans of total policy loans was not very significant in these periods, as the basic thrust of industrial policy was structured to promote HCIs, which required large-scale investment from large firms (Cho and Kim, 1995).
9. Before this change, the constitution (Article 102 Clause 2) focused on promoting organizations that facilitate self-help for farmers, fishermen, and SMEs.

Such emphasis on egalitarianism in the Constitution led to the 1995 overhaul of the 1966 Basic Law of SMEs. The revised Basic Law specifically pinpoints policies to promote SMEs in the areas of: (1) facilitating start-ups, (2) advanced technology, (3) marketing, (4) restructuring SMEs, (5) protecting business domains, (6) nurturing regional SMEs, etc. The SME policy in Korea is like a sanctuary that no one or no administration is willing to disturb (Lee, 2004).

As of now, the extensive government protection of SMEs comprises of various forms: (1) supported by 163 subsidy programs in 2007 (Table 2.3), totaling 0.7 percent of GDP; (2) 50 percent reduction in corporate income tax compared with that levied on larger firms; and (3) considerable government financial support to SMEs via policy loans, credit guarantees, and venture capital investment.

By year-end of 2008, state-owned banks provided a total of 32.8 trillion won in loans to SMEs (24.2 trillion won from the Industrial Bank of Korea and 8.6 trillion won from the Korea Development Bank). The Small Business Corporation (SBC) also provided 2.9 trillion won in policy loans. BoK also operates a discount policy to support SMEs, the so-called "aggregate ceiling loans," interest rates on which are lower than market rates. This BoK's lending facility has a ceiling on its rediscounting credits to commercial banks and allocates quotas to individual banks according to their performance in supporting SMEs. More importantly, by year-end of 2008 the government-run credit guarantee funds were supplied through KODIT (Korea Credit Guarantee Fund: 30.4 trillion won), KOTEC (Korea Technology Credit Guarantee Fund: 12.6 trillion won), and Regional Credit Guarantee Funds (6.0 trillion won). Government credit guarantees increased to 62.7 trillion won by August 2009; credit guarantee funds covered about 16 percent of total loans outstanding to SMEs. Also, the government's support of 3.7 trillion won was poured into venture capital investment through SBC.

Despite the extensive government assistance to SMEs, there has been no significant improvement in their performance. In fact, their performance was weakened due to dampened competitive pressure along with delayed restructuring. In particular, credit guarantees have had the least positive effect on firm performances, suggesting that they have been

Table 2.3

Programs to Assist SMEs (in billion Won) in 2007

	Outlays	*No. of Programs*	*Selected Program*
Small and Medium Business Administration	4,074	65	Restructuring and start-up support Stable operation support Regional SME support Technology development support Venture company support
Ministry of Commerce, Industry and Energy	1,485	44	Industrial technology development Modernization of distribution networks Activation of industrial complexes Energy-saving support
Ministry of Labor	815	22	Workplace accident prevention Workplace environment improvement Vocational training support
Ministry of Information and Communication	236	4	ICT equipment investment support Technology development support Multi-media industry support Software development support
Ministry of Environment	131	5	Anti-pollution facility support Environmental technology development support Recycling development support
Intellectual Property Office	63	4	Technology evaluation support
Ministry of Agriculture and Forestry	45	5	Rice-processing factory support Agricultural product processing Agricultural machine product support
Ministry of Maritime Affairs and Fisheries	44	5	Marine product distribution support Fishing net support
Ministry of Health and Welfare	15	1	New drug development support
Ministry Culture and Tourism	14	3	Film promotion fund support Sporting goods development support
Defense Acquisition Program Administration	5	2	Defense industry R&D support
Ministry of Construction and Transportation	5	2	Construction technology innovation support
Ministry of Science and Technology	1	1	Technology development support
Total	6,933	163	

Source: Presidential Commission on SMEs (2007), quoted from OECD (2008).

used, in part, to rescue unviable firms. According to Kang (2005), the performance of the companies receiving credit guarantees has deteriorated in profitability, and their performance has been significantly worse than that of companies without guarantees. Furthermore, as the guarantee period increases, profitability tends to deteriorate, especially during the post-crisis period (Figure 2.16). In addition, according to Kang and Hyung-Kwon (2006) and Kim (2005), who examined the effects of general SME financial support policy and the government lending programs, there is no significant difference in profitability between the group receiving the benefit and the group that do not. These empirical results show clearly that the policies supporting SMEs have improved neither financial market efficiency nor their profitability. Indeed, these policies are delaying the exit of "zombie" firms and hindering the entry of new innovative firms.

Figure 2.16

Operating Profits to Sales Ratio by Guarantee Periods (%)

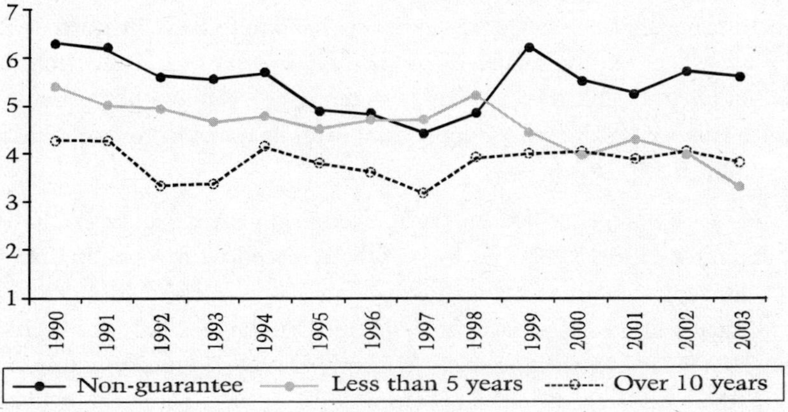

Source: Kang (2005).

Conclusion

One thing Korea has learned from the current global crisis is that to sustain economic growth it needs to diversify where it exports as well as what it exports. It has relied too much on US markets and on manufacturing exports. The collapse of US markets as the demander of last resort combined with inefficiencies in Korea's service industries has had a severe negative impact on its real economy. Fortunately for Korea, China may turn into the largest final destination of Korea's manufacturing exports, substituting the role that the US has played for the past four decades. Whether this prognosis will turn out to be true will depend on whether or not China itself changes its growth strategy from an export-driven to a domestic demand-driven one, a change that is beyond the control of the Korean government. What, however, Korea can do on its own is to diversify its export structure by helping its service industries become globally competitive.

Korea now has some world-class manufacturing firms such as Hyundai and Samsung that compete successfully with other multinational corporations of the world. In services, however, Korea has yet to produce enterprises that can compete in the global market. There may be various reasons for this poor state of Korea's service industries but one of these reasons is, we have argued, government policies that have protected SMEs for too long. These policies have succeeded in protecting SMEs but not in transforming them into globally competitive enterprises. In other words, they have kept the protected firms in their infant stage, hindering their maturation into globally competitive enterprises. Here we offer one policy change that we believe will be more successful in transforming such infants into competitive adults.

We propose that the current credit guarantee scheme, which guarantees existing SMEs indefinitely, be replaced with a policy that sets out a gradual reduction in guarantees. If the firms succeed in meeting the target they will continue to receive specified guarantees but at a declining rate. This means that guarantees are mostly for young promising firms that are in the early stage of their operation with no or a short credit history. These firms would hopefully turn Korea's service industries into leading-edge exporters and sustain its economic growth.

References

Eichengreen, Barry and Poonam Gupta (2009). "The Two Waves of Service-Sector Growth", *Working Paper #235*. Indian Council for Research on International Relation.

Cho, Yoon-Je and Joon-Kyung Kim (1995). "Credit Policies and Industrialization of Korea", *World Bank Discussion Papers* No. 286. Washington, D.C.

Hahn, Chin Hee, Kang Dong Soo, Lim Youngjae and Yang Jeong Sam (2000). *Firm Failures and Re-Crafting of Restructuring Policy* (in Korean). Seoul: KDI.

Jwa, Sung-Hee and Yong Yoon (2004). "A New Look at Development Economics through Korea's Experience: 'United We Stand, Divided We Fall'—Truth or Fallacy?", Paper presented at the 2004 Korea Development Institute(KDI)-Korea-America Economic Association (KAEA) Conference on *Current Economic Issues of Korea*. August 10.

Kang, Dong-Soo (2005). *Distress of Small and Medium-sized Enterprises and Role of Credit Guarantee Scheme in Restructuring: The Case of Korea*. Seoul: KDI.

Kang, Jong-Ku and Chung Hyung-Kwon (2006). "An Analysis of the Effect of Policy Support for Small Medium Enterprises (in Korean)", *Financial and Economic Research*. Seoul: Institute for Monetary and Economic Research, The Bank of Korea.

Kim, Hyeon-Wook (2005). "The Profitability Improving Effects of Korean SME Policy Lending Programs (in Korean)", *Korea Development Research No. 27-2*. Seoul: KDI.

Kim, Joo-Hoon and MoonJoong Tcha (2007). "Advancement of the Service Industry: What do we Need? (in Korean)", *Research Monograph* 2007–04. Seoul: KDI.

Kim, Joon-Kyung and Chung H. Lee (2009a). "Between Two Whales: Korea's Choice in the Post-Crisis Era", in Ashley Tellis, Andrew Marble and Travis Tanner (eds.), *Strategic Asia 2009-2010: Economic Meltdown and Geopolitical Stability*. The National Bureau of Asian Research.

————. (2009b). "Restructuring the Korean Economy in the Post-Crisis Era", Paper presented at *New Growth Strategies for Asian Economies*. Kuala Lumpur, Malaysia. November 24–25.

Korea Federation of Small and Medium Business (2009). *Statistics of Small & Medium Enterprises for 2009*. Press Releases. Seoul: Kbiz.

Lee, Byung-Ki (2004). "Global Competition and New Direction of Policies for Small and Medium Enterprises (in Korean)", *Policy Research Report 2004–07*. Seoul: KERI.

OECD (2008). *Korea Economic Survey*. Paris: OECD.

SERI (2009). "Corporate and Government Tasks for the Development of Service Industry (in Korean)", *CEO Information No.* 706. Seoul: Korea.

3 Financial Sector in India

Challenges, Opportunities and Cooperation with Korea

TAMAL BANDYOPADHYAY

Introduction

Shinhan Bank, the only Korean bank to have branches in India, some time back got the nod of the local banking regulator to open its third branch in Vellore, in Tamil Nadu, which houses about 150 subcontractors of the Korean car maker Hyundai Motors. Till now, it has been operating two branches in New Delhi and India's commercial capital Mumbai. Set up in 1897 and headquartered in Seoul, the oldest financial intermediary in Korea, Shinhan Bank will take nearly 14 years to set up its third branch in Asia's third-largest economy. It opened its Delhi branch in May 1996, shortly after changing its name, and Mumbai in December 2006. It was formerly known as Chohung Bank and changed its name to Shinhan Bank in April 2006.

Another Korean bank, Woori Bank, plans to open a branch in the southern city Chennai after getting approval from the Financial Services Commission, South Korean government's top financial regulator. The country's second-largest lender is waiting for the Reserve Bank of India's nod. Chennai is an ideal location for business for any Korean bank as a Hyundai Motors factory and 50 of its affiliates are located there. Two other players, Korea Exchange Bank and Hana Bank, are planning to expand their liaison offices into local branches before the end of this year.

India seems to be emerging as the hottest destination for Korean banks after the two countries agreed in August 2009 on the Comprehensive Economic Partnership Agreement (CEPA). Under the accord, Korean banks can open up to 10 branches until 2013 after getting approval from Indian regulators.

CEPA was signed on August 7, 2009, ratified in November and became effective from January 2010. Negotiations for the partnership agreement had started in March 2006 and concluded in September 2008, just around the time when an unprecedented economic crisis gripped the world. It consists of six agreements to open up trade in goods, services and customs besides ensuring gradual liberalization in the financial sector. For instance, India has committed to unlimited access of Korean firms in asset management, pension fund management, custodial, depository and trust services. Currently, there is only one Korean entity in the asset management space–Mirae Asset Global Investment (India) Pvt Ltd. It is a very small player, managing just about Rs. 300 crore in the Rs. 7 trillion Indian asset management industry.

The agreement also underlines that India will give "favorable consideration" to the applications for establishment of branches by Korean banks—up to 10 applications over four years. Licenses for ATMs will not be included within the 10 licenses for branches. India also promised Korea entry into the insurance segment where foreign direct investment is currently restricted to 26 percent. The CEPA has eliminated tariffs on 93 percent of Korea's tariff lines and 85 percent of India's tariff lines over 10 years and is expected to boost bilateral trade by as much as $3.3 billion annually. After its implementation, the trade volumes between India and Korea in 2010 increased by 10 percent from the previous year to a historic high of $10.7 billion.

In addition to tariff reduction, South Korea will be able to move into various industrial sectors of the Indian economy, such as food processing, textiles, garments, chemicals, metals and machinery. The deal also opens the service and investment sector, with India accepting South Korean investments in its telecommunications, accounting, medical and advertising markets, as well as allowing South Korean financial firms in the investment market. South Korea expects massive inflows of information technology workers, engineers and English teachers as both sides agreed to allow temporary migration of professional workers. The bilateral trade can be boosted even further by increasing the range of products that are in the list of items that are exempted from duty or have reduced tariff on them.

South Korea is one of the top 10 investing countries in India. South Korean business groups such as LG, Samsung and Hyundai have established their presence in the Indian market. The transportation industry, fuels (power and oil refinery), electrical equipment (computer software and electronics), chemicals (other than fertilizer) and commercial, office and household equipment are the major sectors that have attracted Korean investments. Indian firms have also made their presence felt in South Korea. The acquisition of Daewoo Commercial Vehicles by Tata Motors is an example of this phenomenon.

India's \$1.2 trillion economy expanded 8.67 percent in the first nine months of fiscal 2011 ending March, the second fastest among major economies. Indeed high inflation is a worry and it is highly unlikely that India will be able to sustain the growth momentum but the fact remains that despite monetary tightening (to fight inflation), Indian economy will grow at a higher rate than the rest of the world, except for China, and banks will see big business opportunity here as more and more consumers raise bank loans to buy cars and homes and Indian corporations expand their business and acquire firms.

According to the Financial Supervisory Service or FSS, South Korea's integrated financial regulator that examines and supervises financial institutions under the broad oversight of the FSC, Korean banks' overseas operations suffered a 7.8 percent decline in their 2009 earnings from the year before on increased loan-loss reserves and squeezed commission income. The combined net income of 93 foreign outlets—54 branches and 39 subsidiaries—run by 11 local banks came to \$286.4 million in 2009, compared with \$310.5 million the previous year. Indian banks' overseas operations too were affected as an unprecedented credit crunch hit the global financial system but there was no impact on their domestic operations. They remained safe, well capitalized and there was no problem on the liquidity front. Indeed the government has been infusing fresh capital in some of the state-run banks in phases but in no way did they need to be bailed out. It is being done to cushion against any future shocks. India's state-run banks account for close to 80 percent of the banking industry. Both South Korea and India emerged relatively unscathed from the 2008 global meltdown.

The collapse of the US investment bank Lehman Brothers Holdings Inc. in September 2008 that led to an unprecedented credit crunch in the global financial system was the symptom of an ailment that was first seen in the US housing market. A lot of imprudent loans were given to borrowers who could not afford to repay them. These faulty loans were sliced, mixed with good loans and sold to other banks across the globe. Banks, insurance firms, pension funds, and even state governments bought those rated assets as there was plenty of liquidity and interest rates were low. The bubble burst when interest rates started climbing and house prices started falling. The problem was magnified with the proliferation of derivatives on these loans that were affected by the meltdown in the values of the underlying assets. While most central banks looked the other way and waited for the bubble to burst, the Reserve Bank of India went ahead and pricked the bubble.

Korean Response to Financial Turmoil

On its part, the Korean government too had done its bit to protect the banking system from the impact of the global meltdown and expand the credit supply capacity of banks. The government announced plans to mobilize 20 trillion won and has used the fund to buy subordinated bonds, hybrid loans and redeemable preferred stocks. It also established a 40 trillion won corporate restructuring fund at Korea Asset Management Corp to purchase bad debt and support the restructuring of firms. This fund was modeled on the Non-Performing Loan Resolution Fund, created during the 1997 financial crisis. The non-performing loan ratio of Korean banks in March 2010 was 1.45 percent. The Bank of Korea tried to respond to the financial and economic turmoil through diverse policy instruments. Among other things, it reduced the base rate; broadened eligible collaterals and counterparties for open market operations; provided liquidity to financial institutions subscribing to the Bond Market Stabilization Fund; entered into swap arrangements with central banks of major countries; eased restrictions on foreign currency loans; and supplied foreign currency liquidity to financial institutions.

How did the RBI Ring-fence the Indian Banks from the Turmoil?

A cautious and conservative Reserve Bank has never allowed Indian banks to take excessive risk. The work started a decade back in 2000 when the RBI conducted a stress test of the banks' investment portfolios in an increasing interest rate scenario. That was the first test of its kind to assess the vulnerability of the Indian banking sector in a rising interest rate scenario. With the non-performing assets rising as many corporations turned defaulters, banks were mostly buying government bonds at the beginning of this century. This so-called "narrow" banking was apparently safe as the government would not default but banks were running interest rate risks. For bonds, prices and yields move in opposite directions. In a rising interest rate scenario, banks need to book mark to market or MTM losses. MTM is an accounting practice of valuing the investment portfolio in accordance with the current market price and not the price at which the bonds are bought. So when the yields rise and prices fall, banks need to set aside money or provide for the erosion in the value of the bonds. This affects banks' profits.

The yield on the benchmark 10-year bond dropped to its historic low of 4.97 percent in October 2003 but well before that, in January 2002, the RBI advised banks to meet the adverse impact of interest rate risk by building up an investment fluctuation reserve, or IFR.

(1) When a reversal of rate movement started in late 2004, it helped banks absorb the impact of rising interest rates and MTM losses. In other words, banks used the IFR to take care of the provisions they needed for the MTM losses. Similarly, the Indian central bank also sensed the real estate bubble ahead of other regulators. In June 2005, it directed banks to have a board-mandated policy in respect of their real estate exposure limits, collaterals and margins.

(2) It also increased the risk weight on banks' exposure to commercial real estate from 100 percent to 125 percent in July 2005 and 150 percent in April 2006, to discourage them from aggressively disbursing real estate loans, as higher risk weight called for more capital and made money more expensive. This

discourages lenders as their cost goes up. For instance, with the capital adequacy ratio pegged at 9 percent, for a loan that carries 100 percent risk weight, banks need Rs. 9 for every Rs. 100 lent. But when the risk weight goes up to 150 percent, they need Rs. 13.5 capital for every Rs. 100 lent. Similarly, the risk weight on housing loans to individuals against mortgage of properties was also increased from 50 percent to 75 percent in December 2004.

(3) And not housing loans alone. In an economy which was showing distinct signs of overheating in certain pockets and banks' consumer credit portfolio was growing at a fast pace, the RBI also increased the risk weight for consumer credit and capital market exposures from 100 percent to 125 percent. Unable to rein in the scorching loan growth in the real estate sector, personal loans, credit card receivables, and loans against shares, and apprehending a higher default rate in such loans, the RBI also progressively raised the provisions for standard assets in phases—in November 2005, May 2006 and January 2007.

(4) These loans now attract 2 percent provisions for standard assets, while loans to agriculture and small and medium enterprises continue to attract 0.25 percent provisions and all other loans 0.40 percent. The RBI has also clamped down on inter-bank liabilities and banks are not allowed to borrow more than 200 percent of their net worth or capital and reserves from other banks. The limit for exceptionally well-capitalized banks is 300 percent of their net worth.

(5) At the same time, non-banking finance companies as well as banks and financial institutions were not encouraged to securitize their exposure and create more liquidity. A February 2006 RBI norm on securitization, in fact, virtually killed the market as securitization does not bring down capital requirement any more.

(6) Finally, the RBI has resorted to strong moral suasion to dampen banks' appetite for risk. They now closely monitor unhedged foreign currency exposures of their corporate clients and do not dare venture into selling exotic derivatives to help firms tide over currency fluctuations. As a result, a sophisticated credit

derivatives market and financial innovation in India are still at an embryonic stage, but the country is planning to open up this segment slowly.

Baby Steps toward Reforms

India has taken some baby steps toward financial sector liberalization after the Indian financial system demonstrated its strength and resilience and stayed unaffected by the global meltdown. It expanded the scope of currency futures by allowing stock exchanges to offer future contracts in pairs of euro-rupee, Japanese yen-rupee and pound sterling-rupee in addition to dollar-rupee, and introduced interest rate futures and repurchase or repo corporate bonds. Besides, it also plans to allow banks to offer vanilla cross-currency options on spot US dollar/rupee exchange rate to resident Indians. It has recently formulated the guidelines for trading of currency options. Once this is done, importers and exporters will be allowed to write and sell put options, both in foreign currency-rupee and cross-currencies and earn a premium on them. This will expand the existing menu of exchange traded hedging tools. It is also in the process of introducing plain credit default swaps, or CDS, for corporate bonds, enabling firms to hedge against any possible default by a bond issuer. CDS is a derivative used to offset risks in debt markets. It allows creditors to insure themselves against the possibility that a borrower might default.

The RBI has put up the draft guidelines on its website and invited public comments. This is the third time the RBI has come out with a draft report on CDS; the first was in 2003 and second in 2007. The introduction of CDS got stalled after a credit crunch hit the global financial system in the wake of the collapse of the US investment bank, Lehman Brothers Holdings Inc., in 2008. CDS was blamed for the crisis and the near-collapse of the largest insurance firm in the world, American International Group Inc. Investors were trading CDS as stand-alone instruments and the trade proliferated exponentially. Like all derivatives that reflect the value of an underlying instrument, CDS reflects the value of a bond or a loan. If an investor in a company's bond wants to buy an insurance against a possible default by the issuer, the investor could buy CDS for a price, technically called a CDS spread. The CDS seller, in turn, guarantees to pay the buyer a predetermined amount if the bond issuer defaults on repayment.

To avoid inherent risks, the RBI has suggested that users cannot purchase CDS without having an underlying exposure and the protection can be bought only to the extent (both in terms of quantum and tenure) of such underlying risk. This means CDS cannot be used as a pure trading instrument. The category of users would consist of commercial banks, primary dealers, NBFCs, mutual funds, insurance companies, housing finance companies, provident funds and listed corporations.

The Unfinished Agenda

Of course there are many more things to be done. Successive Union budgets have made many promises on financial sector reforms but very few of them have been kept. Some of the financial sector reform proposals are a decade old and the government's record in implementing them is abysmal.

To begin with, paring the government's stake in public sector banks is one issue that has featured in the wish list of successive finance ministers, but has not moved beyond that. Under the existing norms, the government's stake in public sector banks cannot fall below 51 percent. In 2000, Yashwant Sinha, then finance minister of the Bharatiya Janata Party-led National Democratic Alliance government, made a statement of intent to lower the government's holding in public sector banks to 33 percent. The logic was impeccable: public sector banks should be owned in equal proportion by the government, the Indian public and foreign entities. The ultimate plan was to pare the government stake to 33 percent and raise the foreign ownership limit to the same level from 20 percent.

Indeed, government ownership is a great strength for the banking sector and this was proved in the 2008 crisis but the Indian government does not seem to have any choice other than paring its stake as it does not have the money to keep the banks well capitalized. Banks need huge capital to meet the demand for loans in the world's second fastest growing economy. If the government does not pare its stake, it will stunt the growth of banks, companies and the economy.

Currently, foreign ownership in public sector banks is capped at 20 percent, and for private banks, it is 74 percent. Within the 74 percent limit, foreign direct investment cannot exceed 49 percent. Ditto in the case of portfolio investment. Also under norms, any bank that has more than 50 percent foreign holding is considered a foreign-owned bank. The 20 percent limit on foreign ownership in public sector banks does not seem to make much sense as under corporate law, an investor needs at least a 26 percent stake to play a meaningful role in running a company. So, the government can raise it to at least 25 percent.

Foreign investment in Indian insurance companies is another contentious issue. Currently it is pegged at 26 percent and the government has promised to raise it to 49 percent. Here again, the rise in stake would not make any difference to the role of foreign investors as far as the management of the insurance firms is concerned, but higher foreign stakes will ensure higher capital infusion which they desperately need. Yet another pending issue is the cap on voting rights in banks. Investors do not have voting rights in accordance with their holdings, and, hence, any rise in the foreign holding pattern will not make any radical difference. Successive finance ministers have promised to lift the cap on voting rights, but nothing has happened so far. In private banks, voting rights are capped at 10 percent and in public sector banks at 1 percent. One of the reasons could be the banking regulator's lack of comfort with the idea as an overseas group may end up wielding more power by holding stakes through different firms. For instance, Temasek Holdings Pvt. Ltd and the Government of Singapore Investment Corp. Pte Ltd are both government-owned and if the cap on voting rights is lifted, together they can enjoy substantial power if they hold stakes in a bank. Successive finance ministers announced the removal of the 10 percent cap on voting rights in private sector banks but the necessary amendment to the Banking Regulation Act, 1949 is still awaited. A Bill to make the amendment has recently been tabled in the Indian Parliament.

Larger Role for Foreign Banks

While none of these issues has been addressed yet, the Indian banking regulator is set to open up the sector for more private players as well as foreign banks. Seven years back the RBI had laid down a road map for foreign banks in India and said it would review the ownership norms in 2009, raising expectations that it would encourage a larger play for foreign banks. But it got delayed because of the Lehman crisis. In January 2011 the banking regulator released a discussion paper on its new policy, seeking public comments. The paper has proposed "near-national" treatment for foreign banks provided they opt for local incorporation. Currently, foreign banks are operating as branches of their parents.

The discussion paper has suggested almost doubling the role of foreign banks in the Indian banking system, saying it will "incentivize" foreign players to operate through the wholly-owned subsidiary route in the country. All new overseas entrants in the Indian banking space will have to locally incorporate themselves, and existing players, particularly the "systemically important" ones, will be encouraged to go in for local incorporation and act as subsidiaries of foreign parents, the RBI said. Systemically important banks are those whose assets become 0.25 percent of the total assets of all commercial banks as on March 31, the central bank said. Going by this definition, eight foreign banks, including Citibank NA, HSBC Holdings Plc and Standard Chartered Bank, fall in this category.

As an incentive to set up wholly-owned subsidiaries, the RBI said it might allow them to raise rupee resources in the form of non-equity capital, adding that it will extend a "less restrictive branch expansion policy" to foreign players by allowing them to operate in semi-urban areas. Noting that it may not be possible to mandate conversion of existing players into subsidiaries, the RBI said "the regulatory expectation would be that those foreign banks which meet the conditions and thresholds mandated for subsidiary presence for new entrants...would opt for converting their branches into wholly owned subsidiaries".

Once the policy is in place, the RBI said it will be more liberal in its branch licensing policy, but it is difficult to award "full national treatment" to foreign banks because this "could lead to unintended consequences for the banking sector". They will then be treated virtually on par with their domestic peers in terms of branch expansion regarding which the banking regulator has all along been following a restrictive policy. Currently, there are 34 foreign banks in India and collectively they have at least 310 branches, 0.43 percent of the 71,998-strong branch network across the nation. As of March 31, 2010, the share of foreign banks in total banking assets stood at 10.52 percent, out of which that of the top five was 7.12 percent, the RBI said. Among these, Citibank has 1.6 percent of the total assets of the banking system, while that of HSBC is 1.52 percent and Standard Chartered Bank is 1.5 percent.

Under a 1997 World Trade Organization (WTO) agreement, the total assets of foreign banks in India cannot exceed 15 percent of the total banking system. But the RBI, in its discussion paper, has changed the limit in terms of capital and reserves of banks. As per this, when the capital and reserves of foreign banks in India exceed 25 percent of the capital of the banking system, the regulator will put restrictions on the further entry of new banks and branch expansion, and will make it mandatory to get prior approval for capital infusion, the RBI said. Under the WTO agreement, the RBI needs to give 12 new branch licenses to foreign banks every year, including those given to new entrants and existing players, but the Indian regulator has all along been allowing foreign banks to open more branches, going beyond its commitment, but not as many as the foreign banks want.

New Banks

India's finance minister, Pranab Mukherjee, set the ball rolling, announcing that the central bank would consider new private players, including non-banking finance companies for licenses to set up banks in his February 2010 Budget speech. This marks a clear shift in policy—from consolidation to expansion. In a country where 50 percent of the population does not have access to banking services, this is natural and, in fact, the RBI should have opened its doors earlier. Many Indian business houses cherish the dream of getting into the highly leveraged business, but the RBI had reservations as banks deal with public money and one bad apple can spoil the entire system. A banking license allows a corporation to raise cheap money from the public. Besides, no other business is as leveraged as banking, as for every Rs. 9 worth of capital, banks can build Rs. 100 worth of assets.

The RBI opened the doors for private firms in the banking space in 1993; in 2003, it allowed two more to set up shop. The last time the RBI fine-tuned the ownership norms of private banks was in 2004, when it raised the minimum capital requirement to float a bank from Rs. 100 crore to Rs. 300 crore and focused on the so-called fit-and-proper criterion for the ownership.

The history and performance of the so-called new generation private banks can guide the regulator on selecting the new players. Of the first set of 10 banks that set up shop in 1994–95, three could not survive and got merged with other banks. At least one of them was adventurous and used the bank's money to play in the stock market. In the second lot, Kotak Mahindra Finance Ltd, an NBFC, was converted into a commercial bank in 2003 and a group of private equity investors, professionals and Rabobank International Holding BV were licensed to float Yes Bank Ltd.

In 1993, when India first opened up the banking sector to private firms, the objective was to infuse competition. To a large extent that has been fulfilled, as the so-called new generation private banks such as ICICI Bank Ltd, HDFC Bank Ltd and Axis Bank have forced India's staid public sector banks to become more nimble-footed. But these banks have not been able to spread banking across the country as their focus has all along been on urban India. Apart from financial inclusion, the other critical factor is meeting the credit demand of industry as well as individuals. The Reserve Bank has released a discussion paper on capital, ownership structure, foreign shareholding norms and the business model of new private banks but stayed away from taking any position on the profile of the new players that will be given licences to run such banks.

The Indian banking regulator will soon release its draft guidelines. Going by early indications, it may change its policy and allow big industrial houses to float banks. To be able to control such banks, the RBI is making some changes in the current banking laws. Once the changes are in place, the regulator will get the power to supersede a bank's board for misconduct. It will also be able to supervise group firms of an industrial house that will be allowed to set up banks. This will enable the regulator to check the flow of money, if any, from the bank to the promoter's group firms. According to the RBI, licenses will be granted keeping in mind the larger mandate of financial inclusion apart from introducing competition. It has suggested that apart from mandated 40 percent landings to agriculture and small loans and 25 percent rural branches—the current norms that all banks need to follow—the new banks could be asked to focus on financial inclusion by opening branches in Tier 3 to Tier 6 towns with populations of less than 50,000.

Indeed, financial inclusion is a critical objective for the banking regulator as well as the Indian government. The average population coverage by a commercial bank branch in urban India was 9,400 as on June 30, 2010. In rural and semi-urban India it is far lower, 15,900. Overall, the all-India coverage by a bank branch is 13,400. This is better than 15,500 five years ago but not comparable with developed markets. It will, however, take time for the new players to set up shop. In the first stage, the RBI releases its draft guidelines inviting public comments. Following this, it will finalize the guidelines. Even after that, an external group will examine all applications and "a limited number of licenses" will be given, based on the group's recommendations.

Freeing all Rates

The other critical factor to watch out for is freeing the savings bank interest rate, the last bastion of administered rate. In fact, the next big battle on the Indian banking turf will be fought for savings bank deposits. After freeing all loan rates, the RBI is expected to give banks the freedom to decide on the interest rate they offer customers for money kept in savings accounts. It can happen sooner than later and dramatically change the cost structure of deposits for banks and put pressure on their net interest margins (NIMs). That, in turn, will have a bearing on their valuations.

NIM, a key parameter to judge a bank's operational efficiency, is loosely the margin between the yield on assets, or loans, and the cost of liabilities, or deposits. It will shrink when the cost of deposits goes up. Most bankers feel that if the savings bank rate is freed, there will be a rate war as banks compete fiercely with one another to mobilize savings deposits. Currently, the rate is fixed and hence there is no overt competition, although smarter banks always try to gather as much current and savings accounts (Casa) as possible to bring down their overall cost of deposits.

Current accounts are opened by companies, public enterprises and entrepreneurs who perform many transactions daily. These accounts are check-operated and there is no restriction on the amount or number of times that a customer can deposit or withdraw money. Banks do not pay any interest on such accounts and get the money free but they generally impose service charges for operating a current account. The customers are meant to keep a relatively higher minimum balance in such accounts, as the balance they maintain tends to be volatile because of many transactions.

A savings account is the most common operating account for non-commercial transactions. Banks generally put a ceiling on the number of withdrawals and stipulate a certain minimum balance to be maintained in such accounts. The savings account rate is 3.5 percent, but until recently banks were actually paying less because they used to pay interest only on the lowest balance kept between the 10th and the end of a month. From early 2011, banks are required to calculate the payment of interest on the daily balance kept in a savings bank account, and this will push up the cost of savings bank accounts by about 34 basis points, according to an RBI estimate. One basis point is one-hundredth of a percentage point.

The logic behind the plan to free the savings bank interest rate is not to create grounds for offering higher rates to consumers. There are, in fact, two compelling reasons to free the savings bank rate. First, an administered savings rate reduces the RBI's manoeuvrability in using interest rate signals as a monetary tool. When the Indian central bank was cutting policy rates and flooding the financial system with cheap money to fight the impact of the global crisis, the RBI found it difficult to bring the policy rate below 3.5 percent as the administered savings rate was acting as a floor for all rates. Once the savings rate is freed, it will give more flexibility to the RBI in its policy rate decisions. Second, after freeing all rates for assets (loans), the regulator cannot afford to have an administered rate for liabilities (deposits) as that will create a risk for the system in the long run as banks will face interest rate mismatches.

The Biggest Challenge

Indians have more access to mobile telephony than banking services. About 50 percent of the country's population does not have bank accounts. In rural India, the coverage among the adult population is 39 percent against 60 percent in urban India. This, of course, does not necessarily mean that 60 out of every 100 Indian adults in cities have bank accounts as many people operate multiple accounts.

Some other relevant data will help us understand the criticality of the issue. Only 5.2 percent of India's 650,000 villages have bank branches, even though 39.7 percent of the overall branch network of Indian banks, or 31,727, is in rural India. Overall, the population covered by each branch has come down and the total number of checking accounts held at commercial banks, regional rural banks, primary agricultural credit societies, urban cooperative banks and post offices has risen. Still, very few people in the low-income bracket have access to formal banking channels. Only 34 percent of people with annual earnings less than Rs. 50,000 in urban India had a bank account in 2007. The comparative figure in rural India is even lower at 26.8 percent.

The low coverage is true for other financial services as well. Barely 45 million Indians invest in mutual funds. This is about 4 percent of India's population. The comparable figure for the US is 31 percent. When it comes to direct investment in equities, the number drops drastically and only 15 million Indians hold demat (electronic share) accounts that one needs to buy stocks. Nearly 80 percent of the Indian population is without life, health and non-life insurance coverage. While life insurance penetration is 4 percent, non-life cover is even lower at 0.6 percent. The per capita spend on life and non-life insurance is just about Rs. 2,000 and Rs. 300, respectively, compared with a global average of at least Rs. 18,000 and Rs. 13,000.

The situation is slowly changing with banks aggressively opening "no-frill accounts" that require very low or zero minimum balance. However, a recent study by Skoch Development Foundation, a strategy and management consultancy, says only 11 percent of 25.1 million such basic banking accounts, opened between April 2007 and May 2009, are operational. This means the business correspondent or BC model that the Indian central bank is using to spread banking services across the country has failed. This model allows non-government organizations, self-help groups, microfinance organizations, farmers' clubs, post offices, cooperatives, panchayats and many others, including IT-enabled rural outlets of corporate entities and insurance agents, to act as intermediaries on commission. Fortunately, the banking regulator has widened the scope of the BC model by allowing even village grocery shop owners to facilitate banking services. It is exploring the possibility of using telecommunications companies and non-banking finance companies as

BCs.[1] If that happens, the new model and the use of mobile telephony can change the scenario dramatically.

Collaboration between India and Korea

The relationship between India and Korea dates back to 48 AD However, financial relations have been fairly limited between the two countries. They started in real earnest after the initiation of formal diplomatic relations between the two nations in 1973. Since then, a number of agreements have been signed and the first among them is the Agreement on Trade Promotion and Economic and Technological Cooperation in 1974, which facilitated the growth of trade and financial relations between the two nations. The latest in the relations between the two nations is the historic signing of the CEPA. India and Korea have immense potential for better cooperation in the financial sector. Aware of this, Korea has acknowledged that expanding relations with India should be a major economic and political priority for the country.

Both the nations are part of the G-20, consisting of a group of finance ministers and central bank governors from 20 major economies of the world. Collectively, the G-20 economies constitute 85 percent of global gross national product, 80 percent of world trade (including EU intra-trade) and two-thirds of the world population.

Korea had proposed the setting up of a global financial safety net at the G-20's Seoul Summit in 2010. This was also at the top of India's agenda at the summit. This arrangement is seen as an alternative to the International Monetary Fund's financial rescue mechanism, which had drawn a lot of flak in the 1990s. It is an essential instrument to manage systemic risk faced by an economy by ensuring reliable access to overseas liquidity and would help protect fast-growing emerging economies from destabilizing capital inflows. Sudden bouts of large capital inflows can trigger asset price bubbles and put pressure on local currencies, rendering exports uncompetitive and making monetary management difficult.

1. Discussion paper on *Engagement of 'for-profit' Companies as Business Correspondents. http://rbi.org.in/scripts/bs_viewcontent.aspx?Id=2234*

The financial safety net proposal involved the system of currency swaps. This is another area where India and Korea have potential for mutual cooperation. A currency swap is an agreement to exchange one currency for another and to reverse the transaction at a date in the future. South Korea is currently a part of the Chiang Mai Initiative (CMI), a bilateral currency swap arrangement between ASEAN and three other nations—China, Japan and South Korea—in the wake of the Asian currency crisis. South Korea has signed quite a few bilateral swap agreements with countries such as Japan, China, Thailand, Malaysia and the Philippines. A bilateral swap agreement with India could be ideal for strengthening financial relations between the nations. This will also go a long way toward maintaining regional financial stability.

Both India and South Korea seem to be committed to furthering financial relations as they are aware of the untapped huge potential in this sphere. A bilateral currency swap arrangement between the two and a revision in the CEPA norms at an appropriate time could be two critical steps in that direction.

Notes and References

(1) The two-way movement in interest rates during 2002–03 confirmed that banks should in their interest take steps to build up investment fluctuation reserves in a smooth and phased manner for better risk management. It may be recalled that in January 2002, the RBI proposed that banks should build up investment fluctuation reserve (IFR) to a minimum of 5 percent of their investment portfolio under the "held for trading" and "available for sale" categories, by transferring the gains realized on sale of investments within a period of five years. They were also advised to make adequate provisions for unforeseen contingencies in their business plans, and to fully take into account the implications of changes in the monetary and external environment on their operations. In light of their own risk assessment, banks are free to build up a higher percentage of IFR up to 10 percent of their portfolio depending on the size and composition of their portfolio, with the concurrence of their Boards. Statement by Dr. Bimal Jalan, Governor, Reserve Bank of India on *Monetary and Credit, Policy* for the year 2003–04.

http://rbi.org.in/scripts/NotificationUser.aspx?Id=1153&Mode=0

(2) The RBI directive to banks on exposure to real estate, June 29, 2005. A recent review revealed that though the advances of the banks to the housing sector, particularly to land developers and builders, are on the rise, a corresponding control mechanism required to be in place to manage the risks involved in this sensitive sector has not been adopted by the majority of banks.

http://rbi.org.in/scripts/NotificationUser.aspx?Id=2304&Mode=0

(3) Master Circular on Housing Finance, 1 July, 2008—Risk Weight On Housing Finance

Banks extending housing loans to individuals against the mortgage of residential housing properties were required to assign risk weight of 75 percent on such loans which were fully secured by mortgage of residential properties and investments in Mortgage Backed Securities (MBS) of Housing Finance Companies (HFCs), recognized and supervised by the NHB. In view of the fact that banks have been advised from time to time to tighten their credit administration in this area in particular, it has been decided to reduce the risk weight on residential housing loans to individuals from the existing 75 percent to 50 percent as given below:

LTV Ratio	Sanctioned Amount of loan	Risk weight
LTV Ratio = or < 75%	Up to Rs. 30.00 lakh	50%
LTV Ratio = or < 75%	Above Rs. 30.00 lakh	75%
LTV Ratio > 75%	Irrespective of the amount	100% (unchanged)

Similarly, the risk weight for banks' investment in mortgage backed securities, which are backed by housing loans which would now qualify for 50 percent risk weight, and are issued by the housing finance companies regulated by the National Housing Banks, is also reduced from 75 percent to 50 percent. In all other cases, it will be 100 percent. However the risk weight for commercial real estate exposure was raised to 125 percent on July 26, 2005 and further to 150 percent on May 25, 2006.

http://rbi.org.in/scripts/BS_ViewMasCirculardetails.aspx?Id=4315&Mode=0

(4) Third Quarter Review of the Annual Statement on Monetary Policy for the year 2006–07—Provisioning Requirement for Standard Assets and Risk Weights for Capital Adequacy.

In order to ensure that asset quality is maintained in the light of high credit growth, the general provisioning requirement on standard advances in certain specific sectors, *viz.,* personal loans, loans and advances qualifying as capital market exposure, residential housing loans beyond Rs. 20 lakh and commercial real estate loans was raised from 0.40 percent to 1.0 percent in May 2006. The continued high credit growth in the real estate sector, personal loans, credit card receivables, and loans and advances qualifying as capital market exposure and a higher default rate in regard to personal loans and credit card receivables, as revealed in the data, is a matter of concern. It has, therefore, been decided to increase the provisioning requirement in respect of the standard assets in the following categories of loans and advances from the present level of 1 percent to 2 percent with immediate effect: a) Personal loans (including credit card receivables); b) Loans and advances qualifying as capital market exposure; and c) Real estate loans (excluding residential housing loans).

http://rbi.org.in/scripts/BS_CircularIndexDisplay.aspx?Id=3256

(5) Prudential Limits for Inter-Bank Liabilities (IBL), March 6, 2007.

In India, while the counterparty risk concentration on the assets side has attracted adequate attention and received regulatory policy response, the concentration risk on the liability side of the banks has not received similar attention. Liability-side management has its own merits from the point of view of financial stability. Controlling the concentration risk on the liability side of banks is therefore as important as controlling the concentration risk on the asset side. More particularly, uncontrolled IBL may have systemic implications, even if the individual counterparty banks are within the allocated exposure. Further, uncontrolled liability of a larger bank may also have a domino effect. In view of this, it has become important to put in place a comprehensive framework of liability management so that banks are aware of the risks inherent in following a business model based on a large amount of IBL and the systemic risks such a model may entail.

http://rbi.org.in/scripts/NotificationUser.aspx?Id=3316&Mode=0

(6) Draft Guidelines on Securitisation of Standard Assets, 4 April, 2005.

http://www.rbi.org.in/scripts/NotificationUser.aspx?Mode=0&Id=2180

(7) RBI draft report of the Internal Group on Introduction of Credit Default Swaps (CDS) for Corporate Bonds for Public Comments.

http://rbi.org.in/scripts/BS_PressReleaseDisplay.aspx?prid=22932

(8) Note 6: The voting rights of any person holding shares of a banking company are restricted to 10 percent irrespective of his/her shareholding. The Banking Regulation Act 1949 will be amended to remove this limitation.

Union Budget, 2003–04; *http://indiabudget.nic.in/ub2003-04/bs/speecha.htm*

(9) RBI Discussion Paper on Entry of New Banks in the Private Sector.

http://rbi.org.in/scripts/BS_PressReleaseDisplay.aspx?prid=22964

4 The Recent Performance of the Indian Economy

Recovery and Challenge

AJAY SHANKAR

Introduction

The performance of the Indian economy during the global financial and economic crisis and thereafter has been much better than what most observers expected. The weakest quarterly GDP growth rate was 5.7 percent and the annual rate was 6.7 percent.[1] This paper will attempt to describe the position of the Indian economy prior to the crisis, the impact of the crisis on it, the policy measures adopted to deal with the crisis, the response and performance of the economy thereafter, and the prospects in the future.

Overview of Structural Transformation of Indian Economy until the Recent Financial Crisis

To understand India it is useful to bear in mind that it is a large multilingual, multiethnic, multi-religious federal state of 1.2 billion people. While it has a long and rich civilization, it is a young nation state that got freedom from British colonial rule only in 1947. India's colonization began to be completed when the United States came into existence as a free nation. Further, colonization left an exceedingly poor population and a more or less stagnant economy where in the colonial period starvation deaths in large numbers were not infrequent. Compared to the East Asian economies the performance of the Indian economy in the first few decades of India's independence after the Second World War was modest.

1. International Monetary Fund (IMF). *World Economic Outlook Database. http://www.imf.org/external/ns/cs.aspx?id=28*

Conditioned by its history of having been colonized and impoverished by a trading company, the East India Company; experiencing the short-run effectiveness of government controls and direct management during the mobilization for the Second World War; influenced by the socialist ideas of the Labour Party in England in the 30s and 40s; and impressed by the extraordinary success of centralized planning in the then Soviet Union; India opted for its own model of economic development. Its key features were an emphasis on self-reliance and infant industry protection through increasing barriers to imports and foreign investment, the creation of a dominant role for a government-owned public sector in the economy with the Indian private sector being denied entry into all key industries, a proliferating regime of licenses and controls on private enterprises, and an attempt to steer economic development through centralized planning and government interventions in all spheres of economic activity.

By the 1980s the limitations and weaknesses of India's development model and policies was becoming apparent to the Indian people. India, notwithstanding its initial promise and potential, seemed to have got locked into a low growth equilibrium and into an economy of scarcity, increasing foreign exchange and trade restrictions, controls and distortions. East Asia was beginning to prosper, the Soviet economy was getting visibly dysfunctional and Europe had discovered the limitations of government ownership and control of modern enterprises in terms of innovation and competitiveness. Some measures for liberalization and increasing competition in the economy were undertaken in the 1980s and the results were quite positive. The visible benefits of these modest measures of liberalization contributed to the creation of the national mood in favor of major reforms.

The 1991 Reforms: A Paradigm Shift

An acute balance of payments crisis in 1990 leading to the need for IMF assistance and coinciding with a new government after elections in 1991 that had a clear manifesto for economic reforms saw India move to a new paradigm in its development strategy. This transformation was steered by Dr. Manmohan Singh as the Finance Minister from 1991 to 1996. After being in the Opposition, the Congress Party has been leading India's coalition government since 2004 with Dr. Manmohan Singh as the Prime Minister.

While India' economic reforms were gradual and incremental they have, nevertheless, been quite far-reaching and transformational. These have involved India abandoning self-reliance; seeking greater engagement with the global economy; dismantling barriers to foreign trade; lowering entry barriers; and opening the economy to greater competition. Internally the stifling burden of government controls, restrictions and licenses have been drastically reduced and in many cases eliminated altogether. Tax rates have been progressively lowered. Import duties have come down drastically and are scheduled to reach ASEAN levels shortly. Public sector monopolies have ended, not with privatization but with the facilitation of the entry of new private players. India has gradually reduced restrictions on foreign investment. In fact it has actively pursued and welcomed foreign investment.

Positive Response to Reforms

In the post-reform period India has been conscious of the need for macroeconomic stability and its critical role and importance for sustainable growth over the medium and long run. The difficult challenges have related to containing the fiscal deficit and inflationary tendencies, both of which have periodically tested both the resolve and the skill of the leadership. Containing inflation has been a political necessity for all governments given the democratic nature of the Indian polity and the modest incomes of almost all Indians. A sustained consensus and real political support for containing the deficit has been more difficult. Fortunately for India its modest current account deficits have been more than adequately offset by rising capital inflows into its attractive stock market, Foreign Direct Investment (FDI) into a dynamic and profitable economy and remittances from its growing number of expatriates.

With greater openness, competition and the removal of entry barriers, entrepreneurship in India has blossomed. Starting with a considerable measure of anxiety about globalization in the 90s, this decade has seen the gradual strengthening of the consensus in favor of it. Indian firms have grown rapidly and gained in confidence. Start-ups have grown in number and some have expanded rapidly to reach leading positions in their sectors. Many have become transnational in their operations.

The new economic policies led to a gradual increase in GDP growth rates in the first 10 years of reforms in which the economy had to undergo radical restructuring, reorientation and adjustment. Thereafter, there was a remarkable surge in economic performance. For the five years preceding the impact of the global crisis the Indian economy averaged GDP growth rates of around 9 percent. Foreign Direct Investment (FDI) in these years went up seven times from net inflows of around USD 5 billion a year to around USD 35 billion a year.[2] Surprisingly Indian firms also felt confident enough to go out of India and invest overseas not only in emerging markets but also in the developed markets of the OECD countries as they pursued global competitiveness.

Figure 4.1

GDP Growth: Absolute and %

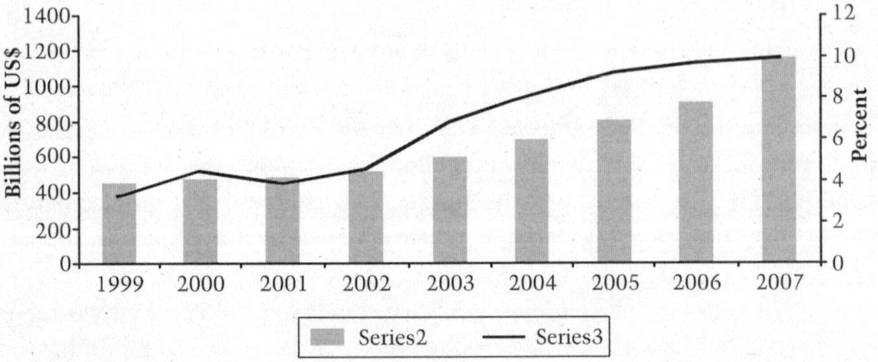

Source: IMF.

In the post-reform period the Indian economy displayed features and characteristics that in many ways were distinct and did not follow the so-called "normal" pattern of development and catching up. The Indian economy first displayed global competitiveness in the services sector and that too in the technologically advanced area of the IT software industry by the late 90s. This went on to encompass the BPO segment. Economic

2. Department of Industrial Policy and Promotion (DIPP), India.

Figure 4.2

Inward FDI

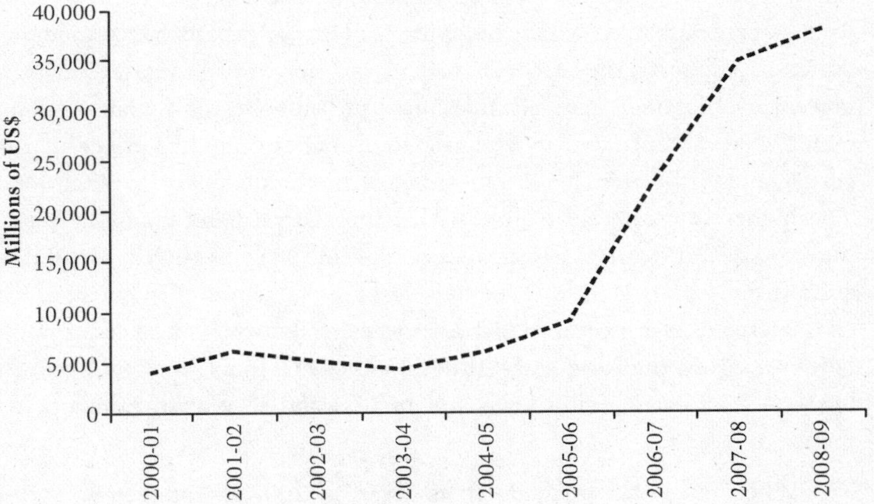

Source: http://dipp.nic.in/fdi_statistics/india_FDI_February2011.pdf

growth was services-led in the early phase of the post-reform period. The Indian manufacturing sector was still adjusting and restructuring, so much so that at the turn of the decade there were some comments to the effect that India could not be competitive in manufacturing and may, perhaps, bypass the manufacturing phase of economic development and go onto becoming a services economy straightaway. However, Indian manufacturing in this decade began to turn around and gradually began to display competitiveness. Even here the development pattern has been unusual. Indian pharmaceutical firms that were manufacturing generic drugs became globally competitive and made their presence felt in international markets. The process of being globally competitive in manufacturing has been underway across a broader spectrum. The results are now noticeable especially in the auto component sector. Consequently India's industrial growth rate began to rise and approach double-digit growth rates, which the services sector had been exhibiting on a sustained basis for quite some time.

Pre-Crisis Period

India's economy in 2006 grew at a record rate of 9.7 percent, steadily rising from a rate of 8.1 percent in 2004.[3] The Reserve Bank of India (India's central bank), which had put in place an expansionary monetary policy to support growth began to feel the need to moderate growth to prevent overheating. Signs of inflationary pressures in the Indian economy, which were accentuated by the rise in global commodity prices in that period, made the case for a tightening of monetary policy even stronger. The higher interest rate regime which the central bank gradually put in place had the desired effect of both moderating growth as well as containing inflation. India seemed to be going through what could be characterized as a normal business cycle in a normal market economy. However, given the early stage of development of India, the bottom of the business cycle was a slowdown and moderation in growth rather than a proper recession.

When the global financial crisis began in 2007 it was seen as a crisis affecting the US and UK where the deregulated financial sector had been the most innovative and with the benefit of hindsight could be said to have been adventurous to the point of being reckless. The financial crisis was expected to have its effect on the real economy in these countries with a lag and through this process have an impact on the global economy. The Europeans who had felt that they had been relatively immune to the charms of financial innovation were soon surprised by the extent to which their banks had been exposed to the new toxic instruments. The global economy was seen as heading toward a major crisis.

In India financial sector, liberalization had moved very gradually. After witnessing the impact of the East Asian economic crisis of 1997–98, which had bypassed India thanks to the restrictions in place on foreign borrowings and the absence of capital account convertibility, opinion in India had crystallized in favor of a more cautious and gradual approach toward financial sector reforms. In fact the slow pace of financial reforms was a constant refrain in Western analyses and comments on the Indian economy: the Reserve Bank of India was usually criticized for being too

3. IMF (2008). *IMF Country Report* No. 08/52.

conservative and was therefore holding India back. Since the Indian financial sector still had restrictions and was not free enough, it had zero holdings of the toxic assets that were causing havoc in the western financial world. Indian banks were well capitalized and in good health with normal and modest levels of non-performing assets. In early 2008, there were some who were optimistic enough to seriously consider the proposition of 'decoupling'. The performance of the Indian economy in the first few quarters after the onset of the financial crisis in the US gave some credence to the decoupling proposition. It was, however, expected that exports would, in due course, take a hit with demand compression in the West as their real economies experienced the full impact of the financial crisis. On the whole business leaders and policy makers were somewhat sanguine about the impact on India as the crisis unfolded through the first half of 2008. In fact the domestic policy debate was India-centric and all about inflationary pressures and the appropriate policy response to it.

The Crisis and the Stimulus Package

Following the collapse of Lehman Brothers there was panic in international financial institutions. These had over the years been investing heavily and profitably in the Indian stock market. In this area the Indian economy was almost fully open and there were hardly any restrictions on entry and exit from the Indian stock market for Foreign Institutional Investors (FIIs). In the prevailing panic situation and seeking enhanced liquidity the FIIs almost overnight began selling their holdings of stocks and converting their Rupees into dollars and taking them out. The scale and speed of these transactions were so massive in relation to the size of the Indian market that almost overnight there was a crisis of liquidity in India. This led to a collapse in market sentiment and confidence. The Indian economy suddenly went into a tailspin.

It then became clear how integrated the Indian financial system had become with the global financial system through this transmission mechanism. This turned out to be the case to the surprise of most observers. The prevailing prognosis had been that with the lack of capital account convertibility, restrictions on what Indian banks could do in international markets as well as on overseas borrowings by Indian firms and the marginal presence of foreign banks in India, the impact of the global crisis would be transmitted through the real economy in the West and certainly not directly and immediately through the financial system.

It took some time to recognize the severity of the liquidity crisis as the banking system did not seem to experience any discontinuity either in terms of deposits or credit off-take. The Non-Banking Financial Companies (NBFCs), which had grown rapidly with light regulation, were the ones to take the real hit. There was some debate in the early days on whether there should be a moderate initial response to see how the situation unfolded before considering further steps. But it soon became clear that the collapse in business confidence and market sentiment was such that immediate and strong measures were required. The global backdrop was one of the real possibility of experiencing something as devastating as the Great Depression. Even the normally conservative IMF was advocating the need for a fiscal stimulus across the board by all economies as a means of preventing the collapse of global demand.

To cope with the crisis the government went into emergency mode with Prime Minister Manmohan Singh personally providing decisive leadership and direction and ensuring a cohesive and coordinated response, both in terms of monetary and fiscal measures and the government and the central bank were able to come out with swift and coordinated stimulus packages within weeks. These were well-designed and calibrated to suit India's specific needs and situation. These measures not only minimized the pain but also facilitated a speedier recovery than was considered likely or feasible. In fact India has now gone back to its earlier high growth trajectory.

The key components of the stimulus packages were the following:

1. Additional funds for expenditure for centrally funded programs for critical rural, infrastructure and social security schemes.
    - Pradhan Mantri Gram Sadak Yojana (PMGSY): a program to provide all-weather roads to all villages in India.
    - Jawaharlal Nehru National Urban Renewal Mission (JNNURM): a program to improve infrastructure in terms of

water supply, sewage treatment, waste management and roads in major cities.

- Accelerated Irrigation Benefit Program for major irrigation projects.
- Indira Awas Yojana: a program to give single-room huts to the homeless rural poor.
- Mahatma Gandhi Rural Employment Guarantee Program (MNREGS): an innovative welfare measure under which 100 days of employment was guaranteed to the rural poor in villages and which was in the process of being extended to cover the whole country.

2. Reduction in taxes to stimulate demand for manufactured goods. CENVAT was reduced by 4 percent.
3. Special measures to give relief and support to specially distressed sectors of exports, Small and Medium Enterprises (SMEs), auto and housing.

Monetary Measures

Monetary measures had the standard dimension of lowering interest rates drastically and injecting liquidity in the market. These are given in Table 4.1.

Table 4.1

Revision in Policy Rates and Movement of Lending Rates (in percent)

	2007–08			*2009*		*2010*	
	*2006–07**	*2007–08**	*Aug 2008*	*Jan*	*June*	*Mar*	*April*
Cash Reserve Ratio	6.50	7.50	9.00	5.00	5.00	5.75	6.00
Reverse Repo Rate	6.00	6.00	6.00	4.00	4.75	3.50	3.75
Repo Rate	7.75	7.75	9.00	5.50	3.25	5.00	5.25

Note: * as on March 30th.

Source: Reserve Bank of India.

In an unorthodox response to a crisis situation the central bank also took the following steps:[4]

A. Rupee Liquidity

- Statutory Liquidity Ratio reduced from 25 percent to 24 percent, with exceptional reductions for specified conditions.
- Repo facility for Rs. 60,000 crore under LAF to banks for lending to Mutual Funds and NBFCs.
- Scheme to advance Rs. 25,000 crore to financial institutions under Agricultural Debt Waiver and Debt Relief Schemes.

B. Forex Liquidity

- Interest rate ceiling on FCNR(B) and NR(E)RA term deposits increased.
- ECB up to $500 million permitted for rupee/foreign currency expenditure for permissible end-use under the automatic route.
- Systemically important non-deposit taking NBFCs and Housing Finance Companies registered with NHB permitted to raise short-term currency borrowing under the approval route.
- Buy back/Pre-payment of Foreign Currency Convertible Bonds permitted.
- Swap facility with Indian banks for foreign currency.

C. Credit Delivery

- Extension of the period of pre-shipment rupee export credit (at concessional rates) from 180 days to 270 days.
- Eligible limit of the ECR facility for banks enhanced to 50 percent of the outstanding export credit eligible for refinance.
- Advance allocation of Rs. 3,000 crore to SIDBI and NHB against estimated shortfall in priority sector lending by banks.

---

4. Government of India press releases, December 7, 2008 and January 2, 2009. *http://www.pib.nic.in/newsite/erelease.aspx?relid=45376* and *http://www.pib.nic.in/newsite/erelease.aspx?relid=46360*, See Appendix A-4.1.

- Provisioning requirement for all types of standard assets reduced to 0.4 percent.
- SPV for providing liquidity support to NBFCs to the amount of Rs. 25,000 crore.

These measures were designed keeping in mind the imperative need for an immediate impact in the real economy rather than trying to come up with an impressive size for the fiscal package which was then the fashion globally. By contrast the size of the Indian stimulus package when computed appeared somewhat modest and its, relatively speaking, modest size was even commented upon by some observers then. In fact the stimulus package was the sum total of a series of carefully considered micro measures.

Macro Policy Adjustment and Sectoral Performance

It was accepted that nothing done in India could possibly have an impact on global demand and, therefore, Indian exporters would need to tide over the crisis period and wait for the global economy to begin recovering. Other than the IT and auto sectors, Indian exports take place through small and medium enterprises. These SMEs were having difficulty getting credit for such export orders that they could get in this difficult period when liquidity and credit in the international market had more or less dried up toward the end of 2008. India having abundant foreign exchange reserves could through its central bank provide additional dollar liquidity to its banks and its EXIM Bank could take care of this problem. Further, many of these SMEs were likely to be in no position to service their existing debt obligations. Indian banks were persuaded to roll over their debt obligations for a year and the central bank facilitated this through guidelines issued for this special situation. This enabled Indian SMEs to weather the global crisis without bankruptcies and with their competitiveness intact. At the end of the day this was also good for Indian banks as their clients remained solvent and once the global recovery began they were again in a position to service their debts. The fact that the Indian banking sector is still dominated by government-owned and controlled public sector banks made it easier to take these decisions and implement them quickly. This swift coordinated action by government, the central bank and public sector banks was critical in sustaining the Indian SME sector.

Positive Wealth Effect and Tax Cuts

India benefited immensely from two major decisions taken earlier for domestic reasons and widely criticized by many conservative economic commentators as being fiscally irresponsible. One was the decision to write off non-recoverable debts of Indian farmers with the banks. With the write-off decision the government decided to pay the banks so that these dodgy loans went off their balance sheets which became healthy. What made the timing of the decision fortuitously just right was the positive wealth effect it created across rural India. Farmers who owed these non-payable debts but lived under the looming danger of losing their lands and properties which had been mortgaged suddenly felt free and richer and were therefore going out and making long delayed purchase and investment decisions. At the height of the crisis, rural demand was buoyant across the board. The write-off was of the order of Rs. 70,000 crore, which was approximately USD 18 billion, not an insignificant sum in the Indian context with the Indian economy being around USD one trillion.[5]

The other major decision was the upward revision in the wages of government employees. India has a system of periodically revising wages upwards at one stroke after an elaborate exercise of determining what the wage hikes should be for different categories of employees through a Pay Commission. These recommendations had been received and were accepted by government shortly before the crisis hit India. Given the historical dominance of the government and government companies in the Indian economy, employees of the public sector constitute a major segment of the organized workforce. They were suddenly getting more disposable incomes in their hands. Further due to a variety of reasons the wage revision had been delayed and as a result all the employees received wage increases from a prior date and therefore got hefty pay arrears. Thus a large section of the workforce felt wealthier and had more income. This translated into greater purchases and investments by these households.

5. Financial Times *http://www.ft.com/cms/s/0/88d9b290-28e4-11dd-96ce-000077b07658.html#axzz1Kkzu9ewg*

Since business confidence and market sentiment had suddenly collapsed, it was essential to take measures to reverse the situation. An across-the-board reduction in excise duty of 4 percent was announced as a temporary measure for a limited period of a few months to boost demand.[6] Excise duties in India are essentially a tax on manufacturing and were still quite high by global standards. A sharp across-the-board reduction had the effect of lowering costs for manufacturers who then had the option of lowering end-prices for consumers and/or increasing their dealers'/retailers' margins to push up sales. They did both. Consumers seeing the prospect of future price increases once the temporary excise duty reduction had been withdrawn had a significant incentive to advance purchase and investment decisions to take advantage of the lower prices. This credible signaling did have an effect and private demand did pick up much sooner than expected.

In looking at measures for increasing demand through public expenditure the material consideration was the speed with which a decision would get translated into actual expenditure creating demand in the market for goods and services. Based on this criterion consideration of big infrastructure projects was ruled out as these require considerable time for assembly of land, firming of detailed technical parameters and selection of parties for execution. The ongoing program of Bharat Nirman to provide essential infrastructure in rural areas of all-weather roads and electricity and improve the provision of water and sanitation to all villages became an ideal choice for providing additional funds as a shelf of projects existed which could be taken up immediately. Short gestation small projects scattered across the country had the advantage of generating demand for cement, steel, pipes and a wide range of electrical goods.

Auto and Housing Sectors

The auto sector in India has over the years evolved into a significant sector of the economy and one of the engines of growth. In 2008 it was going through the downside of a normal business cycle when the crisis hit the Indian economy and sent the sector into a tailspin. The temporary reduction in rates of excise duties was intended to help the auto companies

---

6. Government of India press releases, December 7, 2008 and January 2, 2009 *http://www.pib.nic.in/newsite/erelease.aspx?relid=45376* and *http://www.pib. nic.in/newsite/erelease.aspx?relid=46360*, See Appendix A-4.1.

stimulate demand. Further sector-specific measures were also adopted. A decision was taken to replace the old fuel-inefficient vehicles with government agencies with new fuel-efficient ones. This had the added advantage of lowering greenhouse gas emissions. It was also decided to provide grants to buy 16,000 buses for city bus services. These direct additional measures of demand generation helped the sector move toward recovery.

The housing industry in India had become an engine of growth as in many other economies. It catered to the booming demand for commercial office space, shopping malls and better quality housing as India was experiencing high growth of around 9 percent. It was overleveraged as it tried to assemble large quantities of land in anticipation of rapidly increasing demand. Fortunately for India, housing construction is normally undertaken with the buyer's funds either through upfront payment or payment in installments with the builder' funds getting locked in only for land. With the onset of the crisis and the collapse of business confidence, this industry saw demand disappear in the commercial space and luxury housing segments. When demand as well as flow of funds from overseas collapsed in this overleveraged industry, there was potential for a series of defaults and even bankruptcies. Roll-over of debt was facilitated to enable the industry to cope with the situation. While they were overleveraged, their problem was one of liquidity rather than solvency as their underlying assets in terms of their land banks were valuable enough and they did not have the problem of carrying an inventory of unsold built-up space.

The option of focusing on the demand for affordable housing was encouraged. With the upward pay revision of employees in government agencies the demand for affordable housing for this market segment went up significantly. In any case this was a relatively neglected segment when demand for more expensive housing with higher margins was booming. The housing industry quickly turned its attention to this segment and was therefore able to cope with the crisis much better than expected. The easier monetary policy regime made it possible for banks to lend to home buyers at attractive interest rates. The norms for housing finance in India had been conservative enough, with loans being restricted to only 70 percent of the value of the property and the debt-repaying capacity of the borrower usually being assessed on his income stream independent of the income from the property. Therefore, flow of credit to home buyers was not an issue during the crisis. In fact housing loans tended to be the better-performing and preferred assets in the portfolios of banks.

Political Economy Aspects of Macro Policy to tackle Global Financial Crisis are two dimensions in the evolution of the stimulus package and its implementation which are noteworthy and reflect the growing maturity of the political economy of India. Intense consultations and discussions with all stakeholders and industry segments were the key to the evolution of specific measures of the package that delivered results quickly. Pragmatism was the hallmark of the decision-making process. Such close cooperation with all industry segments was widely appreciated by Indian business. This was noteworthy given India's recent economic history where government and business were not known to work together and where decision-making tended to be driven more by theory than pragmatic business sense and judgment.

The other unusual aspect to be noted is that all this happened when India was going into a fiercely contested general election whose outcome was then uncertain. The measures required to handle the crisis needed and had a broad consensus behind them across civil society and political parties. It also encompassed the states, which was important as India is a federal country. For the conduct of free and fair elections the Election Commission of India, an independent constitutional body, had over time evolved a system where new expenditure by government during the election process was not permitted lest the party in power try to influence voters at the last minute with fresh expenditure. Given the immediate necessity for expenditure for the stimulus package to work it was essential to get the cooperation of the Election Commission and its clearance for fresh expenditure. Due to the broad consensus across the political spectrum it was possible to get the clearances from the Election Commission on the scale required to make the stimulus package effective.

The Economy's Response

The performance of the Indian economy through the crisis and after has been better than expected by most observers.

The Indian economy experienced only a downturn and not a recession. It then recovered quite fast and much earlier than expected. A downturn rather than a recession was primarily due to the fact that exports still comprised a relatively smaller share of GDP in India as it began opening up to freer trade with the global economy only after the reforms in the early 90s. Exports declined by over 30 percent in line with the experience of other economies, but these comprised only 21 percent of GDP as compared to 41 percent in the case of Korea.[7]

Figure 4.3

Exports as Percentage of GDP in 2007

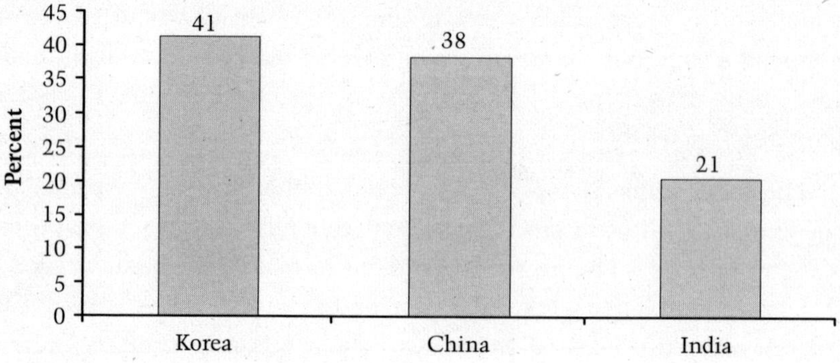

Source: IMF, UNCTAD.

The recovery was quicker as the stimulus package was implemented swiftly and was designed to have the quickest possible transmission mechanism through the economy. The stimulus to domestic demand through the positive wealth effects of the write-off of farmers' non-recoverable loans and higher wages and arrears for government and public sector employees was in any case beginning to have its effect just when the crisis was peaking in terms of loss of liquidity and business confidence. The substantial cut in excise duties on manufacturing gave industry immediate space for stimulating demand. The ability to enhance government spending immediately and across the country through ongoing

7. IMF, *World Economic Outlook Database* and UNCTAD.

programs and projects helped generate demand across a broad spectrum with positive backward linkages. The decision to provide for roll-over debt readily was of immense value in restoring business confidence and facilitating recovery.

Figure 4.4

Impact of Crisis on Growth of GDP and Manufacturing

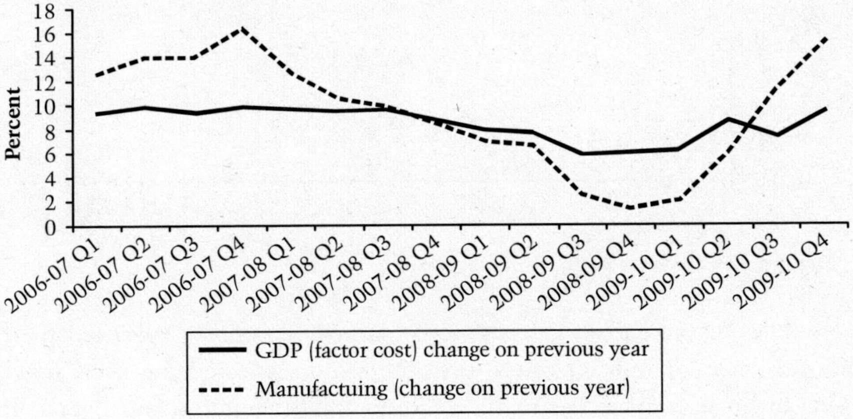

Source: Central Statistical Organisation.[8]

The stimulus package has been gradually phased out as the Indian economy began to return to its normal growth trajectory. It was easier to exit as the tax cuts had been announced as being temporary to stimulate demand. Restricting the expenditure side of the stimulus to ongoing programs and projects and avoiding big ticket items with longer gestation periods had the advantage of having not only a speedier transmission for demand creation but also permitted smooth and easy scaling down of expenditure to normal levels.

The Indian fiscal stimulus was relatively speaking quite modest as can be seen in the following figure.

8. *http://mospi.nic.in/cso_test1.htm*

Figure 4.5

Estimates of Stimulus Measures as Percentage of GDP

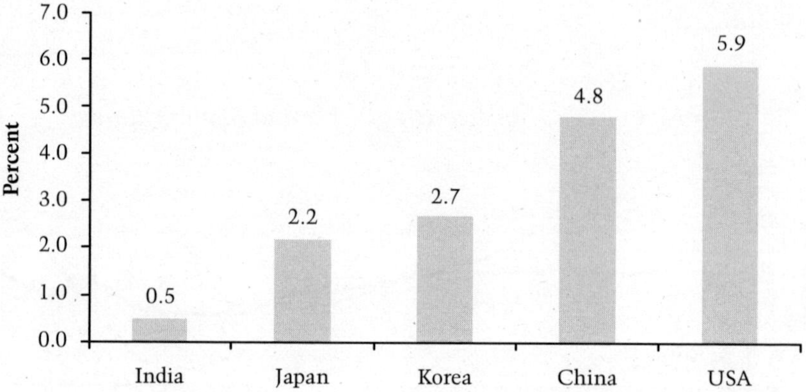

Source: Prasad and Sorkin (2009).

The key concerns in economic management have returned to the normal ones for India, namely, controlling inflation and the fiscal deficit. The authorities have begun to credibly signal their resolve to take the necessary measures to attain both these objectives. Markets have been responding positively. The GDP growth rate of 10.35 percent for 2010 has been particularly encouraging.[9] India would like to sustain its growth trajectory and hopes to reach a growth rate of 8 to 10 percent and sustain it for two decades to overcome poverty and give its people a decent living standard. As the fiscal stimulus was modest, India has been able to revert to the trajectory of a declining debt-to-GDP ratio.

The challenge would be to achieve this growth in an environment where the global economy may experience more sluggish growth in the advanced economies of the US and the EU in the coming years. Further the adjustment process to address global imbalances would make the international economic environment more complex. Volatility in the dollar-euro exchange rate has already been witnessed. Debt issues in member countries of the euro zone have posed difficult challenges. Continued monetary easing in the advanced economics and consequential enhanced

9. IMF, *World Economic Outlook 2011*.

capital inflows to emerging markets have the potential for generating asset price bubbles. Commodity price inflation could also generate difficulties. India for reasons of domestic supply-side constraints has been experiencing higher than expected levels of food price inflation.

Figure 4.6

Government Debt as Percentage of GDP

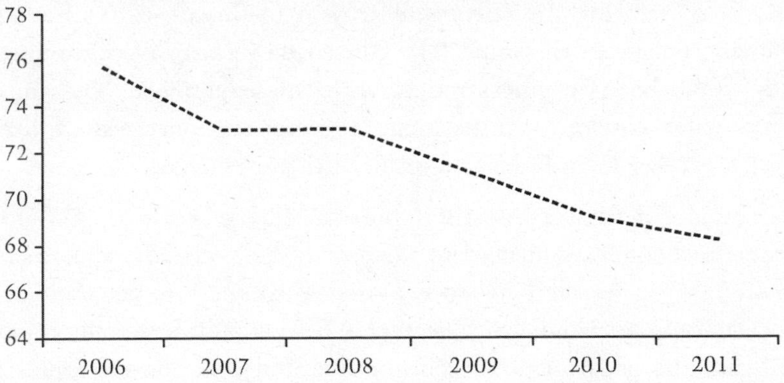

Source: IMF.

Lessons for the Future

In many ways the experience of Korea and India and the rest of Asia has been similar.

- The financial and banking sectors were sound and unaffected.
- Exports fell dramatically because of the crisis in the US and Europe.
- Market and business confidence collapsed.
- Monetary easing and a fiscal stimulus helped.
- G-20 coordination on stimulus and open trade was critical.

The key lesson of this crisis has been that the global economy is now so interconnected that there is no alternative to continued G-20 coordination for the smooth functioning of the global economy. It is also necessary that a consensus emerge on measures to reduce the risk of a similar collapse in the financial markets in the future.

For a country like India the relative autonomy and insulation of the national banking sector from the innovations of Wall Street was a source of strength as it gave India the strength of an unaffected and healthy banking sector at the height of the crisis and permitted a swift response that specifically suited the circumstances in India during the crisis. The existence of public sector government-controlled banks helped in quicker and smoother decisions regarding rolling over of debt. India has had a policy of permitting the entry and growth of private banks but not of privatizing public sector banks. The consensus in favor of continuing this policy would have become stronger with this experience. The voices of caution as far as reforms in the financial sector are concerned are likely to carry greater weight in India as a result of this experience.

The global recovery is still somewhat fragile. Both the US and the European economies still need to undertake the necessary adjustments in terms of correcting their macroeconomic imbalances to get their deficits and debts onto a sustainable trajectory. There is both uncertainty and risk and hence the need for G-20 coordination and cohesion continues to be important. India and Korea have somewhat similar perspectives and need to work together in this endeavor.

References

E. Prasad and I. Sorkin (2009). *Assessing the G-20 Stimulus Plans: A Deeper Look.* Brookings Institution.

Appendix A-4.1

I. Government of India Press Release, December 7, 2008

(http://www.pib.nic.in/newsite/erelease.aspx?relid=45376)

Government announces measures for stimulating the economy.

The Government has been concerned about the impact of the global financial crisis on the Indian economy and a number of steps have been taken to deal with this problem.

The first priority was to re-assure the people of the stability of the financial system in general and of the safety of bank deposits in particular. To this end, steps were taken to infuse liquidity into the banking system and also to address problems being faced by various non-bank financing companies. These steps have ensured that the financial system is functioning effectively without suffering the kind of loss of confidence experienced in the industrialized world.

Having assured the stability of the system, the Government has focused its attention on countering the impact of the global recession on India's economic growth. On the monetary side, the RBI has sought to pump sufficient liquidity into the banking system to enable bank credit to meet the expanded requirements of the economy keeping in mind the contraction in credit from non-bank sources. Banks have been provided adequate liquidity through a series of reductions in the CRR and additional flexibility in meeting the SLR requirement. Interest rate reductions have also been signaled by reductions in the repo and reverse repo rates, the most recent of which was announced on Saturday when both the repo rate and the reverse repo rate were cut by 100 basis points. Access to external commercial borrowings has also been liberalized so that borrowers capable of accessing funds from abroad are allowed to do so. The banks are being encouraged to counter what might otherwise become self-fulfilling negative expectations by enhanced lending to support economic activity.

These measures in the area of money and credit are being supplemented by fiscal measures designed to stimulate the economy. In recognition of the need for a fiscal stimulus, the government had consciously allowed the fiscal deficit to expand beyond the originally targeted level because of the loan waivers, issue of oil and fertilizer bonds and higher levels of food subsidy. In addition, the following steps are being taken:

1. Plan Expenditure

In order to provide a contra-cyclical stimulus via plan expenditure, the Government has decided to seek authorisation for additional plan expenditure of up to Rs. 20,000 crore in the current year. In addition, steps are being taken to ensure full utilization of funds already provided, so that the pace of expenditure is maintained. The total spending program in the balance four months of the current fiscal year, taking Plan and non-Plan expenditure together, is expected to be Rs.300,000 crore.

The economy will continue to need stimulus in 2009–10 also and this can be achieved by ensuring a substantial increase in Plan expenditure as part of the budget for next year.

2. Reduction in Cenvat

As an immediate measure to encourage additional spending, an across-the-board cut of 4 percent in the ad valorem Cenvat rate will be effected for the balance part of the current financial year on all products other than petroleum and those where the current rate is less than 4 percent.

3. Measures to Support Exports

i) Pre- and post-shipment export credit for labor-intensive exports, i.e., textiles (including handlooms, carpets and handicrafts), leather, gems & jewellery, marine products and SME sector is being made more attractive by providing an interest subvention of 2 percent up to 31/3/2009 subject to minimum rate of interest of 7 percent per annum.

ii) Additional funds of Rs.1,100 crore will be provided to ensure full refund of Terminal Excise duty/CST.

iii) An additional allocation for export incentive schemes of Rs.350 crore will be made.

iv) Government back-up guarantee will be made available to EGC to the extent of Rs.350 crore to enable it to provide guarantees for exports to difficult markets/products.

v) Exporters will be allowed refund of service tax on foreign agent commissions of up to 10 percent of FOB value of exports. They will also be allowed refund of service tax on output services while availing of benefits under Duty Drawback Scheme.

4. Housing

Housing is a potentially very important source of employment and demand for critical sectors and there is a large unmet need for housing in the country, especially for middle and low-income groups. The Reserve Bank has announced that it will shortly put in place a refinance facility of Rs.4,000 crore for the National Housing Bank. In addition, one of the areas where Plan expenditure can be increased relatively easily is the Indira Awas Yojana. As a further measure of support for this sector public sector banks will shortly announce a package for borrowers of home loans in two categories: (1) up to Rs.5 lakh and (2) Rs. 5 lakh–Rs. 20 lakh. This sector will be kept under a close watch and additional measures would be taken as necessary to promote an accelerated growth trajectory.

5. MSME Sector

The Government attaches the highest priority to supporting the medium, small and micro enterprises (MSMEs) sector which is critical for employment generation. To facilitate the flow of credit to MSMEs, the RBI has announced a refinance facility of Rs.7,000 crore for SIDBI which will be available to support incremental lending, either directly to MSMEs or indirectly via banks, NBFCs and SFCs. In addition, the following steps are being taken.

(a) To boost collateral free lending, the current guarantee cover under Credit Guarantee Scheme for Micro and Small enterprises on loans will be extended from Rs.50 lakh to Rs.1 crore with guarantee cover of 50 percent.

(b) The lock-in period for loans covered under the existing credit guarantee scheme will be reduced from 24 to 18 months, to encourage banks to cover more loans under the guarantee scheme.

(c) Government will issue an advisory to Central Public Sector Enterprises and request State Public Sector Enterprises to ensure prompt payment of bills of MSMEs. Easing of credit conditions generally should help PSUs to make such payments on schedule.

6. Textiles

(a) An additional allocation of Rs.1,400 crore will be made to clear the entire backlog in TUF Scheme.

(b) All items of handicrafts will be included under 'Vishesh Krishi and Gram Udyog Yojana'.

7. Infrastructure Financing

A large number of infrastructure projects are now being cleared for implementation in the Public Private Partnership mode. These projects may experience difficulty in reaching financial closure given the current uncertainties in the financial world. In order to support financing of such projects, the Government has decided to authorise the India Infrastructure Finance Company Limited (IIFCL) to raise Rs.10,000 crore through tax-free bonds by 31/3/2009. These funds will be used by IIFCL to refinance bank lending of longer maturity to eligible infrastructure projects, particularly in highways and port sectors. In this way it is expected that IIFCL resources used for refinance can leverage bank financing of double the amount. Depending on need, IIFCL will be permitted to raise further resources by issue of such bonds. In particular, these initiatives will support a PPP program of Rs.100,000 crore in the highways sector.

8. Others

(a) Government departments will be allowed to take up replacement of government vehicles within the allowed budget, in relaxation of extant economy instructions.

(b) Import Duty on Naphtha for use in the power sector will be eliminated.

(c) Export duty on iron ore fines will be eliminated and on lumps will be reduced to 5 percent. The Government is keeping a close watch on the evolving economic situation and will not hesitate to take any additional steps that may be needed to counter recessionary trends and maintain the pace of economic activity.

II. Government of India Press Release, January 2, 2009

(http://www.pib.nic.in/newsite/erelease.aspx?relid=46360)

Additional Government Measures for Stimulating the Economy.

The Government is committed to taking steps for minimizing the impact of the global financial crisis on the Indian economy. To this end, Government has taken a number of steps since October 7, the most recent being the measures announced on 7.12.2008. These included:

(i) Additional Plan expenditure up to Rs. 20,000 crore in the current year mainly for critical rural, infrastructure and social security schemes such as Pradhan Mantri Gram Sadak Yojana (PMGSY), Jawaharlal Nehru National Urban Renewal Mission (JNNURM), National Rural Employment Guarantee Scheme (NREGS), Indira Awas Yojana, Accelerated Irrigation Benefit Programme and National Social Assistance Programme (NSAP).

(ii) An across-the-board cut of 4 percent in ad valorem Cenvat rate except for petroleum products.

(iii) Several other measures to support exports, housing, Micro, Small and Medium Enterprises (MSME) and textile sectors.

(iv) Authorizing India Infrastructure Finance Company Limited (IIFCL) to raise Rs.10,000 crore to refinance bank lending for infrastructure projects.

Subsequently, other measures have also been taken such as removal of ban on exort of cement.

2. Additional steps are being taken on the monetary, credit and fiscal front to further strengthen the contra-cyclical stance of policy. The Reserve Bank has today announced a set of measures. In addition, with a view to further liberalizing the policy on External Commercial Borrowing (ECB), the Government and the RBI have decided:

(a) The 'all-in-cost' ceilings on such borrowing would be removed, under the approval route of the RBI;

(b) To facilitate access to funds for the housing sector, the 'development of integrated townships' would be permitted as an eligible end-use of the ECB, under the approval route of the RBI;

(c) NBFCs, dealing exclusively with infrastructure financing, would be permitted to access ECB from multilateral or bilateral financial institutions, under the approval route of the RBI.

(d) In order to give a boost to the corporate bond market, FII investment limit in rupee-denominated corporate bonds in India would be increased from USD 6 billion to USD 15 billion.

The decisions at points (a) to (c) would be reviewed after June 30, 2009.

3. The flow of credit to the economy will be further enhanced by the following:

(i) An SPV will be designated shortly to provide liquidity support against investment grade paper to Non-Banking Finance Companies (NBFCs) fulfilling certain conditions. Details will be announced separately. The scale of liquidity potentially available through this window is Rs.25,000 crore.

(ii) An arrangement will be worked out with leading Public Sector Banks to provide a line of credit to NBFCs specifically for purchase of commercial vehicles.

(iii) Credit targets of Public Sector Banks are being revised upward to reflect the needs of the economy in the present difficult situation. Government will closely monitor, on a fortnightly basis, the provision of sectoral credit by public sector banks.

(iv) Special monthly meetings of State Level Bankers' Committees would be held to oversee the resolution of credit issues of micro, small and medium enterprises by banks. Department of MSME and Department of Financial Services will jointly set up a Cell to monitor progress on this front. Matters of MSMEs remaining unresolved with the Banks-SME Helpline for more than a fortnight may be brought to the notice of this Cell.

(v) Recently the guarantee cover under Credit Guarantee Scheme for micro and small enterprises on loans was extended from Rs.50 lakh to Rs.1 crore with a guarantee cover of 50 percent. In order to enhance flow of credit to micro enterprises, it has been further decided to increase the guarantee cover extended by Credit Guarantee Fund Trust to 85 percent for credit facility up to Rs.5 lakh. This will benefit about 84 percent of the total number of accounts accorded guarantee cover.

4. State Governments are facing constraints in financing expenditure because of slower revenue growth. To help maintain the momentum of expenditure at the state government level, states will be allowed to raise in the current financial year additional market borrowings of 0.5 percent of their Gross State Domestic Product (GSDP), amounting to about Rs. 30,000 crore, for capital expenditures.

5. India Infrastructure Finance Company (IIFCL), which has already been authorized to raise Rs.10,000 crore through tax-free bonds by 31.03.2009 for refinancing bank lending of longer maturity to eligible infrastructure bid-based PPP projects, will be accessing the market next week for raising the first tranche of the amount. This will enable the funding of mainly highways and port projects on hand of about Rs.25,000 crore. To fund additional projects of about Rs.75,000 crore at

competitive rates over the next 18 months, IIFCL is being enabled to access in tranches an additional Rs.30,000 crore by way of tax-free bonds once funds raised in the current year are effectively utilized.

6. Exporters are especially hit by recessionary conditions globally. To support exports a number of steps have been taken. As a further measure:

(i) Taking into account the fact that the rupee has appreciated nearly 4 percent against the dollar since November 2008, it has been decided to restore DEPB rates to those prevailing prior to November 2008. In order to provide predictability and stability of regime in the short term for future contracts, the DEPB Scheme would be extended till 31.12.2009.

(ii) Duty drawback benefits on certain items including knitted fabrics, bicycles, agricultural hand tools and specified categories of yarn are being enhanced. These changes will take effect retrospectively from September 1, 2008.

(iii) Exporters have raised a number of procedural issues where modification of procedures could reduce delays faced by exporters. To consider these and similar problems, Government has decided to constitute a Committee under the chairmanship of the Finance Secretary including Secretaries of the Departments of Revenue and Commerce to look into and resolve these issues on a fast-track basis.

(iv) EXIM Bank has obtained from the RBI a line of credit of Rs.5,000 crore and will provide pre-shipment and post-shipment credit, in rupees or dollars, to Indian exporters at competitive rates.

7. Other measures designed to counter recessionary trends are the following:

(i) Exemptions from CVD on TMT bars and structurals, and from CVD and Special CVD on cement, which were given to contain inflation, are being withdrawn. Full exemption from basic customs duty on zinc and ferro alloys, which was also provided to contain inflation, is being similarly withdrawn.

(ii) Government of India will work with State Governments to encourage them to release land for low-income and middle-income housing schemes.

(iii) States, as a one-time measure up to 30.06.2009, will be provided assistance under the JNNURM for the purchase of buses for their urban transport systems. A scheme towards this end will be announced shortly.

(iv) Accelerated depreciation of 50 percent will be provided for commercial vehicles to be purchased on or after 1.1.2009 up to 31.03.09.

8. Government is closely monitoring its spending to expedite the pace of expenditure for all schemes and programmes. Government will set up a fast-track monitoring committee to ensure expeditious approval and implementation of central projects. Chief Ministers are being advised to do the same.

9. The measures outlined above taken together with steps taken earlier constitute a substantial counter-cyclical stimulus in the current year. Government does not envisage any further measures in the current fiscal year. However, Government is aware that the measures required to provide an economic stimulus to the economy have to extend beyond the current financial year. Toward this end, it is finalizing Plan and non-Plan expenditure that will be required in the next financial year to maintain the tempo. The Plan for the next year will include proposals for recapitalization of the public sector banks. The recapitalization is expected to be of the order of Rs.20,000 crore over the next two years. This will help to ensure that the banking system will not suffer from capital adequacy constraints in order to provide credit growth needed to sustain the economic momentum in 2009–10.

III. Reserve Bank of India Press Release, January 2, 2009

(http://www.rbi.org.in/scripts/BS_PressReleaseDisplay.aspx?prid=19792)

The global financial situation continues to be uncertain. Since the official recognition of recession in the US, the UK, the Euro area and Japan, the downside risks to the global economy have increased. Concomitantly, the policy initiatives in the advanced economies are geared towards managing the recession and defusing potentially deflationary trends. The US has reduced the Federal Funds Rate to 0–0.25 percent. Several other advanced and emerging economies such as Japan, Canada, Republic of Korea, Hong Kong and China too have reduced their policy rates.

2. India's financial sector has remained resilient even in the face of global financial turmoil that is so deep and pervasive. Our financial markets continue to function in an orderly manner. India's growth trajectory has, however, been impacted both by the financial crisis and the follow-on global economic downturn. This impact has turned out to be deeper and wider than earlier anticipated. Concurrently, because of global developments coupled with supply and demand management measures at home, inflation is on the decline.

3. Reflecting these developments, the Reserve Bank has adjusted its policy stance from demand management to arresting the moderation in growth. In particular, the aim of these measures was to augment domestic and forex liquidity and to ensure that credit continues to flow to productive sectors of the economy. Notably, since mid-September 2008, the Reserve Bank has reduced the repo rate under the liquidity adjustment facility (LAF) from 9.0 percent to 6.5 percent, reduced the reverse repo rate under the LAF from 6.0 percent to 5.0 percent and the cash reserve ratio from 9.0 percent to 5.5 percent.

4. The cumulative amount of primary liquidity made available to the financial system through various measures initiated by the Reserve Bank is over Rs. 3,00,000 crore. This sizeable easing has ensured a comfortable liquidity position starting mid-November as evidenced by a number of indicators. Since November 18, 2008, consistent with the policy stance, the LAF window has largely been in the surplus mode. The overnight money market rate has consistently remained within the LAF

corridor since November 3, 2008. The yield on the 10-year benchmark G-Sec has declined from 8.66 percent on September 29, 2008 to 5.31 percent on January 1, 2009. Taking the signal from the reductions in the repo and reverse repo rates, all public sector banks and several private sector and foreign banks have reduced their benchmark prime lending rates (BPLRs). Notably, the top five public sector banks have reduced their BPLRs from a range of 13.75–14.00 percent as on October 1, 2008 to a range of 12.00–12.50 percent presently.

5. The Reserve Bank has been constantly monitoring the global developments and the domestic economic situation. On the positive side, inflationary pressures have eased significantly. Inflation as measured by year-on-year variations in the wholesale price index (WPI) has declined to 6.38 percent as on December 20, 2008, down by more than half from the high of 12.91 percent as on August 2, 2008. However, the consumer price inflation, as reflected in various consumer price indices in the range of 10.38–11.11 percent as of October–November 2008, has yet to show moderation.

6. At the same time, there is evidence of economic activity slowing down. Exports registered a negative growth for the two recent consecutive months, October–November 2008, for the first time since February 2002. The index of industrial production (IIP) registered a negative growth of 0.4 percent during October 2008, with the manufacturing sector registering a negative growth of 1.2 percent, for the first time since April 1994. IIP growth during April–October 2008 at 4.1 percent was less than half of 9.9 percent during the corresponding period of the previous year. The services sector, which has been the main engine of growth during the last several years, has also been slowing down. Business confidence has been dented significantly. There are clear signs of deceleration in investment demand.

7. Even as some public sector and private sector banks have cut lending rates in response to the Reserve Bank's monetary policy stance, concerns over rising credit risk together with the slowing of economic activity appear to have moderated credit growth. The Reserve Bank continues to urge banks to monitor their loan portfolio and take early action, including debt restructuring where warranted, to prevent the rise of bad assets down the road and safeguard the gains of the last several years in improving asset quality. At the same time, banks should price risk appropriately and ensure that quality enterprises continue to get funding. The Reserve Bank appreciates that risk management is difficult even in normal circumstances; it is even more difficult in an environment of uncertainty and downturn.

8. On a review of current global and domestic macroeconomic situation, the Reserve Bank has decided to take the following further measures:

Repo Rate

- To reduce the repo rate under the liquidity adjustment facility (LAF) by 100 basis points from 6.5 percent to 5.5 percent with immediate effect.

Reverse Repo Rate

- To reduce the reverse repo rate under the LAF by 100 basis points from 5.0 percent to 4.0 percent with immediate effect.

Cash Reserve Ratio

- To reduce the cash reserve ratio (CRR) of scheduled banks by 50 basis points from 5.5 percent to 5.0 percent from the fortnight beginning January 17, 2009.

9. The reduction in the CRR will inject additional liquidity of around Rs. 20,000 crore to the financial system. It is expected that the reduction in the policy interest rates and the CRR will further enable banks to provide credit for productive purposes at appropriate interest rates. The Reserve Bank on its part would continue to maintain a comfortable liquidity position in the system.

10. The fundamentals of our economy continue to be strong. Once the crisis is behind us, and calm and confidence are restored in the global markets, economic activity in India would recover sharply. But a period of painful adjustment is inevitable.

Section II

India-Korea Bilateral Economic Cooperation

5 India-Korea Trade and Investment Relations

PRAVAKAR SAHOO, DURGESH KUMAR RAI AND RAJIV KUMAR

Though economic relations between India and Korea have been strengthening, the current size of trade and investment between the two countries is relatively low compared to the size and structural complementarities of the two economies. In this context, the present paper analyzes trade and investment relations. We find that the increase in merchandize trade between the two countries has been mainly because of the changing demand structure and comparative advantages of both the economies in complementary sectors in recent years. The Revealed Comparative Advantage (RCA) analysis at both the aggregated and disaggregated levels shows that while Korea has been specializing in a few, high value-added manufacturing products, India's exports have been more diversified. The analysis also indicates that both countries have comparative advantages in different products in the same industry, revealing the opportunity for intra-industry trade (IIT). Moreover, the increasing trade complementarity index (TCI) shows that Indian and Korean trade gradually became more compatible over the period, indicating that a CEPA between the two countries is likely to enhance trade flows. The trade intensities between the two countries reveal that Korea is doing much better and there is scope for India to improve its export intensity with Korea. Finally, the study reflects upon tariff and non-tariff barriers that affect bilateral trade and investment.

Introduction

Asia has become the growth center of the world economy in recent years. Within the region, India and South Korea are the 3rd and 4th largest economies after China and Japan.[1] Though the Asian growth story mainly revolves around India and China, South Korea has remained a key player for these countries as one of their major trading and investment partners. South Korea adopted outward-oriented economic policies with the beginning of its first five-year economic development plan in 1962, which resulted in high growth, and the integration of the Korean economy with the rest of the world. Subsequently, high and consistent economic growth made South Korea one of the high-income economies in Asia. Korea is still growing at a faster rate than other developed economies. India, on the other hand, adopted an import-substitution policy from its independence until the early 90s. Since 1991, India has introduced wide-ranging economic policy reforms and is moving toward a market-driven economy. This has resulted in consistent high economic growth over the past one-and-a-half decades, making India the 10th largest economy in the world. At present, India is the 2nd fastest growing economy in the world. Both India and Korea have been getting integrated with the world economy, enhancing their role in the international economic order.

The greater openness of the Indian economy has not only enhanced market access for Korean goods but has also provided investment opportunities for internationally competitive Korean companies. This is evident from the fact that bilateral merchandize trade increased from \$0.55 billion[2] in 1991 to \$8.86 billion in 2007.[3] Korea has also emerged as an important source of FDI for India. However, because of several tariff and non-tariff barriers in both economies, the current size of trade and investment is very low compared to the size and structural complementarities of the two economies. There is immense potential to enhance economic cooperation between the two sides. The increasing scale of globalization is posing both opportunities and challenges to the two countries. There is potential not only for greater cooperation at various multilateral forums like the WTO and the IMF, but also immense scope at the regional level to strengthen bilateral ties given the

1. World Bank (2010).
2. All $ figures are in US dollars.
3. UNCOMTRADE, 2008.

deadlock and slow growth of negotiations on the Doha Round in the WTO (Sahoo, 2008). As part of its "Look-East Policy", India has been making efforts to intensify economic relations with the East Asian economies. Consequently, East Asia has become one of India's largest trading partners in recent years. Korea too is looking beyond its traditional trading partners like the US and China to sustain its trade and economic progress.

Against this backdrop and given the fact that there is hardly any comprehensive study on India-Korea economic relations, the present study attempts to investigate the trends, nature and composition of bilateral trade and investment flows. Further, the study highlights barriers/obstacles that hamper trade and investment flows between the two countries.

Economic Profiles of India and Korea

India: Since 1990–91, the structure of the Indian economy has changed substantially (Appendix Table A-5.1, A-5.2[4] and Appendix A-5.1). Higher growth during the past decade and a half was accompanied by substantial growth of the services sector and a marginal improvement in the manufacturing sector. In terms of overall growth performance, the last five years (2002–03 to 2007–08) have been the golden period for the economy according to some experts, with the annual growth rate hovering around 9 percent.[5] The economy has joined the trillion-economy club, both at the official exchange rate ($1.09 trillion 2007 estimate) and on PPP ($2.965 trillion 2007 estimate). There is also sharp acceleration in the annual per capita income growth rate, which almost doubled from a yearly 3.1 and 3.7 percent during the 80s and 90s to a yearly average of 7.2 percent for the period 2003–04 to 2007–08. Most importantly, the Indian economy experienced stable growth with a relatively moderate annual inflation rate (consumer prices) of 3.77 to 5.80 percent during 2002–2006.

---

4. All tables with suffix 'A' are given in the appendix at the end of the paper.
5. See Acharya (2008) for the India's macroeconomic performance for the period 2002-03 to 2007-08.

In the post-reform period, the country's external sector showed vast improvement with considerable growth in exports and foreign exchange reserves and an improvement in the overall balance of payments position (Appendix Table A-5.2). The overall balance of payments also showed a surplus after 2000 because of surplus in the current account and large inflow of foreign capital in the capital account. However, a growing deficiency of infrastructural facilities, increasing labor costs, rising income, regional inequalities and slow agricultural growth are some of the challenges that threaten to slow down the growth momentum the Indian economy achieved in the past five years.

South Korea: South Korea is the 11th largest economy in the world[6] and is considered one of the most dynamic economies. South Korea joined the trillion-dollar club of world economies in 2007 (World Bank, 2008) with an estimated GDP of $1.206 trillion (PPP). In 2006, South Korea's GDP per capita was roughly equivalent to some of the developed economies. The growing economic prowess of Korea saw it enter the OECD on December 12, 1996. Rapid economic growth changed the structure of the economy, making it one of the most advanced countries in Asia after Japan (Appendix Table A-5.1). The industrial and services sectors account for a major part of Korea's GDP.

After the 1997–98 Asian financial crisis, South Korea moved away from a centrally planned, government-directed investment model and introduced extensive structural reforms in four main sectors—corporate, financial, labor and public sectors. However, the restructuring of Korean conglomerates, privatizing banks, and creating a more liberalized economy with an exit mechanism for bankrupt firms remain among the most important, unfinished reform tasks. For Korea, the challenges in sustaining its high growth rate will come from the decrease in its current account surplus,[7] because of a rapid increase in the negative balance in services, an aging population that could result in a labor shortage and necessitate higher public expenditure on pensions and

6. *http://www.nytimes.com/2007/04/03/business/worldbusiness/03trade.html?_r=1&oref=slogin*

7. The current account balance has decreased from $11,950 million in 2003 to $6,092 million in 2006. However, Korea's international reserves are continuously increasing and reached $238,956 million in 2006 compared to $155,355 million in 2003.

healthcare, the rapid shift of labor from the manufacturing to the service sector where productivity is low and increasing income inequalities (Schiff, 2007).

India-Korea Trade Relations

Korea is very well integrated with the global economy with a trade/GDP ratio of more than 85 percent in 2006. The Korean economy has followed an export-led growth strategy with exports contributing 43 percent of GDP in 2006. Comparatively, India is far less integrated, despite the increasing openness of its economy since 1991, with a trade/GDP ratio of around 45 percent in 2006. Korea also has a higher share in total world merchandize trade compared to India. It is also a major importer of services (Appendix Table A-5.3) while India has emerged since 2001 as a significant exporter of services. In this section we analyze merchandize trade between the two countries.

Merchandize Trade between India and Korea

Indian economic reforms were considered timely by Korean companies that were looking for alternative destinations for trade and investments. Between 1991 and 2007, the value of Indian exports to Korea increased from a mere $0.24 billion to $2.46 billion while Indian imports from Korea increased from $0.314 billion to $5.4 billion (UNCOMTRADE, 2008). In 2007, India ranked 11th among export destinations and 16th among sources of imports for the Korean economy. Korea's share in Indian imports touched a peak in 2003 and declined thereafter, whereas Korea's share in India's total exports remained almost stable till 2000 but increased to around 2 percent in 2006[8] (Appendix Figure A-5.1a). During the same period, India's share in total Korean exports and imports rose from 0.67 and 0.41 percent in 1990 to 1.70 and 1.15 percent respectively in 2007 (Appendix Figure A-5.1b). An important feature of India-Korea trade relations is that the trade balance has always been in favor of South Korea and has continuously increased over the period 1990–2007. In fact, between 1991 and 2007, India's exports to South Korea increased 10 times, while imports rose more

8. However, it went down significantly in 2007 compared to 2006.

than 17 times, resulting in an increase in the trade deficit (Appendix Figure A-5.1c).

The increase in merchandize trade between the two countries has been attributed to the changing demand structures and comparative advantages of both economies in different sectors (Sahoo, 2009; Sahoo *et al.*, 2009). The Indian export basket has traditionally consisted of a few low value-added products (Appendix Table A-5.4). For instance, in 1990, ores, slag and the ash product group alone constituted more than 40 percent of Indian exports to Korea followed by cotton and other product groups. However, the composition of India's exports to Korea has undergone significant changes after 2000. In 2006, the Indian export basket consisted of a wider range of industrial products. Mineral fuels, oils and products of their distillation group have now become an important export group, with a 35 percent share in total exports in 2006, followed by ores, slag and ash, and cotton and other product groups. However, some conventional export commodity groups such as cotton have lost their dominant position from a 17.4 percent share in total Indian exports in 1990 to 8.7 percent in 2006. Other products that lost their weight substantially in India's export basket are ores, slag and ash, cereals, aluminium and articles thereof, etc. Similarly, India's import basket from Korea has undergone changes over time. The top 10 major product groups that constituted more than 79 percent of Indian imports from Korea in 1990 were industrial products (Appendix Table A-5.5). In 2006, the Indian import basket mainly consisted of relatively high-value-added products such as electrical machinery and equipment; nuclear reactors, boilers, machinery and mechanical appliances, etc.

Revealed Comparative Advantage (RCA) of India and Korea

Export competitiveness is an important determinant of successful integration of a country in the rapidly globalizing world economy. A high degree of competitiveness reflects relative cost advantages, superior product attributes and fewer trade restrictions.[9] In this study we

9. The determinants of export competitiveness include price-related factors such as domestic wages or material costs; availability of labor; exchange rate; Foreign Direct Investment (FDI) and management; and reduced cost of communication and transportation (Adams *et al.*, 2006) as well as qualitative attributes.

compute comparative advantage using the Balassa Index (1965) to calculate the export competitiveness of Korea's and India's exports to the world. We also calculate an index derived from the Balassa Index to suit the bilateral context[10] for the reference years.

Summary of IRCA

Table 5.1 presents a summary of the comparative advantages in the products of India and Korea in the world market at the HS 2-, 4- and 6-digit levels of classification for the triennium ending (TE) 1998,[11] 2003 and 2007. Table 5.1 shows that for India, at the HS 2-digit level of classification, the number of products with an RCA value of more than 1 has remained almost constant between TE 1998 and TE 2007. However, the share of these commodities in total exports has gone down from 72.82 percent in TE 1998 to 67.34 percent in TE 2007, perhaps because India may be exporting products that have low RCAs but their share in total exports is significant. This has been happening since India started exporting mineral-related products after 2001. At the 4-digit level, although the number of commodities having RCA>1 has increased from 385 in TE 1998 to 440 in TE 2007, the share of these commodities has remained almost the same during the period. At the HS 6-digit level, both the number of commodities having RCA>1 and their share in total exports have increased substantially between TE 1998 and 2007. The RCA analysis of India shows that due to structural changes and changing global demand, the composition of Indian exports has changed and become more diversified, both at the horizontal and vertical levels, especially since TE 2003.

In contrast, Korea has shown a different trend in its RCA. During TE 1998 and 2006,[12] the number of products being exported at the 2-, 4- and 6-digit levels has been decreasing. However, the share of products having RCA>1 in Korea's total exports to the world has been increasing. This indicates that Korea is specializing in a few sectors and products.

10. See Werner (2002).

11. Triennium Ending (TE) 1998, 2003 and 2007 refer to the average RCA for three years: 1996-1998, 2001-2003 and 2005-2007, respectively.

12. The analysis for Korea is up to 2006 instead of 2007 due to unavailability of data for some products for 2007.

It can also be interpreted as an indication that Korea is losing its competitiveness in some sectors/products in which it had traditionally been competitive in the world market, to new emerging countries, especially China.[13]

Table 5.1

Number and Share (in Total Exports) of Products with RCA>1

Year		*India*			*Korea*		
		TE 1998	*TE 2003*	*TE 2007*	*TE 1998*	*TE 2003*	*TE 2006*
Number of products	2-digit	41 (72.82)	39 (74.65)	42 (67.34)	26 (65.1)	20 (80.66)	20 (70.71)
	4-digit	384 (81.35)	311 (81.48)	440 (82.06)	246 (80.28)	240 (80.85)	205 (83.59)
	6-digit	1524 (84.12)	1224 (86.86)	2024 (93.41)	870 (82.87)	849 (81.82)	797 (86.32)

Note: Figures in parentheses show share in total merchandize exports.

Source: WITS Database.

IRCA of India's Top Exports to Korea

Here we look at the movements in the IRCA values of top export commodities from India. In TE 1998, the top 10 products were mainly low value-added products such as stones and metals (HS 71), articles of apparel and clothing accessories (HS 62), cotton (HS 52), etc. (Appendix Table A-5.6). In TE 2007, new product groups like mineral fuels (HS 27) and vehicles (HS 87) have become part of the top commodities exported from India. Though these products do not exhibit comparative advantages in the world market, they are becoming important segments of the Indian export basket. Due to the changing global demand and supply environment, and substantial addition to refining capacity in the country, mineral fuel has become the most prominent export commodity from India (from 5.32 percent in 2003 to 14.22 percent in 2007). The other product group that has demonstrated an increase in both its RCA and share between TE 1998 and 2007 is organic chemicals. Though apparel and clothing has improved its share and RCA from TE 1998 to TE 2003, it slowed down in TE 2007. It is important to note

13. *http://www.hani.co.kr/arti/english_edition/e_business/144265.html*

that India's competitiveness in cotton is declining, which has resulted in its share in total exports declining.

The RCA analysis of India's top export commodities at both the 4- and 6-digit level[14] of classifications shows almost similar trends. Overall, India was found to be very competitive in sectors like cotton and textiles, products related to diamond and pearls, and rice during TE 1998. In TE 2007, the petroleum products group (HS 2710), with a relatively higher RCA value of 3.16, had become an important export item. India has become very competitive in new products after TE 2003 such as iron ore and concentrates (HS 2601), other organic compounds (HS 2942), etc. In contrast, cotton yarn export is losing its place in terms of export share though its competitiveness improved between TE 1998 and 2007. In some products, such as rice, there has been deterioration in both the RCA value and share in total Indian exports. Analysis at the 6-digit level shows that the competitive commodities are "non-industrial: other" (HS 710239) within the category of "diamonds" followed by Milled rice (HS 100630), and frozen shrimps and prawns (HS 030613). However, as reflected in 2- and 4-digit levels of classifications, in TE 2007, petroleum (HS 271000) had become the top export commodity with an RCA value of 3.25 that was higher than in TE 2003. In products such as iron ores and concentrates (HS 260111), non-industrial (HS 710239), and men's or boys' shirts of cotton (HS 620520), both the RCA value and hence the share in its total exports have increased between TE 1998 and 2007.

IRCA of Korea's Top Exports

Korean exports to the world are more concentrated on some product groups compared to India with the top 10 exports (Appendix Table A-5.7). Electrical machinery equipment parts (HS 85) was the top export that constituted more than one-fourth of total Korean exports. The other top commodity groups were nuclear reactors and related machinery (HS 84) and vehicles (HS 87), even though Korea does not have a comparative advantage in these industries. In TE 2007, the

14. For details of top products and respective IRCA values at 4- and 6-digit levels, see Sahoo *et al.* (2009).

composition of the top 10 exported commodity groups remained almost the same. However, there is an improvement in Korean competitiveness and hence, in the share of the top four exported commodities in total exports. This indicates increasing specialization of Korean companies in certain groups of products. New product groups like optical, photographic, cinematographic products, etc. (HS 90) have also gained importance in the Korean export basket with a high RCA value of 1.5.

At the 4-digit level[15] also, in TE 1998 products related to electrical equipment (HS 85) such as electronic integrated circuits (HS 8542) etc. figured among the top 10 exports from Korea. In all these product groups, Korean competitiveness was quite high. Since TE 2003, Korean competitiveness and share in total exports have improved significantly for the category "motor cars and motor vehicles", pushing electronic integrated circuits to second position. A new entry into the top 10 exports since TE 2003 has been transmission apparatus for radio and television (HS 8525). Korea's RCA analysis at the 6-digit level shows that in TE 1998, all the top 10 exports belonged to a few categories from the top export items at the 2- and 4-digit levels. Korea exhibited the highest comparative advantages in monolithic digital integrated circuits, other woven fabrics, and tankers and other vessels for transport. In TE 2006, Korea has been able to enhance its competitiveness in products like transmission apparatus incorporation (HS 852520), petroleum oils and oils obtained from bituminous minerals. With an increase in the RCA value of the product category "other vehicles with spark ignition", its share has risen in Korea's exports. Other devices, appliances and instruments (HS 901380) have also become important in the Korean export basket with a high RCA value. All this indicates that the policy emphasis of the Korean government on specializing in high-value products has resulted in an upward trend in share and RCA of high-end products in the Korean export basket.

RCAs of India and Korea in Each Other's Markets

The patterns of India's RCA in Korea are different from its RCA in the world market. In contrast to its RCA in the world market, where

15. For details at 4- and 6-digit levels of top products and respective IRCA values, see Sahoo *et al.*, (2009).

India's exports are getting diversified, its RCA in the Korean market shows that there is a decline in the number of commodities having RCAs greater than 1 at all digit levels of classification. As can be seen from Table 5.2, the number of products that have an RCA>1 at all three levels—2-, 4- and 6-digit—has gone down between TE 1998 and 2006 but total exports are increasing, indicating concentration/specialization of Indian exports. The same trend is found for Korea as well at the 4- and 6-digit levels, but their share has been increasing.

Table 5.2

Number and Share (in Total Exports to Each Other's Market) of the Products with RCA>1

		India in Korea			*Korea in India*		
Year		*TE 1998*	*TE 2003*	*TE 2007*	*TE 1998*	*TE 2003*	*TE 2006*
Number of Products	2-digit	27 (86.61)	20 (82.01)	26 (89.89)	23 (63.43)	30 (86.01)	24 (85.75)
	4-digit	227 (93.76)	267 (90.83)	182 (90.22)	221 (86.08)	226 (86.86)	196 (87.78)
	6-digit	673 (96.65)	533 (88.05)	668 (94.44)	707 (91.83)	743 (89.94)	655 (92.09)

Note: Figures in parentheses show share in total merchandize exports.

Source: WITS Database.

India's RCA in Korea

The RCA analysis of India's top 10 export commodity groups (at the 2-digit level) to Korea shows that cotton (HS 52) had been the top commodity group in the Indian export basket to Korea followed by the food industry (HS 23), organic chemicals (HS 23), ores, slag and ash (HS 26), and iron and steel (HS 72) until 2003 (Appendix Table A-5.8). However, in TE 2006, India has become less competitive in two of its traditionally important exports to the Korean markets, viz., cotton and residues and waste from the food industry as both their share in total export and their RCA value have gone down. Now, mineral fuels and related products (HS 27) and ore, slag and ash (HS 26) have become very prominent in India's export to Korea. This has happened despite the fact that India's competitiveness for this group has marginally deteriorated. Except for pharmaceutical products, all other product groups have remained among the top 10 exports to Korea over this period. Pharmaceutical products have lost both their share in total exports and their RCA value during the period 1996–2006, which can be a disturbing phenomenon since it was a good performing sector in the recent past.

The RCA of 10 export commodity groups (at the 4-digit level, Appendix Table A-5.9) to Korea shows that India exhibited high competitiveness in cotton yarn (HS 5207) followed by organic compounds, oil cake and other solid residues, sulphonated and nitrated goods, etc. An almost similar composition of products was found in 2003 but in most of the items, India's competitiveness was found to have declined when compared to TE 1998. In TE 2006, India's composition of top export items has partially changed and it has become competitive in new products like petroleum oils, motor parts and accessories, waste and scrap of precious metals and cyclic hydrocarbon.

The RCAs of India's top 10 commodity exports (at the 6-digit level) to Korea show that in TE 1998, oil cake and other solid residues (HS 230400) was the top export item with very strong competitiveness followed by cotton-related goods, such as "multiple or cabled yarn" and "single yarn of uncombed fibres" that have shown the highest RCA (Appendix Table A-5.10). Items from the broad category of cotton remained significantly competitive till TE 2003, although in most of them India's competitiveness has been deteriorating in the Korean market. However, as reflected at a broader level of classifications (2- and 4-digit levels), India's competitiveness has increased sharply in petroleum products as both the RCA value and share in total Indian export to Korea have increased significantly. With the significant value of RCAs, products related to iron ore have become the second-most important items of export from India. Among these zinc ores and concentrates (HS 260800) and iron ores and concentrates (HS 260111) are the chief ones. The next most important items are from the broad category of "residues and waste" including oil cake and solid residues (HS 230400), where India's comparative advantages increased significantly. Although India remained quite competitive in cotton-related products like single yarn of combed (HS 520521) and uncombed fibres (HS 520511), their share has declined significantly over the period.

Korea's RCA in India

If one looks at the RCA values of the top 10 commodities exported from Korea to India at the 2-digit level, nuclear reactors, boilers and machinery (HS 84) was the top commodity group, accounting for more than a fifth of total exports to India in TE 1998 (Appendix Table A-5.11). This was despite the fact that Korea was less competitive in the Indian market (RCA value was 0.9) compared to the rest of the world. Except for the "electrical machinery equipment parts thereof" group (HS 85) and nuclear reactors, boilers and machinery (HS 84), Korea was competitive in all the top 10 export commodity groups. Between TE 1998 and 2006, Korea's export structure changed. An increase in the RCA value of electrical machinery equipment parts thereof (HS 85) resulted in an impressive increase in its share of total exports. Its share rose to almost a third of Korea's total exports to India and its RCA reached 2.98 in the same year. Korea has also significantly improved its competitiveness in product groups such as nuclear reactors, boilers, machinery (HS 84), vehicles, rail/tram roll-stock (HS 87), iron and steel (HS 72), etc. However, it has been losing its competitiveness in product groups like plastic and articles thereof (HS 39), ships, boats and floating structures (HS 89) and man-made filaments (HS 54). At the 4-digit level, Korea was very competitive in all the top 10 export commodities in TE 1998 (Appendix Table A-5.12 for details). Since TE 2003, Korea has developed competitiveness in new product groups such as transmission apparatus for radiotelephony, etc. televisions, cameras, cordless telephones (HS 8525), motor parts and accessories (HS 8708), parts for television, radio and radar apparatus (HS 8529), petroleum oil and oils obtained from bituminous minerals (excluding crude) (HS 2710), flat-rolled products of iron (HS 7209), newsprint in rolls or sheets (HS 4801), etc.

At the 6-digit level also (Appendix Table A-5.13), the top competitive exports in TE 1998 was other machines and mechanical appliances (HS 847989), followed by polypropylene (HS 390210), aromatic policorboxilic acids, etc. The competitive structure of Korean exports has changed after TE 2003; now transmission apparatus incorporation (HS 852520) and other parts and accessories (HS 870899) under motor parts and accessories have become the top exports from

Korea to India with quite impressive RCAs of 8.89 and 12.03, respectively, in TE 2006. Petroleum oils and oils obtained from bituminous minerals, preparations thereof (HS 271000) have become the third most important export commodity to India from Korea and exhibited a high level of competitiveness in comparison to previous years. It is interesting to note that the same product—petroleum oils and oils obtained from bituminous minerals, preparations thereof (HS 271000)—has become the top commodity export from India to Korea during the same period. This indicates the possibility of intra-industry trade between the two countries in this industry.

Intra-Industry Trade between India and Korea

In this section, the Intra-Industry Trade (IIT) index is computed, which shows the gains derived from international trade over and above those associated with comparative advantage. IIT refers to simultaneous exports and imports of products within the same product category. The Grubel-Lloyd (G-L) index is commonly used to measure intra-industry trade. The G-L index takes a value of 0 if there are no exports or imports of a particular product group, i.e., no IIT in that particular product category. If exports exactly match imports, both being positive, the G-L index value equals 100. IIT is driven by economies of scale and productivity gains. By being engaged in IIT, a country can reduce the number of similar products it produces and benefit from scale economies and specialization. Based on the Grubel-Lloyd (G-L) formula, the IIT index between India and Korea can be calculated as follows:

$$IITi_k = 1 - \{|\ X_{jik} - M_{jik}\ |\ /\ (X_{jik} + M_{jik})\} \text{ or}$$
$$\{X_{jik} + M_{jik} - |\ X_{jik} - M_{jik}\ |\}/\ X_{jik} + M_{jik} \qquad \ldots(1)$$

where X_{jik} and M_{jik} represent exports and imports of products from industry j in country i (India) to and from country k (Korea).

Since there are significant differences in the economic structures and the level of development, the possibility of intra-industry trade between the two countries is not very high though it has been increasing in recent years. Table 5.3 highlights the changes in value of the intra-industry trade index from TE 1998 to TE 2007. In TE 2007, sectors with high value of intra-industry trade include mineral products, chemical products, wood and wood products, textiles and textile articles, articles of stone, plaster, cement, asbestos, pearls, precious or semi-precious stones, metals, base metals and articles thereof, and miscellaneous products.

Table 5.3

Intra-Industry Trade (IIT) between India and Korea in Different Sectors

Sectors	*IIT*			*Share in Trade in TE'07*
	TE'98	*TE'03*	*TE'07*	
Animal and animal products	0.03	0.02	0.03	0.25
Vegetable products	0.15	0.22	0.09	0.58
Animal/veg fats and oils & their clea	0.12	0.46	0.02	0.08
Prepared foodstuff	0.01	0.06	0.03	2.56
Mineral products	0.73	0.04	0.50	18.25
Chemical products	0.60	0.90	0.96	7.31
Plastic and rubber	0.02	0.07	0.07	5.42
Hides and skins	0.64	0.26	0.13	0.51
Wood and wood products	0.87	0.59	0.54	0.03
Wood and pulp products	0.02	0.07	0.03	1.26
Textiles and textile articles	0.73	0.70	0.56	4.68
Footwear, headwear	0.28	0.15	0.26	0.02
Articles of stones, plaster, cement, asbestos	0.86	0.99	0.49	0.39
Pearls, precious or semi-precious stones, metals	0.70	0.60	0.44	1.59
Base metals and articles thereof	0.41	0.54	0.42	16.87
Machinery and mechanical appliances	0.12	0.05	0.08	31.83
Transportation equipment	0.10	0.04	0.19	6.71
Instruments: measuring, musical	0.14	0.09	0.20	1.47
Arms and ammunition; parts and accessories	0.00	–	0.02	0.00
Miscellaneous	0.66	0.59	0.38	0.18
Works of art, collectors' pieces and	0.00	0.04	0.12	0.01

Source: WITS Database.

Intra-industry trade in products with the highest share in bilateral trade between the two countries is presented in Table 5.4. In TE 1998, intra-industry trade was minimal for the top traded commodities except for one product group (iron and steel) with a value of 0.54. However in TE 2007, overall intra-industry trade increased for all the top traded product groups. Intra-industry trade in other top traded product groups is very low and offers a huge opportunity for intra-industry trade if sector-specific barriers, along with general barriers, are removed. These products include electrical machinery, equipment and parts thereof (HS 85), ores, slag and ash (HS 26), plastics and articles thereof (HS 39), cotton (HS 52), etc. A careful observation reveals that most of the products with very high IITs are not top traded commodities, indicating that there is potential for higher trade in these products which would reduce cost and enhance the benefits for both countries.

Table 5.4

Value of Intra-Industry Trade of Top 10 Traded Products

TE 1998				*TE 2007*			
HS Code	*Product*	*IIT*	*Share*	*HS Code*	*Product*	*IIT*	*Share*
29	Organic chemicals	0.48	14.88	85	Electrical mchy equipment, parts thereof	0.03	18.44
84	Nuclear reactors, boilers, mchy & m	0.11	13.13	27	Mineral fuels, oils, waxes and bituminous	0.63	13.95
39	Plastics and articles thereof	0.02	8.81	84	Nuclear reactors, boilers, mchy & m	0.15	13.39
52	Cotton	0.02	7.98	72	Iron and steel	0.42	10.37
72	Iron and steel	0.54	7.35	87	Vehicles o/t railw/tramw roll-stock	0.22	5.65
85	Electrical mchy equip parts thereof	0.14	7.11	29	Organic chemicals	0.97	4.77
23	Residues & waste from the food industry	0.01	6.32	26	Ores, slag and ash	0.05	4.21
26	Ores, slag and ash	0.08	2.68	39	Plastics and articles thereof	0.06	3.79
87	Vehicles o/t railway/ tramway roll-stock	0.06	2.64	52	Cotton	0.05	2.96
74	Copper and articles thereof	0.01	2.60	73	Articles of iron or steel	0.37	2.55

Source: WITS Database.

Trade Complementarity between India and Korea

The trade complementarity index (TCI) provides useful insights on prospects for trade and shows the degree of match between the structures of the two countries' imports and exports. A change in the TCI over time indicates whether the trade profiles of the two countries are becoming more or less compatible. To measure India's trade complementarity with Korea, we used the UNESCAP formula:

$$TCI = \left(1 - \left(\Sigma\left|\frac{\sum_w m_{iwd}}{\sum_w M_{wd}} - \frac{\sum_w x_{isw}}{\sum_w X_{sw}}\right|\right) \div 2\right) \times 100 \qquad ...(2)$$

where d = importing country of interest

s = exporting country of interest

w = set of all countries in the world

i = set of industries

x = commodity export flow

X = total export flow

m = commodity import flow

M = the total import flow

In this study, the overall TCI for India is calculated for the period 1995–2006. Figure 5.1, which depicts trends in the overall trade complementarity index for India over the period, shows that the trade complementarity of India increased from 37.9 in 1995 to 59.8 in 2006. This indicates that the Indian export pattern is becoming more compatible with Korea's import pattern. In 1995, India's trade complementarity was around 38 percent. It touched 40 in 1996 but decreased in subsequent years to reach 34.3 percent in 1998. However, after 1998, India's trade complementarity index has continuously increased and reached around 60 in 2006. This signals that any agreement between the two countries is likely to enhance trade and investment flows.

Trade Intensity between India and Korea

We measured the intensity of trade between the two countries to identify trade potential. The trade intensity index is used to determine whether the value of trade between the two countries is greater or smaller than would be expected on the basis of their importance in world trade. The trade intensity index is defined as a ratio of the share of one country's trade with another country to the other country's share of world trade (Kaliranjan and Bhattacharya, 2007; Sahoo *et al.*, 2009). The trade intensity of a country is calculated in terms of export and import intensity indices (Appendix A-5.1).

Figure 5.1

India's Overall TCI with respect to Korea (1995–2006)

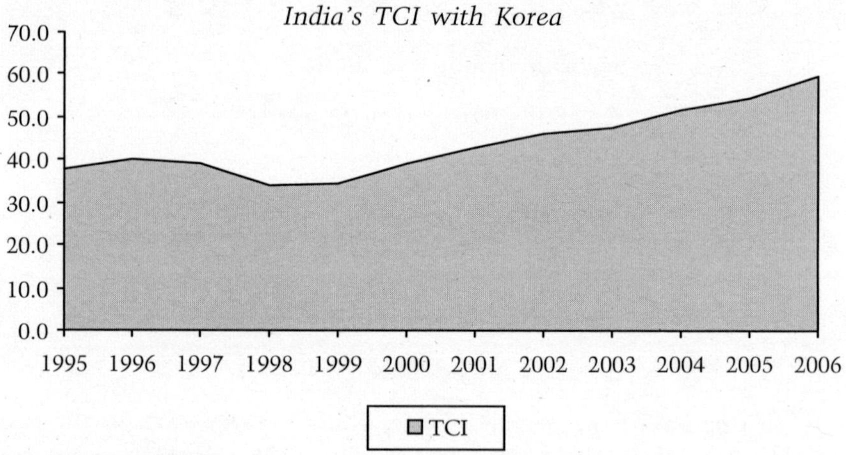

Source: WITS Database.

Figure 5.2 highlights changing trends in the export and import intensities of India and Korea during 1996–2006. Though India's export intensity improved from 52 to 80 during 1996 and 2006 with Korea, it has always been below 1, indicating that Indian exports to Korea have been much below the world average. Contrary to India's export intensity, Korea's export intensity has been greater than unity in most of the years since 1996, indicating Korean exports to India have been greater than its exports to the world on average. Although there has been a decline in the past few years, it still remains higher than Indian export intensity to Korea.

During 1996–2006, Indian import intensity varied widely. In 1996, the value was around 90. It touched 130 in 1998 but has since then continuously declined to reach 60 in 2000. Subsequently, it started to increase up to 2003 but after that it again declined in successive years. On the other hand, Korean import intensity has been quite stable during this period and its value has been around unity. This shows that Korean imports from India have been equivalent to its average imports from the rest of the world.

Figure 5.2

Trade Intensity of India and Korea

(Export and Import Intensity Indexes of India and Korea with Each Other)

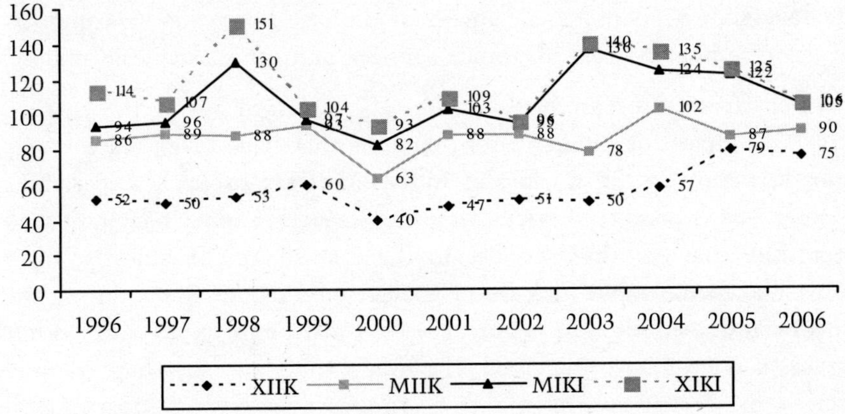

Source: WITS Database.

Trade in Services

Unlike the case of merchandize trade, where Korea ranks ahead of India, India has been performing slightly better than Korea in services. India's exports of commercial services have been increasing by more than 20 percent annually in the past five years. India's export of commercial services has grown steadily and increased by more than five times, from $16 billion in 2000 to $89.7 billion in 2007. Korea, on the other hand, has witnessed fluctuations in its exports of services though it has grown steadily after 2002. In 2007, the annual growth of Korea's services exports was higher than that of India. The total value of Korea's exports of commercial services in 2000 was $29.7 billion, which fell consecutively over the next two years to $27.3 billion in 2002. But since then, it has been increasing continuously and touched $ 61.5 billion in 2007.[16] In 2007, India's share in world exports and imports of commercial services was 2.7 percent and 2.5 percent, respectively, compared to Korea's shares of 1.9 percent and 2.7 percent.[17] Moreover,

16. WTO, *International Trade Statistics, 2008.*

17. *Ibid.*

India has the highest share of commercial services in total exports (both goods and services)—even more than high-income countries. In 2006, the share of commercial services in total exports from India was around 36 percent, whereas it was 13 percent for Korea. Some of the services that have shown phenomenal growth in the last few years are computer and information services, insurance services and other business services.

The export structure of Korea has also changed during the past 15 years. This change is different from changes that have taken place in the export structure of the world and India. Contrary to world experience, the share of transport services in total services export has increased faster than that of other services in the case of Korea. This has been mainly due to the rapid increase of goods exports from Korea during the same period. Among the other services, although exports of "other business services" have increased, the total export and the share in total services export of communication and computer and information services have increased slower than that of India.[18] As far as bilateral trade in services between India and Korea is concerned, there is little data it is believed that trade in services between the two countries is increasing rapidly, at least in some sub-sectors especially in IT/software services and travel services. According to the Electronic and Computer Software Export Council (ESC), software exports from India to South Korea in 2001–02 were $27.53 million compared to $8.67 million in 2000–01. According to industry sources, Korea is not only a market for Indian software companies, but it can also be used as a platform to establish a stronger presence in the APEC region.

India-Korea Investment Relations

Economic reforms that started in the early 90s in India offered a conducive investment environment for potential foreign investors, including Korean companies. Many Korean companies started entering the Indian market aggressively and, within a short period of time, many of them became household names in the country. At present, many Korean enterprises such as LG, Samsung, and Hyundai have not only established their presence but have been able to diversify their

18. UNCTAD, *Handbook of Statistics, 2008.*

businesses to various sectors in the economy. The share of Korea in total actual cumulative FDI received and approved by India were 3.56 and 5.18, respectively during 1991 and 1999. However, after 2000, the share of Korea has been declining not only in actual FDI inflow but also in terms of approvals. This can be observed from Table 5.5.

Table 5.5

Year-wise FDI Inflow (Actual and Approved) in India (USD million)

Year (Jan–Dec)	Actual Inflow			Approvals		
	From S. Korea	From all Countries	Share of Korea in Total Investment (%)	From S. Korea	From All Countries	Share of Korea in Total Investment (%)
August 1991–December 1999	571.7	16019.7	3.56	2605.4	53245.7	5.18
2000	17.7	2873.0	0.61	9.6	4008.6	0.24
2001	4.5	3728.4	0.12	14.8	4653.3	0.32
2002	37.8	3790.7	0.99	6.0	2303.8	0.26
2003	24.5	2525.5	0.97	13.4	1177.5	1.4
2004	26.7	3753.4	0.71	3.5	1900.3	0.66
2005	66.0	4360.2	1.51	15.3	1795.4	0.85
2006	64.7	11108.4	0.58	23.1	5,111.2	0.45
2007	67.95	19309.892	0.35	15.7	4772.8	0.32

Source: Directorate of Industrial Policy and Promotion, Ministry of Commerce and Industry, Government of India.

The major sectors for which approvals were given for FDI (Table 5.6) from South Korea were transport, fuels (power and oil refinery), and electrical equipment (including computer software and electronics). In terms of actual inflows (Table 5.7), sectors like electrical equipment (including computer software and electronics), metallurgy, and food processing have attracted the maximum investment.

Contrary to its trade performance, South Korea does not fare well in terms of attracting foreign investment into the country. Compared to other East Asian economies, Korean policy makers gave preference to loan-based investments over direct investment. However, Korean policymakers have realized the importance of foreign investment in economic growth and enacted a new foreign investment promotion act in 1998. Korea has also created several new institutions such as Invest

KOREA and the Office of the Foreign Investment Ombudsman to facilitate foreign investment in the country.[19] Since 1998, Korea has had a liberal FDI regime, under which all kinds of FDI including establishment, stock acquisitions, mergers, and long-term loans are allowed.[20] Subsequently, FDI flows into Korea have increased mainly from the EU, followed by the US and Japan and accounting for more than 80 percent of total FDI inflow to Korea (Ahn, 2008).

Table 5.6

Share of Top Sectors in FDI Approvals (August 1991 to June 2006)

Rank	*Sector*	*No. of FDI Approvals (USD million)*	*Amount of FDI Approved*	*%age with FDI Approved for Korea*
1.	Transportation industry	69	995.7	38.17
2.	Fuels (power & oil refinery)	8	832.3	32.46
3.	Electrical Equipment (including computer software & electronics)	72	303.6	10.62
4.	Chemicals (other than fertilizers)	32	175.4	6.07
5.	Commercial office & household equipment	11	110.1	3.94
	Total	192	2,417.1	91.26

Source: DIPP.

Although Indian investment in South Korea is almost negligible and India does not figure among the major investors in the country, due to the growing prowess of Indian companies and their eagerness to expand their global presence, many Indian companies have begun to invest in Korea through different means including mergers and acquisition (M&A). For instance, in February 2004, Tata Motors signed an agreement to acquire Daewoo Commercial Vehicles, Kunsan (South Korea) for $102 million.[21] The Indian IT industry sees a lot of opportunities in South Korea and, according to industry sources, Korea is seen as a stable plank for those looking to establish a stronger presence in the APEC region. Some IT companies, such as Aptech, have already set up centers in Korea.[22]

19. Ahn (2008).
20. WTO *(2004)*.
21. FICCI (2004).
22. *http://www.expresscomputeronline.com/20021216/newsan1.shtml*

Table 5.7

Share of Top Sectors Attracting FDI Inflows from South Korea (January 2000 to June 2006)

Ranks	*Sector*	*FDI Inflows (US$ million)*	*Percentage in Total FDI Inflows from Korea*
1.	Electrical Equipment (including computer software & electronics)	78.7	41.49
2.	Metallurgical industries	51.0	26.13
3.	Food processing industries	18.7	9.81
4.	Transportation industry	12.8	6.69
5.	Industrial machinery	3.2	1.68
	Total	164.4	85.8

Note:

1. Amount includes the inflows received through FIPB/SIA route, acquisition of existing shares and the RBI's automatic route only.
2. The amount and sector-specific FDI inflows are not provided by the RBI prior to January 2000.

Source: DIPP.

Technical Collaboration

Technological collaboration between the developed and developing world has been a major source of technology acquisition for companies in developing countries. In the case of India-South Korea investment relations, Korea has been a major partner of India for technological collaboration. According to DIPP, 228 technical collaborations have been approved from South Korea which accounts for 2.93 percent of the total collaboration approved between August 1991 and June 2006. The highest number of technical collaborations (Table 5.8) has been in the transportation industry followed by electrical equipment (including computer software and electronics) and chemicals (other than fertilizers).

There is significant potential for small and medium-sized (SMEs) Korean companies to synergize with Indian SMEs in the areas of semi-conductors, plastics, auto parts, agricultural instruments, textiles, multi-media, ceramic products, software, etc. Korean participation can also be invited in the Special Economic Zones (SEZs) in India. Since the development of infrastructure in India is a priority and requires both advanced technology and huge investment, there is tremendous scope for Korean companies to participate and collaborate in infrastructure sectors such as power, ports, telecommunications, etc. There are also opportunities in ship-building and ship repair, petrochemicals, automobile ancillaries, electrical and electronics, office equipment, banking and financial services, software as well as iron and steel.[23]

Table 5.8

Share of Top Five Sectors Attracting Technology Transfer (August 1999–June 2006)

Rank	*Sector*	*No. of Technical Collaboration Approved*	*% of Technical Collaborations Approved for Korea*
1.	Transportation industry	55	24.12
2.	Electrical Equipment (including computer software & electronics)	48	21.05
3.	Chemicals (other than fertilizers)	19	8.33
4.	Misc. Mechanical & Engg.	14	6.14
5.	Metallurgical industries	13	5.70

Source: DIPP.

Barriers to Bilateral Trade and Investment

As has been highlighted in the trade analysis part of this paper, trade flows between India and Korea, though on the rise in the past few years, remain much below potential. Apart from natural and structural factors like distance and differences in economic structures, the non-realization of potential is mainly due to barriers/problems in both the countries. These barriers exist for merchandize and services trade as well as investment.

Barriers in India

Since the early 90s, tariff rates on most of non-agricultural commodities have been significantly reduced in India. However, India has bound only 70 percent of its non-agriculture tariff lines. India's tariff rates are very high on some product categories that constitute a major proportion of Korea's exports. For instance, in 2007, the weighted

23. In recent years, the participation of Korean companies in the infrastructure sector in India has increased substantially. Of 44 contracts awarded for national highway development projects, nine have been won by Korean companies, either in collaboration with Indian companies or independently. Recently, Hyundai Heavy Industries has won two mega projects, including one pipeline project worth $600 million.

average of the MFN tariff rate on vehicles, rail/tram rolling stock, and access group, was 18.8 percent with a maximum rate of 100 percent. Tariff rates are also high on products in which Korea is competitive. For example, Korea has high RCA values for the iron and steel group but the weighted average of the MFN tariff rate in India is 20 percent, which is equal to the maximum tariff. Further, the import of automotive products is subject to cumbersome customs procedures. For example, motor vehicles can be imported only through a limited number of ports and only from the country of manufacture.[24]

One problem that has generally been felt by exporters to India is the lack of an official publication or a searchable database setting forth applied tariff and other customs duty rates. Also, due to a complex tariff structure and multiple exemptions, Indian customs requires extensive documentation, which leads to frequent processing delay and inhibits the free flow of trade.[25] Non-transparency and unpredictability in the unofficial policy of the government have also been highlighted as constraints in exporting to India.[26] Apart from these tariff-related barriers, there are several non-tariff barriers in India. These include poor infrastructure, the hiring, management and dispute settlement mechanism in the case of labor, high production costs, credit retrieval, local financing and binding system, relatively limited demand, high competitiveness, government intervention, customs and clearance procedures and visa problems.[27]

Imports of certain products, like electrical appliances, where Korea is very competitive, are subject to a license from the Bureau of Indian Standards (BIS). For this, BIS needs to first inspect the production facility and then issue a license to the exporter. According to some foreign companies, licensing and inspection costs imposed on foreign companies are very high. In the case of copyright, the proposed amendments in the copyright laws have major deficiencies like the lack

24. Office of USTR (2008).

25. *Ibid.* (2008).

26. For instance, unofficial policies of revising edible oil reference prices every two weeks and maintaining a reference price system for soybean oil to address alleged under-invoicing.

27. From a presentation of by Soon C. Lee (2007).

of a clear path toward implementation of the world intellectual property organization Internet treaties. Another related issue is the weak enforcement efforts against copyright piracy in India. Other issues that have come up in the United States Trade Representative (USTR) 2008 are the lack of an efficient regulatory device regime, India's failure to notify sanitary and phytosanitary (SPS) measures to the WTO, non-transparency and bias in government procurement practices and procedures, lack of clarity on tax holidays for export-oriented units and exporters in Special Economic Zones (SEZs) and ambiguity in India's patent law regarding the scope of patentable inventions. In services, the barriers are regulatory. These barriers include limitations on foreign ownership, excessive regulation, nationality or residency requirements, bias in award of projects, and compulsory registration with local, specific, and service provider associations.

Barriers in South Korea

Trade and investment barriers exist in Korea too, despite the continuous rationalization of its tariff structure and other external sector reforms. Korea maintains high tariffs on several agricultural and fishery products, which are of interest to India. It imposes a 30 percent or higher tariff rate on most commodities in this group. Korea has established tariff rate quotas (TRQs) in a bid to minimize access to previously closed markets to maintain pre-Uruguay Round access. In-quota tariff rates may be very low or zero but over-quota tariff rates are very high and prohibitive.[28] Another tariff-related problem in Korea is the use of adjustment tariffs and compound taxes on some agricultural, fishery and plywood products, which raise the applied tariff rates in the country.

Another sector of interest to India is textiles and apparel products. Bound tariffs on these products in Korea is significantly high at 30 percent on several man-made fibres and yarns, many fabrics and most made-up and miscellaneous goods like pillow cases and floor coverings and 35 percent on most apparel items.[29] Also, Korean tariff rates are very

28. For instance barley is subject to an over-quota tariff rate of 324 percent; malted barley, 513 percent; potatoes and potato preparations more than 304 percent, etc. (USTR, 2008).

29. USTR (2008).

high on some products where India exhibits maximum RCA. For example, lac, gums, resins and other vegetable group of products are among the groups with the highest RCA for India but the weighted average bound tariff rate in Korea is as high as 142.83 percent, while the MFN rate is 136.63.

South Korea maintains some standards, technical regulations and conformity assessment procedures that are burdensome. These barriers mainly restrict the export of food items that are of interest to India. For instance, the Korean Food and Drug Administration (KFDA) defines product categories narrowly for specific food additives, making it difficult to obtain approval. Another related problem faced by exporters is that Korea has non-transparent and onerous labeling requirements, with frequent changes for health foods which create a lot of difficulty and enhance the cost of compliance.

Foreign companies face a number of trade barriers in exporting services to Korea. A relatively high threshold is maintained/imposed for procurement of construction services by sub-central and government enterprises. Korea imposes several restrictions on the film and broadcast industry. The lack of transparency in the regulatory system, the lack of a mechanism to raise concerns regarding these and market access issues in the financial sector are major concerns in the financial services. In the telecommunications sector, where Indian companies may be interested, Korea imposes a number of restrictions on foreign service providers. There is prohibition on foreign satellite service providers from selling services directly to end-users, lack of transparency in investment-related regulatory decisions, limits on foreign shareholding of facilities-based telecommunication operators, restrictions on foreign investment in terrestrial broadcast television operations, etc.

Other barriers faced by foreign suppliers in the Korean market include government assistance to targeted domestic industries like the semiconductor industry, a weak legal regime to protect intellectual property, lack of data protection, issues related to its copyright act, protection of temporary copies and technological protection measures, sale of pirated audio-visual DVDs by unlicensed vendors, and burdensome and detailed product information requirements to get registration and certification.

Conclusion

The increase in merchandize trade between the two countries has been mainly because of the changing demand structures and comparative advantages of both economies in complementary sectors. The analysis of revealed comparative advantage shows that Korea has been specializing in a few products that are highly competitive as India's exports have become more diversified. Moreover, India shows a declining comparative advantage in cotton and textiles, rice and other primary products. The analysis at the disaggregated level shows that there are some industries where both countries have a comparative advantage in different products, pointing to opportunities for intra-industry trade. The intra-industry trade (IIT) analysis shows that IIT is low in the top traded product groups and high in some products where trading is low. This offers huge opportunity for intra-industry trade if sector-specific barriers are removed along with general barriers. Further, the increasing trade complementarity index (TCI) shows that Indian and Korean trade gradually became more compatible over the period under review. This indicates that the CEPA agreement between the two countries is likely to enhance trade flows. The trade intensities between the two countries show that Korea is doing much better and there is scope for India to improve its export intensity with Korea.

Though foreign investment from Korea has increased over the years, the share in total FDI inflows to India has declined. Further, Korean investment is concentrated in a few sectors such as electrical equipment and metallurgical industries. There are opportunities for small and medium-sized Korean companies to synergize with Indian SMEs. Further, there is tremendous scope for improving trade in services between the two countries, particularly for India. The analysis also shows that there are both tariff and non-tariff barriers and both countries need to remove sector-specific barriers to improve trade and investment relations.

In this context, the successful conclusion of the CEPA is timely and supported by increasing the trade complementarity index (TCI), which shows Indian and Korean trade has gradually become more compatible over the period. Therefore, CEPA provisions to reduce and eliminate tariffs and non-tariff barriers on a large number of product categories would make their exports competitive in each other's markets.

References

Acharya, Shankar (2008). "India's Macroeconomic Performance and Policies since 2000", *ICRIER Working Paper* No. 225. October. New Delhi.

Adam, F., G. Gangnes and Y. Sachmurore (2006). "Why China so Competitive? Measuring and Explaining China's Competitiveness", *The World Economy* 29(2): 95-122.

Ahn, Choong Yong (2008). "New Direction of Korea's Foreign Direct Investment Policy in the Multi-Track FTA Era: Inducement And Aftercare Services", *OECD Global Forum on International Investment VII*. March 27–28.

Balassa, B. (1965). "Trade Liberalization and Revealed Comparative Advantage", *Manchester School of Economic and Social Studies* 33: 99–123.

Department of Industrial Policy & Promotion (DIPP) (n.d.). *Fact Sheet on Foreign Direct Investment (FDI)*. New Delhi: Ministry of Commerce and Industry, Government of India.

Economist Intelligence Unit (2008). *Country Report*. South Korea. February.

Federation of Indian Chambers of Commerce and Industry (FICCI) (2004). "India - Korea Economic and Commercial Relations", *http://www.ficci.com/*

Government of India (2007–08). *Economic Survey*. New Delhi: The Ministry of Finance, Economic Division.

Kaliranjan, K. and S. Bhattacharya (2007). "Free Trade Arrangement between India and Japan: An Exploratory Analysis", *ASARC Working Paper* 2007/2009.

Lee, Soon C. (2007). "Promoting Economic Co-operation Between India and Korea from a Business Perspective", Paper presented at *RIS-ISEAS-IDE Sixth High-Level Conference on Asian Economic Integration*. New Delhi. 12–13 November.

Office of the United States Trade Representative (2008). *2008 National Trade Estimate Report on Foreign Trade Barriers*.

Sahoo, P. (2008), "Driving Korea-India Ties on Trade and Investment", in *A New National Strategy for Korea* (ed.), *The Korea Herald* 4: 66–73.

———. (2009). "India-Korea CEPA: A step in right direction", *Korea Herald*, 17th September.

Sahoo, P., D.K. Rai and R. Kumar (2009). "India-Korea Trade and Investment Relations", *Indian Council for Research on International Economic Relations (ICRIER) WP No.* 242.

Schiff, Jerarld (2007). "Korea's Economic Prospects and Challenges", *Korea's Economy*, Volume 23. Korea Economic Institute and the Korea Institute of International Economic Policy Trade Barriers. March 28.

UNCTAD (2007). *World Investment Report*.

———. *Handbook of Statistics*.

———. *UNCOMTRADE Database*.

United States Trade Representatives (USTR) (2008). *USTR Report on Korea*. United States of America.

Werner, P. (2002). *Economic Relations Between Germany and Japan: An Analysis of Recent Data.* Duisburg, Germany: Duisburg University.

World Bank (2010). *World Development Indicators*. Washington D.C.

———. *World Development Indicators.* Washington DC.

———. *World Development Indicators* (various issues).

———. WITS Database.

World Trade Organization (2004). *Trade Policy Review: Republic of Korea.* Report by the Secretariat. WTO.

———. (2008). *World Tariff Profiles, 2008.*

———. *International Trade Statistics* (various issues), Geneva.

Websites:

http://comtrade.un.org/

http://dipp.nic.in/fdi_statistics/india_fdi_index.htm

http://www.andhranews.net/India/2008/January/17-China-Korea-30055.asp

http://www.expresscomputeronline.com/20021216/newsan1.shtml

http://www.keia.org/Publications/Insight/2006/december%2006.pdf

http://www.nytimes.com/2007/04/03/business/worldbusiness/03trade.html?_r=1&oref=slogin

http://www.oecd.org/dataoecd/24/37/40400795.pdf

http://www.unctad.org/Templates/Page.asp?intItemID=1465

http://www.ustr.gov/Document_Library/Reports_Publications/2008/2008_NTE_Report/Section_Index.html?ht=

http://www.wto.org/english/res_e/statis_e/statis_e.htm

http://www.wto.org/english/tratop_e/tpr_e/tpr_e.htm

Appendix A-5.1

A. Trade Intensity Indices

Export Intensity of Korea with respect to India

$XI_{KI} = [X_{KI} / X_K] / [M_I / (M_W - M_K)]]$ ...(i)

Where:

XI_{KI} = Export intensity of Korea with India

X_{KI} = Export of Korea to India

X_K = Total Export of Korea

M_I = Total Import of India

M_W = Total World Imports

M_K = Total Import of Korea

Import Intensity of Korea with respect to India

$MI_{KI} = [M_{KI} / M_K] / [X_I / (X_W - X_K)]$ ...(ii)

Where:

MI_{KI} = Import intensity of Korea with India

M_{KI} = Import of Korea to India

M_K = Total Import of Korea

X_I = Total Export of India

X_W = Total World Exports

X_K = Total Export of Korea

Export Intensity of India with respect to Korea

$XI_{IK} = [X_{IK} / X_I] / [MK / (M_W - M_I)]$ ...(iii)

Where:

XI_{IK} = Export intensity of India with Korea

X_{IK} = Export of India to Korea

X_I = Total Export of India

M_K = Total Import of Korea

M_W = Total World Imports

M_I = Total Import of India

Import Intensity of India with respect to Korea

$MI_{IK} = [M_{IK} / M_I] / [X_K / (X_W - X_I)]$ ...(iv)

Where:

MI_{IK} = Import intensity of India with Korea

M_{IK} = Import of India from Korea

M_I = Total Import of India

X_K = Total Export of Korea

X_W = Total World Exports

X_I = Total Export of India

Appendix Figure A-5.1a

Korea's Share in India's Total Merchandize Exports and Imports (Korea's Importance in India's External Trade)

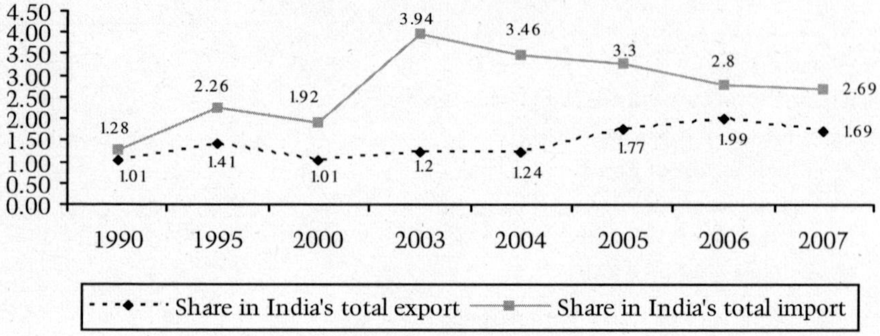

Appendix Figure A-5.1b

Korea's Share in India's Total Merchandize Exports and Imports (Importance of India in Korea's Trade)

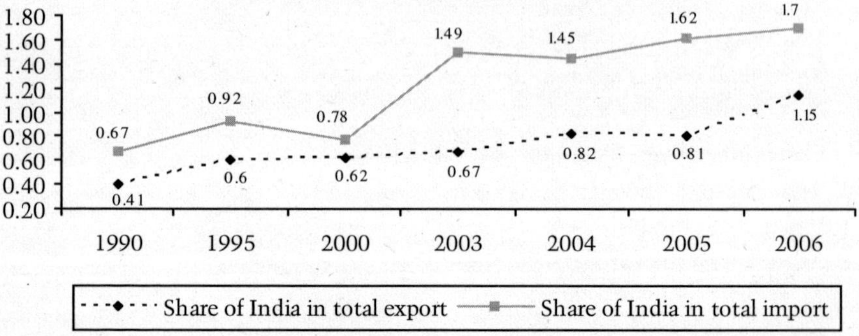

Appendix Figure A-5.1c

India-Korea Trade Relation (US$ million)

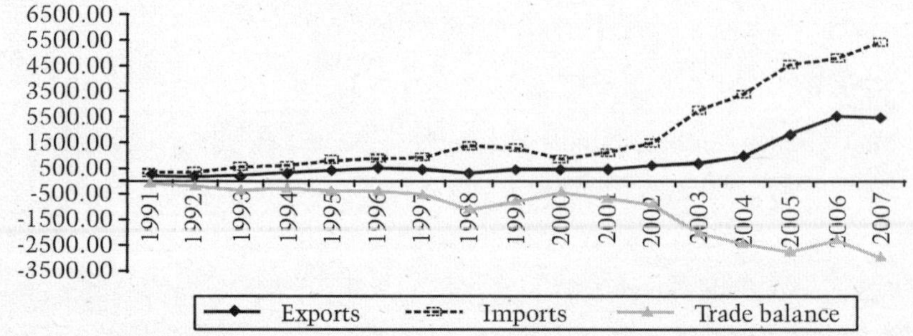

Source: WITS Database.

Appendix Table A-5.1

Macroeconomic Trends in India and Korea

Sector	*Korea Growth Rates*				*India Growth Rates*			
	1990–99 (CAGR)	*2000–04 (CAGR)*	*2005*	*2006*	*1990–99 (CAGR)*	*2000–04 (CAGR)**	*2005*	*2006*
GDP	5.22	3.70	3.9	4.9	5.04	5.08	9.2	9.2
GDP per capita	4.34	3.23	3.74	4.72	3.35	3.81	7.75	7.70
Agriculture	1.64	0.18	–0.1	–2.6	2.77	1.63	6.0	2.7
Industry	5.28	4.85	5.6	4.9	4.88	5.32	9.6	10.6
Manufacturing	6.40	5.20	7.07	8.39	5.01	4.88	9.09	12.32
Services	5.14	3.19	3.0	4.16	6.73	6.46	9.8	11.2

Note: * CAGR implies compound average growth rate per annum.
Source: WDI, 2008.

Appendix Table A-5.2

Major Trend of Major Macroeconomic Indicators of Korea and India

(As percentage of GDP)

	Korea						*India*					
	1991	*2002*	*2003*	*2004*	*2005*	*2006*	*1991*	*2002*	*2003*	*2004*	*2005*	*2006*
Agriculture	7.9	4.1	3.4	3.8	3.8	3.3	29.6	20.9	20.9	18.8	18.3	17.5
Industry	42.6	38.5	40.3	39.1	40.7	39.6	25.7	26.4	26.2	27.5	27.6	27.9
Manufacturing	27.39	27.6	26.9	28.4	26.4	28.6	15.7	15.3	15.3	15.9	16.0	16.3
Services	49.43	56.3	57.5	56.3	57.2	55.6	44.5	52.7	52.9	53.7	54.1	54.6
Gross domestic saving	37.0	30.5	32.3	34.6	32.4	30.9	21.9	24.6	26.2	29.2	30.4	31.1
Gross capital formation	39.73	29.1	30.0	30.4	30.1	29.8	21.9	25.6	27.5	31.0	33.4	33.9
FDI (net inflow)	0.38	0.4	0.6	1.4	0.8	0.4	0.03	1.1	0.7	0.8	0.8	1.9
Exports (goods & services)	26.33	35.3	37.9	44.0	42.3	43.2	8.59	14.5	14.7	18.2	20.3	23.0
Imports (goods & services)	28.99	33.9	35.6	39.7	39.9	42.1	8.59	15.5	16.0	20.0	23.3	25.8

Source: WDI, 2008.

Appendix Table A-5.3

Trade Integration of India and Korea with World

Indicators	*India*					*South Korea*				
	1991	*2001*	*2005*	*2006*	*2007*	*1991*	*2001*	*2005*	*2006*	*2007*
Share in World Merchandize Exports	0.5	0.7	1.0	1.0	1.1	2.1	2.4	2.7	2.7	2.7
Share in World Merchandize Imports	0.6	0.8	1.3	1.4	1.5	2.3	2.2	2.4	2.5	2.5
Share in World Services Exports	0.6	1.1	2.2	2.7	2.5(1)	1.1	1.9	1.8	1.8	1.9(1)
Share in World Services Imports	0.7	1.3	2.0	2.3	1.5(1)	1.3	2.1	2.4	2.6	2.8(1)

Note: (1) Estimated figures.
Source: WDI, 2008.

Appendix Table A-5.4

India's Top 10 Export Commodities to Korea

Rank	*2006*	*2005*	*2000*	*1995*	*1990*
1	Mineral fuels, oils & product of their distillation (34.59)	Mineral fuels, oils & product of their distillation (27.06)	Cotton (28.65)	Cotton (20.51)	Ores, slag and ash (40.07)
2	Ores, slag and ash (12.07)	Ores, slag and ash (14.14)	Residues & waste from the food industries (10.22)	Residues & waste from the food industries (18.97)	Cotton (17.40)
3	Cotton (8.70)	Cotton (11.93)	Organic chemicals (7.82)	Ores, slag and ash (10.84)	Organic chemicals (7.66)
4	Organic chemicals (6.56)	Residues & waste from the food industries (7.52)	Ores, slag and ash (6.97)	Organic chemicals (10.20)	Aluminium and Aluminium articles (4.39)
5	Residues & waste from the food industries (6.42)	Organic chemicals (7.32)	Iron and steel (5.53)	Iron and steel (6.66)	Tanning/dyeing extract; tannins & derives (3.90)
6	Iron and steel (6.28)	Iron and steel (6.93)	Cereals(5.28)	Cereals (3.61)	Iron and steel.(3.82)
7	Natural/cultured pearls, precious stones & metals, co. (4.82)	Vehicles o/t rail/tram roll-stock, pts. & acc. (2.80)	Raw hides and skins (other than fur skins) and lea (3.47)	Tanning/dyeing extract; tannins & derives (3.34)	Raw hides and skins (other than fur skins) and lea (3.45)
8	Nuclear reactors, boilers, machinery & mechanical appliance (2.95)	Copper and articles thereof (2.51)	Aluminium and articles thereof (2.53)	Electrical machinery equipment parts and sound recording (2.03)	Salt; sulphur; earth & stone; plastering materials (3.05)
9	Vehicles o/t rail/tram roll-stock, pts. & acc. (1.84)	Nuclear reactors, boilers, machinery & mechanical appliances (2.21	Tanning/dyeing extract; tannins & derives (2.31)	Nuclear reactors, boilers, machinery & mechanical appliances (1.63)	Beverages, spirits and. vinegar (2.48)
10	Raw hides and skins (other than fur skins) and lea (1.41)	Raw hides and skins (other than fur skins) and lea (1.85)	Electrical machinery equipment parts thereof; sound recording (2.29)	Miscellaneous chemical products (1.61)	Electrical machinery equipment parts and sound recording (1.76)

Note: Figures in parentheses show percent of total.

Source: WITS Database.

Appendix Table A-5.5

India's Top 10 Import Commodities from Korea

Rank	*2006*	*2005*	*2000*	*1995*	*1990*
1	Electrical machinery equipment parts and sound recording (24.084)	Electrical machinery equipment parts and sound recording (40.82)	Nuclear reacts, boilers, machinery and & mechanical appliances(18.39)	Plastics and articles thereof (17.90)	Plastics and articles thereof (17.91)
2	Nuclear reactors, boilers, machinery and & mechanical appliances (18.565)	Nuclear reactors, machinery and & mechanical appliances (14.02)	Electrical machinery equipment parts and sound recording (16.69)	Organic chemicals (15.27)	Iron and steel (16.48)
3	Iron and steel (11.720)	Iron and steel (8.72)	Electrical machinery equipment parts and sound recording 99 (14.48)	Nuclear reactors, boilers, machinery and & mechanical appliances (12.07)	Man-made filaments (8.89)
4	Mineral fuels, oils & product of their distillation (10.191)	Vehicles o/t rail/tra roll-stock (6.17)	Iron and steel (7.43)	Miscellaneous goods (8.79)	Nuclear reactors, boilers, machinery and mechanical appliances (8.84)
5	Vehicles o/t rail/tram roll-stock, pts. & acc. (6.546)	Plastics and articles thereof (6.12)	Plastics and articles thereof (7.28)	Electrical machinery equipment parts and sound recording (7.76)	Electrical machinery equipment parts and sound recording (7.01)
6	Plastics and articles thereof (4.878)	Ships, boats and floating structures (3.24)	Organic chemicals (5.66)	Iron and steel (5.93)	Organic chemicals (5.83)
7	Organic chemicals (3.037)	Organic chemicals (2.98)	Man-made filaments (3.79)	Copper and articles thereof (5.01)	Man-made staple fibres (4.31)
8	Rubber and articles thereof (2.211)	Optical, photo, cine, meas, checking, precision (1.75)	Optical, photo, cine, meas, checking, precision (2.99)	Man-made staple fibres (4.47)	Articles of iron or steel (3.70)
9	Articles of iron or steel (2.196)	Rubber and articles thereof (1.70)	Paper & paperboard; art of paper pulp, paper (2.47)	Vehicles o/t rail/tram roll-stock pts. & acc. (4.33)	Zinc and Zinc articles (3.17)
10	Paper & paperboard; art of paper pulp, paper (2.164)	Articles of iron or steel (1.64)	Rubber and articles thereof (1.81)	Man-made filaments (2.54)	Wool, fine/coarse animal hair, horsehair yarn (2.98)

Note: Figures in parentheses show percent of total.
Source: WITS Database.

Appendix Table A-5.6

India's IRCA (at 2-digit) for Top 10 Export Commodities (in Terms of Volume)

TE 1998				TE 2003				TE 2007			
HS Code	*Product Description*	*Average Share in Total Exp.*	*Average RCA*	*HS Code*	*Product Description*	*Average Share in Total Exp.*	*Average RCA*	*HS Code*	*Product Description*	*Average Share in Total Exp.*	*Average RCA*
71	Natural/cultured pearls, prec. stone	15.66	7.99	71	Natural/cultured pearls, prec. stone	16.94	8.67	27	Mineral fuels, oils & product of th	14.22	0.99
62	Art of apparel & clothing access, n	8.56	4.85	62	Art of apparel & clothing access, n	6.36	3.81	71	Natural/cultured pearls, prec. stone	13.71	6.02
52	Cotton	7.36	11.43	27	Mineral fuels, oils & product of th	5.32	0.58	29	Organic chemicals	4.57	1.92
10	Cereals	3.47	4.51	61	Art of apparel & clothing access,	4.34	3.17	62	Art of apparel & clothing access, n	4.35	3.01
29	Organic chemicals	3.30	1.29	52	Cotton	4.20	7.59	84	Nuclear reactors, boilers, mchy. & m	4.10	0.34
03	Fish & crustacean, mollusc & other	3.29	5.28	29	Organic chemicals	4.03	1.52	72	Iron and steel	4.08	1.30
61	Art of apparel & clothing access,	3.27	2.46	84	Nuclear reactors, boilers, mchy. & m	3.59	0.24	26	Ores, slag and ash	4.07	4.32
84	Nuclear reactors, boilers, mchy. & m	3.12	0.20	72	Iron and steel	3.28	1.56	85	Electrical mchy equip. parts thereof	3.05	0.19
85	Electrical mchy equip parts thereof	2.52	0.18	85	Electrical mchy. equip. parts thereof	2.87	0.20	52	Cotton	3.01	5.80
42	Articles of leather; saddlery/harness	2.51	5.85	10	Cereals	2.54	4.52	87	Vehicles o/t railw/tramw roll-stock	2.99	0.41

Source: WITS Database.

Appendix Table A-5.7

Korea's IRCA (at 2-digit) for Top 10 Export Commodities (in Terms of Volume)

TE 1998				TE 2003				TE 2006			
HS Code	Product Description	Average Share in Total Exp.	Average RCA	HS Code	Product Description	Average Share in Total Exp.	Average RCA	HS Code	Product Description	Average Share in Total Exp.	Average RCA
85	Electrical mchy equip. parts thereof	25.37	1.85	85	Electrical mchy equip. parts thereof	26.86	1.84	85	Electrical mchy equip. parts thereof	27.30	1.92
84	Nuclear reactors, boilers, mchy. & m	10.26	0.64	84	Nuclear reactors, boilers, mchy. & m	16.37	1.09	84	Nuclear reactors, boilers, mchy. & m	13.28	0.95
87	Vehicles o/t railw/ tramw roll-stock	8.91	0.86	87	Vehicles o/t railw/ tramw roll-stock	10.91	1.11	87	Vehicles o/t railw/ tramw roll-stock	13.14	1.46
89	Ships, boats and floating structure	5.45	6.96	89	Ships, boats and floating structure	6.25	8.36	89	Ships, boats and floating structure	6.33	8.82
71	Natural/cultured pearls, prec. stone	5.15	2.63	39	Plastics and articles thereof	4.51	1.38	27	Mineral fuels, oils & product of th	5.98	0.45
54	Man-made filaments	4.40	7.27	27	Mineral fuels, oils & product of th	4.31	0.47	90	Optical, photo, cine, meas, checking	4.94	1.51
39	Plastics and articles thereof	4.13	1.25	72	Iron and steel	3.40	1.64	39	Plastics and articles thereof	4.87	1.44
72	Iron and steel	4.01	1.73	29	Organic chemicals	2.87	1.08	72	Iron and steel	4.40	1.55
27	Mineral fuels, oils & product of th	3.46	0.66	54	Man-made filaments.	2.21	4.49	29	Organic chemicals	3.81	1.43
29	Organic chemicals	2.43	0.95	60	Knitted or crocheted fabrics	1.58	6.21	73	Articles of iron or steel	1.68	0.94

Source: WITS Database.

Appendix Table A-5.8

India's RCA (at 2-digit) for Top 10 Export Commodities to Korea (in Terms of Volume)

TE 1998				TE 2003				TE 2006			
HS Code	Product Description	Average Share in Total Exp.	Average RCA	HS Code	Product Description	Average Share in Total Exp.	Average RCA	HS Code	Product Description	Average Share in Total Exp.	Average RCA
52	Cotton	25.04	33.81	52	Cotton	28.43	38.25	27	Mineral fuels, oils & product of th	31.55	1.72
23	Residues & waste from the food indu.	20.02	51.48	72	Iron and steel	8.38	1.94	26	Ores, slag and ash	12.99	5.60
29	Organic chemicals	11.30	2.92	23	Residues & waste from the food indu.	8.29	23.97	52	Cotton	10.10	20.69
26	Ores, slag and ash	8.18	6.48	26	Ores, slag and ash	8.14	5.76	23	Residues & waste from the food indu.	6.91	23.10
72	Iron and steel	6.30	1.38	29	Organic chemicals	7.60	2.12	29	Organic chemicals	6.90	1.76
32	Tanning/dyeing extract; tannins & derives	3.89	4.85	27	Mineral fuels, oils & product of th	4.67	0.40	72	Iron and steel	6.57	1.05
84	Nuclear reactors, boilers, mchy & m	2.28	0.13	41	Raw hides and skins (other than furs)	4.16	5.14	71	Natural/cultured pearls, prec. stone	3.21	3.96
76	Aluminium and articles thereof	1.79	1.40	84	Nuclear reactors, boilers, mchy & m	2.46	0.18	84	Nuclear reactors, boilers, mchy & m	2.65	0.21
85	Electrical mchy equip. parts thereof	1.56	0.08	10	Cereals	2.41	2.40	87	Vehicles o/t railw/ tramw roll-stock	2.26	1.10
30	Pharmaceutical products	1.50	3.39	32	Tanning/dyeing extract; tannins & derives	2.19	2.69	74	Copper and articles thereof	1.77	1.00

Source: WITS Database.

Appendix Table A-5.9

India's RCA (at 4-digit) for Top 10 Export Commodities to Korea (in Terms of Volume)

TE 1998				TE 2003				TE 2006			
HS Code	*Product Description*	*Average Share in Total Exp.*	*Average RCA*	*HS Code*	*Product Description*	*Average Share in Total Exp.*	*Average RCA*	*HS Code*	*Product Description*	*Average Share in Total Exp.*	*Average RCA*
5205	Cotton yarh (other than sewing thread)	19.21	149.84	5205	Cotton yarn (other than sewing thread)	16.44	90.46	2710	Petroleum oils and oils obtained fr	30.75	18.61
2304	Oil-cake and other solid residues,	11.69	92.27	5207	Cotton yarn (other than sewing thread)	9.69	170.43	2608	Zinc ores and concentrates	7.50	20.55
2306	Oil-cake and other solid residues,	7.36	61.62	2304	Oil-cake and other solid residues,	7.02	43.27	5205	Cotton yarn (other than sewing thread)	7.33	43.60
2601	Iron ores and concentrates, including	6.87	11.33	2601	Iron ores and concentrates, including	5.31	9.40	2304	Oil-cake and other solid residues	5.28	34.78
7202	Ferro-alloys	4.70	15.60	2710	Petroleum oils and oils obtained fr	3.74	2.48	2601	Iron ores and concentrates, including	3.14	4.59
3204	Synthetic organic colouring matter,	3.73	11.65	7208	Flat-rolled products of iron or non	3.40	2.89	7202	Ferro-alloys	2.31	4.62
5207	Cotton yarn (other than sewing thread)	3.62	194.48	4106	Goat or kid skin leather, without h	2.65	133.21	8708	Parts and accessories of the motor	2.10	1.96
2922	Oxygen-function amino-compounds	2.20	21.39	1001	Wheat and meslin	2.00	7.73	7112	Waste and scrap of precious metal o	2.04	79.13
2942	Other organic compounds	2.03	116.96	3204	Synthetic organic colouring matter	1.94	9.33	5207	Cotton yarn (other than sewing thread)	2.01	95.61
2904	Sulphonated, nitrated or nitrosated	1.74	85.56	2942	Other organic compounds	1.72	123.01	2902	Cyclic hydrocarbons	1.91	1.79

Source: WITS Database.

Appendix Table A-5.10

India's RCA (at 6-digit) for Top 10 Export Commodities to Korea (in Terms of Volume)

TE 1998				TE 2003				TE 2006			
HS Code	*Product Description*	*Average Share in Total Exp.*	*Average RCA*	*HS Code*	*Product Description*	*Average Share in Total Exp.*	*Average RCA*	*HS Code*	*Product Description*	*Average Share in Total Exp.*	*Average RCA*
230400	Oil-cake and other solid residues,	11.69	92.27	520710	Containing 85% or more by weight o	7.63	56.58	271000	Petroleum oils and oils obtained fr	30.75	18.61
520521	Single yarn, of combed fibres : — M	8.12	198.53	230400	Oil-cake and , other solid residues	7.02	14.77	260800	Zinc ores and concentrates	7.50	20.55
230640	Of rape or colza seeds	7.03	139.24	260111	Iron ores and concentrates, other t	5.31	4.12	230400	Oil-cake and other solid residues,	5.28	34.78
260111	Iron ores and concentrates, other t	6.87	13.50	271000	Petroleum oils and oils obtained fr	3.74	1.02	260111	Iron ores and concentrates, other t	3.14	5.58
520511	Single yarn, of uncombed fibres :—	5.46	194.96	520521	Single yarn, of combed fibres :— M	3.73	59.28	520521	Single yarn, of combed fibres :— M	2.13	95.95
720249	Ferro-chromium :— Other	2.91	113.65	520511	Single yarn, of uncombed fibres :—	3.57	54.66	711290	Other	2.03	82.87
520790	Other	2.38	194.80	720825	Other, in coils, not further worked	3.00	53.23	870899	Other parts and accessories :— Oth	1.99	5.70
294200	Other organic compounds	2.03	116.96	520523	Single yarn, of combed fibres :— M	2.36	39.88	294200	Other organic compounds	1.87	80.77
760110	Aluminium, not alloyed	1.68	2.98	520524	Single yarn, of combed fibres :— M	2.33	33.40	720241	Ferro-chromium :— Containing by we	1.87	13.92
520535	Multiple (folded) or cabled yarn, o	1.60	199.58	520790	Other	2.06	64.87	520511	Single yarn, of uncombed fibres :—	1.66	74.43

Source: WITS Database.

Appendix Table A-5.11

Korea's RCA (at 2-digit) for Top 10 Export Commodities to India (in Terms of Volume)

TE 1998				TE 2003				TE 2006			
HS Code	*Product Description*	*Average Share in Total Exp*	*Average RCA*	*HS Code*	*Product Description*	*Average Share in Total Exp.*	*Average RCA*	*HS Code*	*Product Description*	*Average Share in Total Exp.*	*Average RCA*
84	Nuclear reactors, boilers, mchy. & m	20.42	0.90	85	Electrical mchy equip. parts thereof	29.04	2.58	85	Electrical mchy. equip. parts thereof	30.64	2.98
29	Organic chemicals boilers, mchy. & m	12.48	2.27	84	Nuclear reactors, boilers, mechy. & m	15.47	1.15	84	Nuclear reactors, boilers, mchy. & m	16.47	1.19
39	Plastics and articles thereof	11.30	4.60	87	Vehicles o/t railw/ tramw roll-stock	8.95	5.57	87	Vehicles o/t railw/ tramw roll-stock	10.29	6.63
85	Electrical mchy. equip. parts thereof	8.69	0.89	89	Ships, boats and floating structure	7.53	15.14	72	Iron and steel	9.71	2.44
89	Ships, boats and floating structure	8.45	13.29	39	Plastics and articles thereof	4.84	2.33	27	Mineral fuels, oils & product of th	6.44	0.31
72	Iron and steel	6.90	1.82	72	Iron and steel	4.64	2.00	39	Plastics and articles thereof	5.25	2.33
87	Vehicles o/t railw/ tramw roll-stock	5.64	3.07	54	Man-made filaments	3.44	4.24	29	Organic chemicals	2.57	0.63
73	Articles of iron or steel	5.09	2.39	29	Organic chemicals	3.41	0.75	89	Ships, boats and floating structure	2.11	7.54
74	Copper and articles thereof	3.32	2.69	27	Mineral fuels, oils & product of th	2.49	0.16	48	Paper & paper board; art of paper pulp.	1.84	2.16
54	Man-made filaments	2.34	8.09	88	Aircraft, spacecraft, and parts the	2.14	1.25	73	Articles of iron or steel	1.83	1.27

Appendix Table A-5.12

Korea's RCA (at 4-digit) for Top 10 Export Commodities to India (in Terms of Volume)

TE 1998				TE 2003				TE 2006			
HS Code	*Product Description*	*Average Share in Total Exp.*	*Average RCA*	*HS Code*	*Product Description*	*Average Share in Total Exp.*	*Average RCA*	*HS Code*	*Product Description*	*Average Share in Total Exp.*	*Average RCA*
8479	Machines and mechanical appliances	5.95	4.50 for	8525	Transmission apparatus for radio-tel	16.62	8.38	8525	Transmission apparatus radio-tel	21.25	8.51
2902	Cyclic hydrocarbons	5.17	6.17	8708	Parts and accessories of the motor	8.74	8.13	8708	Parts and accessories of the motor	9.84	8.66
8905	Light-vessels, fire-floats, dredger	4.75	19.96	8901	Cruise ships, excursion boats, ferries	5.33	17.72	2710	Petroleum oils and oils obtained fr	6.43	3.12
3901	Polymers of ethylene, in primary fo	4.08	6.71	8529	Parts suitable for use solely or pr	3.90	3.83	7208	Flat-rolled products of iron or non	3.42	3.02
2917	Polycarboxylic acids, their anhydri.	3.99	9.32	8540	Thermionic, cold cathode or photo-c	2.51	6.51	8479	Machines and mechanical appliances	3.30	5.57
3902	Polymers of propylene or of other o	3.92	8.37	2710	Petroleum oils and oils obtained fr	2.48	2.53	7209	Flat-rolled products of iron or non	2.32	11.10
8901	Cruise ships, excursion boats, ferries	3.67	11.03	8471	Automatic data processing machines	2.47	1.25	8529	Parts suitable for use solely or pr	2.29	3.17
8703	Motor cars and other motor vehicles	3.46	6.90	8905	Light-vessels, fire-floats, dredger	2.20	21.18	8901	Cruise ships, excursion boats, ferries	2.10	8.64
7408	Copper wire	3.04	10.24	8802	Other aircraft (for example, helicopter	2.13	2.45	8540	Thermionic, cold cathode or photo-c	1.77	6.76
7208	Flat-rolled products of iron or non	2.34	2.86	7209	Flat-rolled products of iron or non	2.13	12.22	4801	Newsprint, in rolls or sheets	1.75	4.39

Source: WITS Database.

Appendix Table A-5.13

Korea's RCA (at 6-digit) for Top 10 Export Commodities to India (in Terms of Volume)

TE 1998				TE 2003				TE 2006			
HS Code	*Product Description*	*Average Share in Total Exp.*	*Average RCA*	*HS Code*	*Product Description*	*Average Share in Total Exp.*	*Average RCA*	*HS Code*	*Product Description*	*Average Share in Total Exp.*	*Average RCA*
847989	Other machines and mechanical appliances	5.03	6.57	852520	Transmission apparatus incorporating	16.58	8.87	852520	Transmission apparatus incorporating	21.20	8.93
390210	Polypropylene	3.86	9.45	870899	Other parts and accessories :— Oth	8.58	11.19	870899	Other parts and accessories :— Oth	9.30	12.07
291736	Aromatic polycarboxylic acids, their	3.59	10.19	890120	Tankers	4.40	23.86	271000	Petroleum oils and oils obtained fr	6.43	3.13
870322	Other vehicles, with spark-ignition	3.44	15.51	852990	Other	3.88	4.39	852990	Other	2.28	3.85
390120	Polyethylene having a specific grav	3.22	10.52	271000	Petroleum oils and oils obtained fr	2.48	2.93	720836	Other, in coils, not further worked	2.17	18.70
740811	Of refined copper :— Of which the	3.03	11.03	890590	Other	2.20	22.23	890120	Tankers	2.09	12.30
890590	Other	2.85	20.19	880240	Aeroplanes and other aircraft, of a	2.13	2.98	720917	In coils, not further worked than c	1.84	17.73
290243	Xylenes:— p-Xylene	2.54	6.10	847170	Storage units	2.05	3.98	480100	Newsprint, in rolls or sheets.	1.75	4.40
890120	Tankers	2.00	11.05	841430	Compressors of a kind used in refrigerator	1.66	11.11	847989	Other machines and mechanical appliances	1.64	5.13
890520	Floating or submersible drilling or	1.91	20.20	720917	In coils, not further worked than c	1.58	15.81	840290	Parts	1.58	11.74

Source: WITS Database.

6 India-Korea CEPA

Likely Impact on Bilateral Economic Relations

PRAVAKAR SAHOO, DURGESH KUMAR RAI AND RAJIV KUMAR

The signing of the India-Korea CEPA on August 7, 2009 has been welcomed and rightly so, by both the business community and policy makers from both countries. The substantial reduction of both tariffs and non-tariff barriers in a phased manner would take India-Korea relations to a higher level and also India's presence in East Asia. Further, the agreement offers a huge opportunity for intra-industry trade between the two countries. The provisions in CEPA are expected to further investment and technology collaboration between the two countries. In the coming years, higher trade in services and in areas such as information technology, science and technology, pharmaceuticals, healthcare, human resource development, etc. may occur. Apart from increase in trade, the two positive results expected due to the agreement are an increase in Korean FDI inflows into Indian manufacturing due to a reduction in tariffs on specific sectors and movements of professionals from India to Korea.

Introduction

Against the background of the prolonged Doha Round with no consensus being reached on several issues in the WTO, both developed and developing countries are left with no option but to pursue regionalism in a rigorous way to cater to their development needs. In today's age, almost every country in the world is a party to signing an advanced form of regional Trading Agreements (RTAs) such as Comprehensive Economic Partnership Agreements (CEPA). India is no exception to this trend and has signed several agreements in the past five years, and CEPA with Korea being the recent one in line. The signing of the India-Korea CEPA on August 7, 2009 has been welcomed by the business community and policy makers from both the countries. This agreement bearing provisions for substantial reduction of both tariff and non-tariff barriers in a phased manner would take India-Korea relations to a higher level and also strengthen India's presence in East Asia.

India and Korea have shared a close relationship since the establishment of formal diplomatic ties in 1973. The last three-and-a-half decades have seen high-level exchanges and the signing of several crucial agreements[1] leading to continuous strengthening of bilateral economic relations (Sahoo, 2008). The opening up of the Indian economy since 1991 not only enhanced the market access for Korean goods but also provided investment opportunities for the internationally competitive Korean companies. Today, Korean companies like LG, Samsung, and Hyundai have become household names in India. This is evident from the fact that bilateral trade increased from USD 0.55 billion in 1991 to more than USD 12 billion in 2008 (UN Comtrade Data, 2008). Korea has also emerged as an important source of foreign direct investment (FDI) for India. However, the current size of trade and investment is low compared to the size and structural complementarities of the two economies due to several tariff and non-tariff barriers in both the economies (Lee, 2007; Sahoo, 2009).

Realizing the need for greater economic cooperation, both countries agreed in 2005 to establish a Joint Study Group (JSG) to comprehensively evaluate their economic relations and the feasibility of an India-Korea Comprehensive Economic Partnership Agreement (CEPA). After several rounds of negotiations, the CEPA was finally signed on August 7, 2009.[2] It is India's second comprehensive deal with any country, the first being with Singapore in 2005. This is also India's first Free Trade Agreement (FTA) with an Organisation for Economic Co-operation and Development (OECD) country. The CEPA is more than a free trade agreement as it covers not only trade in goods but also investments, services and bilateral cooperation in other areas of common interest.

---

1. Such as Agreement on Trade Promotion and Economic and Technological Cooperation in 1974; Agreement on Cooperation in Science & Technology in 1976; Convention on Double Taxation Avoidance in 1985; and Bilateral Investment Promotion/Protection Agreement in 1996.
2. Ministry of Commerce and Industry, Government of India.

The India-Korea CEPA 2009 addresses most of these qualitative and quantitative barriers to trade and Investment and provides an adequate platform for bilateral cooperation. Apart from improving trade and investment, the CEPA is expected to contribute to greater bilateral cooperation between the two countries at various multilateral forums like the WTO and the IMF. In addition, it will substantially strengthen the growing regional economic integration in the Asian region. The CEPA is the right step in support of India's 'Look-East Policy'. On the other hand, Korea is looking beyond its traditional trading partners like US and China to sustain its trade and economic progress.

India's and Korea's Trade Policy and Policy toward Economic Regionalism

India

Trade policy reform has formed a major part of India's economic reforms agenda and has contributed significantly to the impressive performance of the economy's external sector. Export-import policies have seen progressive liberalization and its tariff regime has continuously been rationalized. (Table 6.1). The average tariff rates have been brought down substantially in recent years from 32.3 percent in 2001-02 to 15.8 percent in 2006-07. Being an original member of WTO India is an active participant in its deliberations and strong supporter of the multilateral process. However, due to continued failures of multilateral negotiations at the WTO and rising trends of regionalism, especially in Asia, India has also started taking a keen interest in the growing phenomenon of economic regionalism in terms of forging RATs/FTAs/CEPA with various countries or economic blocks.

India no longer sees bilateral and regional trade arrangements as building blocks to multilateral trade regime. It recognizes them as important instruments to liberalize its economy apart from securing market access and enhancing foreign investment in the country. Currently, India is among the top most countries having FTAs/RTAs either in place or under negotiations. As of now the total cumulative number of India's FTAs/ RTAs was 32. Of this 11 were proposed, for 5 either the framework agreement have been signed or being negotiated, 6 FTAs have been under negotiation without having a framework agreement, 4 were signed and 5 are under negotiations. Majority of its RTAs are with the Asian countries. Along with Korea, India is one of the founding members of Bangkok Agreement, 1975, which is one of the first preferential trading arrangements in Asia. Thereafter, India has joined various other regional trading arrangements such as India-Sri Lanka FTA, SAFTA, India-Thailand FTA, Indian-ASEAN FTA and India-Singapore CECA. Currently, India is in process of negotiating several other regional and bilateral trade agreements such as BIMSTEC FTA, and India-GCC framework agreement on economic cooperation, India-Australia Trade and Economic framework agreement, India-Israel PTA, India-Japan CEPA etc. Apart, India has set up various joint study groups to see the possibilities of economic cooperation with several countries like China, Malaysia, Indonesia, Turkey etc. Table 6.2, highlights major RTAs/PTAs that India has either signed or in the process of negotiation.

Table 6.1

Tariff Structures of India and Korea

(Figures in Percentages)

	Years	*India*			*Korea*		
		Total	*Agriculture*	*Non-Agriculture*	*Total*	*Agriculture*	*Non-Agriculture*
Simple Average Final Bound		50.2	114.2	36.2	17.0	59.3	10.2
Simple Average MFN Applied	2007	14.5	34.4	11.5	12.2	49.0	6.6
Trade Weighted Average	2006	8.0	41.9	6.5	7.0	91.6	3.6

Source: WTO World Tariff Profiles, 2008.

Korea

Korea has continuously (more so in recent years) liberalized its trade and investment policies and business related regulations to enhance and sustain its economic development. Since the Korean economy is highly dependent on the external sector and export has been identified as a growth engine to double its per capita income by 2010, the main objective of Korean trade policy has always been to promote structural reform and efficiency. Expansion of high-technology industries, high value-added exports and making Korea a Northeast Asian business and financial hub are the main priorities. Though Korea actively participates[3] in the multilateral trading system, like India, it has increasingly focused on regional and bilateral trading arrangements after the Asian financial crisis. In response to the growing trend of regionalism, Korea considers these agreements as a means to liberalize its trade and investment regimes to rejuvenate the economy, secure export markets and promote regional integration. Korea's first such agreement was with Chile, which came into effect from April 2004. Other important countries and blocs with whom Korea has agreements are Singapore, Peru, EFTA, the US and ASEAN. Korea is also in the process of negotiating several other trade agreements with other countries/blocs such as Canada, Mexico, EU, MERCOSUR, China, Gulf Cooperation Council (GCC) and Japan (Table 6.3).

Major Provisions in CEPA and Likely Impact on Goods Trade

In the backdrop of growing economic exchanges between the two countries and rising number of FTAs/PTAs in the world, especially in Asia, the CEPA negotiation was initiated by the declaration at the India-Korea summit in February 2006. After 13 rounds of negotiations in more than three years period the interim agreement was signed in February 2009 and the final agreement was signed on 7 August 2009.

The principle objectives of the CEPA are to liberalize and facilitate trade in goods and services and expand investment, and establish a cooperative framework for strengthening and enhancing the economic relations between the two sides. It emphasizes on establishing a framework conducive for a more favorable environment for the businesses and to promote conditions of fair competition in the free trade area. Both countries have also committed to explore new areas of economic

3. It took part in the extended GATS negotiations on financial services and basic telecommunications, and is a member and observer of the plurilateral Agreements on Government Procurement and Trade in Civil Aircraft, respectively. It resolves trade disagreements using the WTO dispute settlement system, and has complied on time with the Dispute Settlement Body (DSB) findings in cases brought against it since its last Review.

cooperation and develop appropriate measures for closer economic partnership and to establish a framework for further regional and multilateral cooperation to expand and enhance the benefits of this Agreement throughout Asia, and thereby, to encourage the economic integration of Asian economies.

Table 6.2

India's Engagements in RTAs

Partner Country/Countries	*Type of RTA*	*Status*
BIMTEC, GCC,	FTA	Under Negotiation
Asia-Pacific Agreement	Trade Agreement	Under Implementation
China, Australia, New Zealand	FTA	Under consultation and study
Afghanistan, Chile, MERCOSUR	PTA	Signed
Columbia, Israel, Uruguay, Venezuela	PTA	Under Consultation and Study
Egypt, Southern African Customs Union (SACU)	PTA	Under Negotiation
European Union	Trade and Investment Agreement (TIA)	Under Negotiation
Indonesia	Comprehensive Economic Cooperation	Under Consultation and Study
Japan	Comprehensive Economic Partnership Agreement (CEPA)	Under Negotiation
Mauritius	Comprehensive Economic Cooperation and Partnership Agreement	Under Negotiation
Russia	Federation Comprehensive Economic Cooperation Agreement	Under Consultation and Study
Singapore	CECA	Under Implementation
Sri Lanka, South Asia	FTA	Under Implementation
Nepal	Treaty of Trade	Under Implementation
Malaysia	CECA	Under Consultation and Study
India-Korea	CEPA	Signed
India-ASEAN	FTA	Singed in goods. Being negotiated in services and investment.

Source: Department of Commerce, Ministry of Commerce and Industry, Government of India.

Table 6.3

Korea's Multi-track Free Trade Agreements

Nations	*Status*	*Effectiveness*
Chile	April 2004, Effectuation	Assuming that accumulation must occur by both domestic and foreign investors
Singapore	March 2006, Effectuation	
ASEAN 10	May 2006, Liberalized manufacturing sector service industry to be concluded in 2007	
EFTA (Switzerland, Norway, Ireland, Liechtenstein)	September 2006, Effective	
Japan	Negotiations suspended	
Canada, Mexico, India	M to conclude within 1-2 years	
EU	Six rounds of negotiations completed	
USA	Concluded on April 2, 2007	Inward FDI will rise to USD 23-32 billion over 10 years

Source: Ministry of Foreign Affairs and Trade, Korea; Taken from Ahn (2009).

For India this is the first with an OECD member country and perfectly fits into its "Look-East Policy" to strengthen its ties with East Asian region, of which Korea is an important part. For Korea this agreement is first with a BRIC country which is an emerging source of global economic growth and likely to remain so in next couple of decades. It also fits into the present government's "New Asia Policy, to rejuvenate its relations with Asian countries.

CEPA has come into effect from January 1, 2010. It has provisions to cut tariff and non-tariff barriers in a phased manner. Almost all the major sectors that are of mutual interest to both the countries are subject to the tariff reduction or elimination. Given the low levels of existing tariff rates in Korea and relatively high level of competitiveness in many of the manufacturing sectors, Korea is likely to gain more than India in goods. According to Korea Institute for International Economic Policy estimates, bilateral trade is expected to soar to USD 3.3 billion annually. India has committed to reduce or eliminate tariffs from 85 percent of its tariff lines, Korea has taken commitment to reduce or eliminate tariffs from 93 percent of its tariff lines. Farm products, automobiles and textiles have been kept outside the ambit of tariff elimination while some of them will be scaled down gradually in future. Hence, while India maintains a negative list of 15 percent of items, South Korea has included 7 percent of the items in the negative list. India's negative list includes agricultural, textiles and auto sectors items. In 10 percent of items, tariff will be reduced up to 5 percent, while in 10 percent of the items the tariff will be halved from their current rate. For rules of origin both countries have agreed to follow both rules of origin criteria-tariff sub-heading change (HS 6-digit) and the level of local content should be a minimum of 35 percent. Table 6.4 reports the tariff reduction schedule for Indian and Korea wherein Korea would eliminate tariffs on large number of tariff lines. India also would reduce tariffs on a substantial number within five to eight years. Though Korea will reduce or eliminate tariffs on more tariff lines, it is expected that exports from Korea would benefit more than India's exports as tariff rates in India are relatively higher than in Korea.

Table 6.4

CEPA Tariff Reduction Schedule

	India				*Korea*			
	No. of Tariff Lines (HS 6-digit)	*Share of Trade*	*Import Value*	*Share of Trade*	*No. of Tariff Lines (HS 6-digit)*	*Share of Trade*	*Import Value*	*Share of Trade*
1. Elimination of tariffs	3739	71.5	2984	74.5	9984	88.6	1679	84.8
1.a Immediately	202	3.9	1538	38.4	6824	60.6	1248	63.0
1.b Within 5 years	180	3.4	560	14.0	2310	20.5	205	10.3
1.c Within 8 years	3357	64.2	886	22.1	850	7.5	226	11.4
2. Cut to 1-5 % within 8 years	559	8.8	342	8.5	34	0.3	3	0.2
3. Cut to 50% within 8 or 10 years	261	5.0	96	2.4	478	4.2	94	4.8
4. Exceptions	768	14.7	580	14.5	765	6.8	205	10.3
Total	5,227	100.0	4,001	100.0	11,261	100.0	1,981	100.0

Source: Bank of Tokyo Mitsubishi UFJ, 2009.

Table 6.5 highlights the major product groups of India's exports to Korea and the weighted average tariff rate on those categories of products in Korea. Mineral and oil product is the largest group that goes from India to Korea. Although the tariff rate is not high, it is substantial compared to product groups like iron and steel, and ores, slag and ash. Some other product groups that constitute the major share in total Indian exports to Korea and have relatively high tariff rates include cotton, vehicles, cereals, and tanning/dying extracts.

Table 6.5

Major Items of Indian Export to Korea and Tariff Rates

HS Code	*Products*	*Share in Total Indian Export to Korea (2008)*	*Tariff Rate in Korea (Weighted Average)*
27	Mineral Fuels, Mineral Oils and Products of their Distillation; Bituminous Substances; Mineral Waxes	41.82	2.41
72	Iron and steel	12.28	0.13
23	Residues and Waste from the Food Industries; Prepared Animal Fodder	6.85	3.82
29	Organic chemicals	6.29	3.99
73	Articles of iron or steel	4.87	3.95
52	Cotton	4.27	6.34
84	Nuclear reactors, boilers, machinery and mechanical appliance; parts thereof	2.86	5.14
87	Vehicles other than railway or tramway rolling stock, and parts and accessories thereof	2.74	7.89
26	Ores, slag and ash	2.03	0.02
12	Oil Seeds and Oleaginous Fruits; Miscellaneous Grains, Seeds and Fruit; Industrial or Medicinal Plants; Straw and Fodder	1.64	32.02
71	Natural/cultured pearls, precious stone	1.56	3.58
10	Cereals	1.38	282.07
85	Electrical machinery equip parts thereof	1.35	2.15
32	Tanning/dyeing extracts etc..	1.14	6.72

Source: UN Comtrade Data; UNCTAD TRAINS Database.

Table 6.6 highlights various manufacturing sectors in India that are likely to benefit from tariff concession/elimination in Korea in various phases within eight years. Although Korea tariff concessions are more active than that of India, they are passive compared to FTAs with other countries. Korea has offered concessions where the country is relatively more competitive. These sectors include electricity and electronics, automobiles, steel, and chemicals, etc. Given its share in the Korean market and the existing tariff rates in Korea, India stands to gain in sectors like vehicles other than railway or tramway rolling stock, and parts and accessories (HS87), natural/cultured pearls, precious stones (HS71), product groups relating to cotton and textiles, nuclear reactors, boilers, machinery etc.(HS84), and in chemical-related groups like organic chemicals (HS29) and tanning/dyeing extracts (HS32), etc.

Table 6.6

Korea's Tariff Concession by Industry (Unit: Number of Items)

Sectors/Tariff Concessions	*Immediately*	*Within 5 Years*	*Within 8 Years*	*Exception*	*Reduction Stage by 5%*	*Reduction Stage by 50%*	*Total*
Chemicals	1868	256	87	3	0	1	2215
Textiles	304	818	84	4	0	81	1291
Steel	315	23	7	0	0	0	345
Machinery	932	248	36	0	0	0	1216
Electricity and electronic	1022	204	42	0	0	1	1269
Automobiles	92	85	4	0	0	0	181
Daily products	447	198	49	0	0	1	695
Other manufacturing	1764	346	131	41	10	48	2340
Total	6744	2178	440	48	10	132	9552

Source: Do Hoon (2009a).

As can be observed from Table 6.7, many categories that are major import items of India from Korea are also subject to high tariff rates in India. Product groups like vehicles, parts and accessories (HS87) that constituted around 10 percent of total exports to India were subject to substantially high tariff rates. Other major groups with high tariffs include Articles of iron or steel (HS73), Rubber and articles thereof (HS40), Paper and paperboard products (HS48), etc. Given the relatively high level of applied tariffs in India on the major product groups, which constitute a big proportion of Korean export to India, South Korea stands to benefit immensely and will get more than what India may benefit in absolute terms. The biggest beneficiary in Korea would be many of the manufacturing sectors. According to one estimate exports of Korean manufacturing are expected to grow annually by USD 177 million on average for a decade after the CEPA becomes operational; this represents an increased 3.9 percent in growth over the average growth for the 2004–2006 period (Do Hoon, 2009b).

Table 6.7

Major Items of Indian Import from Korea and Tariff Rates

HS Code	*Products*	*Share in Total Indian Import to Korea (2008)*	*Tariff Rate in Korea (Weighted Average)*
84	Nuclear reactors, boilers, machinery and mechanical appliance; parts thereof	16.66	6.84
85	Electrical machinery equipment parts thereof	16.37	4.62
72	Iron and steel	14.78	5.00
27	Mineral Fuels, Mineral Oils and Products of their Distillation; Bituminous Substances; Mineral Waxes	9.72	3.74
87	Vehicles other than railway or tramway rolling stock, and parts and accessories thereof	9.71	19.62
39	Plastics and articles thereof	5.49	7.97
73	Articles of iron or steel	5.27	10.00
29	Organic chemicals	3.82	7.31
40	Rubber and articles thereof	3.16	11.04
48	Paper and paperboard; articles of Paper pulp, of paper or of paperboard	2.34	10.00
90	Optical, Photographic, Cinematographic, measuring, checking, precision, medical or surgical instruments and parts and accessories	2.18	6.70
31	Fertilizers	1.24	6.43
82	Tools, implements, cutlery, spoons and forks, of base metal; parts thereof of base metal	1.22	10.00
28	Inorganic Chemicals; Organic or Inorganic Compounds of Precious Metals, of Rare-Earth Metals, of Radioactive Elements or of Isotopes	1.00	6.83

Source: UN Comtrade Data.

If we examine Table 6.8 that highlights the concession in various sectors, keeping in mind major importing product groups from Korea to India and the applied tariff rate on those product groups in India, we get a broader idea of Korea's potential gain. Although the list of exception products in the case of India's commitment is relatively bigger than that of Korea's, Korea is likely to gain substantially in sectors like electrical and electronic, machinery, chemicals etc. However, realization of benefits would be at different points of time for different sectors. The electricity and electronics sector will benefit immediately but gains in the steel sector would arise mostly in the 8th year of implementation. Given its sensitivity, India has listed a large number of items under the exception clauses such as the textiles and automobile sectors. One sector which would benefit substantially is the Korean automobile sector. Given the high rate of existing tariffs in India in the pre-CEPA period and a highly competitive automobile industry, Korea's gains would be substantial in the automobile sector in the post-CEPA period. Tariffs on Korean auto parts, the biggest export item to India, are to be reduced to 1 percent over an eight-year period from the current average of 12.5 percent. This will consolidate the Korean auto industry's share in India. Due to the least products put in the exception category from the steel industry, Korea's gains are likely to be substantial in this also.

Table 6.8

India's Tariff Concession by Industry (Unit: Number of Items)

Sectors/Tariff Concessions	*Immediately*	*Within 5 Years*	*Within 8 Years*	*Exception*	*Reduction Stage by 5%*	*Reduction Stage by 50%*	*Total*
Chemicals	3	12	642	80	9	52	798
Textiles	7	6	609	144	0	12	778
Steel	0	18	216	3	12	1	250
Machinery	28	27	410	40	70	6	581
Electricity and electronic	136	37	225	40	23	5	466
Automobiles	0	0	11	40	3	4	58
Daily products	1	10	269	37	1	6	324
Other manufacturing	27	70	976	101	29	40	1243
Total	202	180	3358	485	147	126	4498

Source: Do Hoon (2009a).

CEPA has also indicated opportunities for collaboration between small and medium-sized Korean companies to synergize with Indian Small and Medium Enterprises (SMEs) in the areas of auto parts, textiles, leather, electronics, IT, semi-conductors, plastics, agricultural instruments, multi-media and ceramic products. In the electronics market where Korean-based giants such as LG and Samsung are leaders, Indian SMEs in electronic component manufacturing can probably expand their trade basket by supplying electronic parts to big players in this sector.

Major Provisions in CEPA and Likely Impact on Trade in Services

Services are an important component of the CEPA, which is the fast growing sector in both the economies, especially in India. Given its demographic advantage with a large pool of trained professionals, India is likely to gain significantly in the services sector. India has emerged as a major services exporter in the world in recent years. Its competitiveness in IT services is well recognized all over the world. India's services exports have increased much faster than that of imports. It is a net service exporter to the world. Korea, on the other hand, is a net importer of services and import of services has increased faster than that of exports during 1998–2008. The services trade structure of both countries is very complementary. For instance, in India the share of transportation services has decreased and the share of other services in total services export of India increased during 1998-2008. In contrast, the share of transportation services has substantially increased and the share of other services in total services exports from Korea decreased during the same period. India seems to enjoy a comparative advantage in 'other commercial services', while Korea's advantage lies in transportation services. Hence, there exists substantial scope for increasing trade in services between the two countries.

However, there are a number of barriers in both countries that restrict the flow of services between them. For instance, India has an interest in exporting audio-visual services to Korea. However, Korea maintains a screen quota for films requiring that any movie screen show domestic films at least 73 days per year.[4] Other sectors where India has an interest in supplying services to the Korean market but face some barriers include insurance and banking, telecommunications, etc. Similarly, Korean companies face a variety of trade barriers in India, including a cap on

---

4. It also maintains a variety of foreign content quotas for terrestrial, cable and satellite television, radio broadcasting, and Internet Protocol television. Overall, foreign programs may not exceed 20 percent of terrestrial television or radio broadcast time or 50 percent of cable or satellite broadcast time on a quarterly basis.

foreign equity participation in sectors such as insurance and retail. The CEPA will help to address a number of these issues that will ultimately will help in enhancing services trade flows between the two countries. For instance, the newly passed Foreign Legal Consultant Act (FLCA), 2009 in Korea says that law firms from countries that have a free trade agreement with South Korea will be able to start consultancy businesses in Korea.

Both countries have taken substantial commitment to open the services sector for trade. Commitments are taken for both market access and national treatment. In services, India's interest lies mainly in Mode 1 (cross-border supply) and Mode 4 (movement of natural persons). On the other hand, Korea is more interested in Mode 3 (commercial presence). Apart from taking horizontal and sector-specific commitments, commitments for movement of natural persons is taken in a separate chapter by both countries. In fact, India is the only country, among Korea's FTA partners, to obtain a commitment for temporary migration of professional workers under Mode 4 of WTO rules. South Korea has not offered such a commitment in any other bilateral agreement.

In sector-specific commitments, Korea has offered market access and national treatment in many of the professional services without any limitation on Mode 1 and Mode 2. These services include legal, accounting, auditing and book-keeping, taxation services, architectural services, engineering, integrated engineering services, veterinary services, etc. Korea has also offered commitments under various computer and related services in Mode 1 and Mode 2 that are of prime interest to India. These services include consultancy services related to computer hardware, software implementation services, and data processing services. In all these services categories market access is also provided through Mode 3 without any conditions. In research and development services, market access and national treatment is provided in all the categories but commercial presence is allowed in only one category, namely, R&D in social sciences and humanities. Other services categories which are of interest to India and where Korea has offered substantial commitment include advertising services, market research services, management consultancy services, printing and publishing services, etc. It has also given commitments in audio-visual services that are of interest to India. Further, Korea's commitments are also in construction, distribution (excluding retail), advertizing, leisure/culture, and transport services.

As mentioned before, for services trade under the movement of natural persons, CEPA has a separate chapter. This reflects the desire of both countries to facilitate temporary entry of natural persons on a comparable basis and to establish transparent criteria and streamlined procedures for temporary entry. Commitment in this chapter is related to service sellers, service suppliers, sellers of goods, investors and employees of investors. Both countries have to grant temporary entry to natural persons of other country and process the applications on priority for temporary entry. This is particularly in the case of applications from members of professions for which a mutual recognition agreement has been concluded. Natural persons of either country who are granted temporary entry into the territory of the other country shall not be required to make contributions to social security funds in the host country.

Commitments have been made by both countries under the categories for business visitors, intra-corporate transferees, and independent professionals. As many as 163 such professions are allowed to access the Indian and Korean services market. Some of the important professions which are important to Indian suppliers include assistant English teachers for primary and secondary schools, different types of engineers, programers, public relations consultants, information system operators, database managers, database designers and analysts, IT consultants, general management consultants, financial management consultants, and human resources management consultants.

CEPA contains mutual recognition agreements in professional services to facilitate the entry of Indian professionals. In this context it is stated that if a request is made in writing by one country to the other, in any regulated service sector, both countries shall encourage their respective professional bodies to negotiate and conclude. This should be done within 12 months of the date of entry into force of this Agreement. Both countries also committed for mutual recognition of education, or experience obtained, requirements met, or licenses or certifications granted in the service sector for early outcomes such as clearances and registration.

CEPA and Implications for Bilateral Investment

The India-Korea CEPA also covers investment. In fact, one of the principle objectives of the CEPA is to expand bilateral investment. Both countries have committed to accord investors of the other country treatment no less favorable than that it accords to its own investors with respect to the establishment, acquisition, expansion, management, conduct, operation, and sale or other disposition of investments in its territory. The CEPA also ensures that both sides will provide a minimum standard of treatment and has committed that each country will accord the investor of the other Party in its territory fair and equitable treatment and provide full protection and security. It is stipulated that neither country will impose any kind of restriction on the investors of the other country in terms of performance requirements such as to achieve a given level or percentage of domestic content and to export a given level or percentage of goods or services, etc. The CEPA also ensures that neither Party may require that an investor of the other Party appoint in senior management positions individuals of any particular nationality. It is India's first FTA with a negative list in the area of investment where performance requirement is prohibited.

Diversified investment opportunities in almost all Indian manufacturing and infrastructure sectors exist. Given Korea's competitiveness in many manufacturing sectors, India is likely to get substantial investment and become a manufacturing hub. The CEPA will encourage more Korean investments in consumer goods and physical infrastructure and construction sectors; modernization of railways stands out as one of the sectors where stellar Korean engineering and innovation expertise can be used to India's benefit. The easing of restrictions on Korean FDI in fields such as automotive and electronics manufacturing will lead to significant increase in investment in these sectors. The agreement will eventually allow Korean firms to invest in many sectors where Koreans are competitive such as automotive manufacturing, machinery and electronics. This is a potentially lucrative opportunity for Korean manufacturers to reposition their global supply chains to leverage India's low-cost structure and abundance of skilled human resources. India can be used as a platform for Korea to facilitate its exports to Europe, Africa and the Middle East.[5] Already the Indian electronics industry is a major recipient of Korean FDI but more Korean investment is expected in SMEs in the electronics component sector in the post-CEPA period. Overall, the CEPA will strengthen the case for foreign direct investment into India's Special Economic Zones, for whom Korea will now form another potential export market.

In this context, it may be mentioned that Korea Land Corporation (KLC), an agency of the South Korea government, signed a memorandum of association (MOA) to set up an industrial park and technology zone in Gujarat Vittal Innovation City (GVIC), a multi-product special economic zone (SEZ) being jointly developed by Gujarat Industrial Development Corporation (GIDC) and GVIC. Around 60 medium-sized Korean companies engaged in manufacturing, IT and automobiles have shown an interest in setting up their units or R&D activities in the industrial complex. A Korean township will be set up in the first phase with an investment of Rs.8,000 crore. GVIC is a proposed ecosystem for knowledge-based services, industry, manufacturing, research & development and incubation activities.[6] It is expected that more such projects will come in future.

Although Indian investment in South Korea is negligible, the CEPA has come at the right time for the growing prowess and eagerness of Indian companies to expand in Korea. This is a good opportunity for the Indian IT industry that is looking to establish a stronger presence in the APEC region.

Areas of Future Cooperation in CEPA

The most promising part of the India-Korea CEPA is the area of mutual interest for future cooperation. The CEPA explicitly recognizes that exchange and collaboration between the enterprises of both countries will act as a catalyst to promote trade and investment. CEPA has laid out 12 areas of bilateral economic cooperation. Various forms of cooperation are

5. *http://www.biztechreport.com/story/219-cepa-marking-new-era-indo-korean-partnership*
6. *http://gujaratmoney.com/2009/08/04/south-korea-to-set-up-industrial-parktechnology-zone-in-gujarat-sez/*

proposed in each area. The important areas and forms of cooperation are as follows:

Information and Communications Technology (ICT): Promote the development of ICT and ICT-related services; promote cooperation between public and private sectors for ICT development; and promote cooperation in development, processing, management, distribution and trade of digital contents. It also emphasizes cooperation for exploring markets in third countries. Since Korea's strength lies in manufacturing and product development of hardware and India's strength is in software, future collaboration in the ICT sector is expected to gain momentum after CEPA. Since the cost of production and competition for Korean companies has been increasing and India has become an attractive destination for outsourcing services, there is greater scope for outsourcing/subcontracting from Korea to India, both in IT products and services. Another area of cooperation in the IT sector is IT education and training. Indian companies are endowed with a wide network of world-class training institutions. Korea's strength lies in manufacturing, product development and marketing. If this is combined with India's strength in related services, it would be advantageous for both countries.

Energy: Facilitate cooperation between public and private sectors of both countries for exploration of oil, gas and mineral resources; strategic storage of crude oil; and conservation and development of alternative fuels. The pact also emphasizes cooperation between research institutes and universities of both countries for research and development in the energy sector. Since there is a widening gap between demand-supply of energy in India, cooperation in research, design and development of various renewable energy technologies, including solar, wind and bio-energy would be beneficial to India.

Science and Technology: Cooperation in this sector includes exchange of scientists, researchers, and experts; joint organization of seminars, symposia, conferences and other scientific and technological meetings including technology summits; cooperation in the commercialization of the results of scientific and technological activities. The areas of cooperation include: (a) nano-science and technology, (b) biotechnology, (c) information technology, (d) advanced materials, (e) high-energy physics, (f) space technology, and (g) science and technology policy and research and development systems. Science and technology (S&T) is an area which both countries are already seriously engaged in. India is endowed with well-educated S&T personnel and Korea has the financial resources; therefore cooperation in this area will be mutually beneficial in the coming years.

Small and Medium Enterprises: The agreement has provision for cooperation in establishing networking opportunities for SMEs of the parties to facilitate collaboration or sharing of best practices in the field of management skill, technology transfers, product quality improvements, supply-chain linkages, information technology, access to financing and technical assistance. Apart from promoting investment and supporting organization of fairs and exhibitions, CEPA is to encourage the relevant agencies to cooperate and share information and experiences in the development of SMEs policies and programs. In pursuant of the above provision, an MoU between the Ministry of Micro, Small and Medium Enterprises of India and the Small and Medium Business Administration of South Korea on cooperation in the field of small and medium enterprises has recently been signed. Besides, the CEPA will encourage collaboration between small and medium-sized Korean companies to synergize with Indian SMEs in the areas of semi-conductors, plastics, auto parts, agricultural instruments, textiles, multi-media, ceramic products, etc.

Infrastructure and Transportation: Cooperation in this area includes developing and promoting cooperative activities such as: (a) highways, power plants, ports and airport construction; (b) infrastructure development and industrial plant construction; (c) development of infrastructure of roads and railroads; and (d) maritime transportation. Development of infrastructure in India is a priority and requires both advanced technology and huge investment; there is tremendous scope for Korean companies to participate and collaborate in the infrastructure and construction sectors. In the past few years, the construction sector has been one of the fastest growing sectors in India. Given the growing infrastructure demand, the sector is likely to continue its growth momentum in the coming future. However, because of the Indian construction industry's limited capability and exposure to various kinds of construction requirements, the government is very keen to enhance the participation of foreign players. This is expected to not only enhance the industry's capacity to deliver high-quality projects within tight timelines but also provide opportunities to Indian companies to acquire new construction techniques/know-how. Korean companies are well endowed with technological capability and their global exposure is also high. Hence, there is tremendous scope for cooperation in the construction industry.

Audio-Visual Content: Promoting regular exchange of views on general audio-visual issues; encouraging cooperation and exchange between audio-visual industries of both the countries; encouraging visits and participation in international audio-visual events held in the territory of the other country. The emphasis on bilateral cooperation in audio-visual and broadcasting is timely as broadcasting is a growing industry in both countries and there are complementarities in the industry. India is well recognized among Asian countries for its content, whereas Korea is specialized in drama, digital and mobile broadcasting technologies. Hence, it would be in the interests of both countries to initiate cooperation in the broadcasting industry.

Pharmaceuticals: This includes: (a) cooperation in the development of traditional medicinal products based on herbs; (b) collaboration in research and development of pharmaceuticals including generic drugs; and (c) exchange of information on domestic regulations in the fields of pharmaceuticals, clinical trials, vaccine and blood products. From being a major importer of pharmaceutical products, the Indian pharmaceutical industry has today become a net exporter of these products. Indian export destinations not only include developing countries in Asia and Africa but also developed countries such as the US, Canada and European countries. This proves the strength and overall competitiveness of the industry. India has both R&D facilities and human capital to leverage. Since Korea is focusing on R&D in pharmaceutical-related areas, there is scope for cooperation between the two countries in the areas of clinical trials, vaccines, biotech goods, traditional medicinal products, etc.

Tourism: The agreement proposes to promote the field of tourism by facilitating the development of tourism infrastructure and facilities; organizing familiarization trips for leading tour operators and travel agents/agencies, tourism journalists and other media representatives; encouraging tourist traffic between the Parties for medical treatment, international conferences and conventions, and entertainment, etc. Since tourism is an important industry, it is one of the areas of bilateral cooperation in the

India-Korea CEPA. There are possibilities that not only tourist inflows from Korea to India would increase, but also there can be substantial inflow of investment in the development of various Buddhist sites spread across the country. Due to the strong, ancient historical and cultural linkages between the two countries, there is huge potential for enhancing tourism-related trade and investment flows.

Textiles and Leather: Facilitating collaboration, including training for textile and leather products in the areas of product development, quality upgrading, fashion design and textile engineering, and holding of fairs and exhibitions. Cooperation in the textiles industry will be very important for Indian textiles to understand the needs of the international market and to raise their quality with the help of Korean technology.

Healthcare: CEPA emphasizes the promotion of cooperative activities in the fields of healthcare by the organization of conferences for health professionals, exchange of programs between medical educational institutions, sharing of information and experience in the modern and traditional healthcare systems, and collaborative research in the fields of preventive and curative medicine and healthcare. In the health sector, cooperation is going to be significant given the size and capability of the healthcare industry and quality health professionals in India. India has also been gaining in importance as a health-related tourism services destination not only among developing countries but also in developed countries. Korea's healthcare system has significantly improved in the recent past due to remarkable progress in the medical sciences, quality professionals and appropriate government policies. However, there have been concerns about a glut of health professionals in Korea. Given the complementarities in the healthcare industry, enhanced cooperation will help both countries realize the vast opportunities in this sector.

Cooperation in Science, Technology and Human Resource Development: Science and technology (S&T) is an area which both countries are already seriously engaged in. CEPA once again further emphasizes S&T collaboration. The importance of knowledge in the world economy has been growing at a fast pace in recent years. The backbone of the knowledge economy is the supply of quality human resources. However, due to differences in their demographic stages and investment in human resources, developing countries differ significantly in their human resource endowments. Though India has a vast workforce, due to its rapid economic growth in the past few years, many industries face a shortage of skilled manpower. Korea, on the other hand, because of its different demographics and development stage, faces a shortage of overall manpower. Korea has long experience in certain industries, such as electronics, construction and engineering and hence is better endowed with skills in these industries. And these are the industries, as mentioned earlier, where the growth rate has been quite impressive in the past few years in India. Therefore if cooperation is enhanced during the post-CEPA period, it will benefit both countries.

References

Ahn, C.Y. (2009). "India-Korea Economic Relations", Presentation made at 8th *India-Korea Dialogue, 2009.* New Delhi, May 24-25.

Bank of Tokyo Mitsubishi UFJ (2009). "Free Trade Agreements in Asia: A Progress Report", *Economic Report* 4(6), October.

Do Hoon, Kim (2009a). "Effects of Korea-India CEPA on Korean Manufacturing", *KIET News Brief* 450, September 16.

———. (2009b). "The Impact of a Korean-India CEPA on the Manufacturing", *News Brief.* Korea: Korea Institute for Industrial Economic and Trade.

Lee, Soon C. (2007). "Promoting Economic Cooperation Between India and Korea from a Business Perspective", Paper presented at RIS-ISEAS-IDE Sixth Sixth High-Level Conference on *Asian Economic Integration*, New Delhi. .

Sahoo, P. (2008). "Driving Korea-India Ties on Trade and Investment", in *A New national Strategy for Korea* (ed.), *The Korea Herald* 4: 66-73.

———. (2009). "India-Korea CEPA: A Step in Right Direction", *Korea Herald*.

Sahoo, P., D.K. Rai and R. Kumar (2009). "India-Korea Trade and Investment Relations", *Indian Council for Research on International Economic Relations (ICRIER) WP* No 242.

UNCTAD (2008). *Handbook of Statistics.*

World Bank. *WITS Database.*

7

India-Korea Strategic Dialogue in Technology and Climate Change

SURESH P. PRABHU

Introduction

Lately the climate change phenomenon seems to have engaged policy makers worldwide. Arguably, this has become one of the most important public policy issues today. All countries—rich as well as poor, developed as well as developing—are equally concerned with this phenomenon. Emerging economies in Asia, Africa and Latin America think this is one issue they must all factor into their own growth strategies. All global events, whether organized under the United Nations (UN) umbrella or by groupings of nations like G-8 or G-20, are focusing on this particular issue, which is emerging as one of the most lethal threats to the very existence of the mankind. The years 2009-10 were landmark years for the global economy, as one after another economic crisis—be it the increasing monetary instability or the rising intensity of trade wars—threatened the sustainability of the present global economic order. Interestingly, despite these developments, the importance of climate change issues on the global stage did not diminish.

Cooperation in Technology and Climate Change

Not only the governments of various countries, but also a large number of civil society organizations have been simultaneously working on the issue—individually as well collectively. Many of these NGOs have created transnational alliances to deal with climate change. Although primarily a platform for discussions for inter-government organizations, almost all United Nations Framework Convention on Climate Change (UNFCC) negotiations were held in the presence of an overwhelming number of NGOs, which participated as observers. Heavy security measures had to be taken at most places to contain the wrath of these angry congregations, which expressed similar sentiments. Their anger stemmed from the belief that the various governments and politicians of the world were not serious about climate change issues—that governments the world over did not act with as much urgency and commitment as this volatile issue, which is being hotly discussed in the corridors power as having posed a serious threat to the very existence of this planet, warranted.

Public opinion in most countries—from Australia to Argentina, and USA and Canada to Zambia—favors very strong action to combat climate change. In Europe, countries compete to make laws to address climate change in their respective national parliaments, and, in the US, presidential elections are fought on this issue. In a report of a meeting organized to assess public attitude about climate change, famous environmentalist Tom Bowman states that results across many surveys and over many years reveal some important trends and reliable data points. It observes:

> most notably, the public's sense of urgency has grown significantly. In the simplest terms, an overwhelming majority of Americans now believes that global warming is happening, that humans are at least partly responsible for causing it, and that the net effects will be harmful. The majority favors starting immediately to reduce greenhouse gas (GHG) emissions and is willing to pay at least some higher costs for energy and even higher taxes if they directly enable emissions reductions.

The report was sponsored by the National Oceanic and Atmospheric Administration and the George Mason University Center for Climate Change Communication. It is obvious that people today see climate change as posing a serious risk to humanity. There seems to be a change of perception and this is clearly a recent phenomenon. That global warming is occurring and that human beings are at least partly responsible for this problem is now well accepted.

The Bowman report further observes, "The American public expresses a greater sense of urgency than policymakers seem to realize. Public support for national mitigation policies (e.g., higher CAFE and renewable energy standards) and international agreements to reduce GHG emissions is higher than it is among members of Congress."

Another report on the world's first climate change election prepared by the School of Social and Political Sciences, University of Melbourne says that people's knowledge about climate change mostly came from media sources but most people also referred to their own experiences, such as flowers in the garden blooming out of season and the extent of the drought, to support their view that climate change was real. It further states that there were not just local climatic reasons for increased anxiety. Public consciousness about climate change was impacted by Al Gore's book and film 'An Inconvenient Truth' (Gore, 2006) and the publication by the British government of the report prepared by its leading economic adviser, Sir Nicholas Stern (Stern 2006), which accepted the scientific consensus that global warming was real and elaborated upon the necessary economic challenges to mitigate its drastic effects.

In Australia, opinion polls in 2007 confirmed that levels of concern about climate change had recently risen dramatically. Most people believed that global warming was a serious and pressing problem and that it was imperative for them to begin taking steps now even if this involved significant cost. People were of the opinion that the federal government should be doing more to tackle the issue of climate change.

Clearly, the concern about climate change is at an all-time high and the vast majority of people no longer doubt that it is real or that it is caused by greenhouse gases created by human activity. More importantly, climate change now ranks as more important to people than a wide range of issues including housing affordability and national security.

Many people are worried about the legacy they will be leaving for their children's futures. Some even feel that it may be too late to solve climate change. Questions of adaptation are also of concern with the perceived speed of change a major factor in influencing how urgently people feel the need to take action. "There is a passionate enthusiasm in many people who want to do their bit to reduce greenhouse pollution... People now expect concerted action on the part of their political leaders and they want a way to be able to make a direct and useful contribution themselves" (Climate Institute, 2007a: 17).

A survey was conducted by the Chicago Council on Global Public Affairs and World Public Opinion, which included China, India, the US,

Indonesia, Russia, Thailand, Ukraine, Poland, Iran, Mexico, South Korea, the Philippines, Australia, Argentina, Peru, Israel, Armenia and the Palestinian territories. In this survey, 12 countries were asked whether steps should be taken to combat climate change and the majority favored action. The largest majorities favoring action were 92 percent in Australia, 83 percent in China and Israel and 80 percent in the US, the world's largest producer of greenhouse gases.

Public opinion in Canada has consistently favored taking action on climate change. Support has grown even stronger since the federal government signed the Kyoto Protocol in 2002 and committed the country to reducing its greenhouse gas emissions to 6 percent below 1990 levels by 2012.

Canadians were rightly proud when the federal government signed and then ratified the Kyoto treaty. But somehow, that public pride and concern about climate change has not convinced successive governments to make progress on reducing greenhouse gas emissions. The European parliament is always at the vanguard of dealing with various aspects of climate change. Brazil, South Africa, India and China have formed a group now called BASIC as they consider it the most important policy preoccupation. North and south are all at the forefront of action on this. So climate change is a great leveler and all feel very strongly about it.

There are several disagreements on the ways to deal with climate change but almost unanimity on the issue that technology is the key to address climate change in a significant manner. For instance, one of Europe's key instruments in tackling global warming is its emissions trading scheme (EU ETS), a system first envisaged in the 1997 Kyoto Protocol. The EU ETS encourages the uptake of climate-friendly technologies by rewarding businesses investing in green technologies, thus turning their investments into quick, short-term profits. With its EU ETS in place, Europe has opted for a "market pull" approach to bringing low-carbon technologies onto the market. However, policy makers have realized that new breakthrough technologies are also needed if deeper emission cuts are to be achieved in the long run (2020-2050 and beyond). In an attempt to match the US, the EU has greatly increased its research and development (R&D) funding for climate change technologies in the past few years.

But the biggest challenge lies outside Europe. Energy-related CO2 emissions alone are expected to surge by 57 percent by 2030, largely due to emerging economies such as China and India (*IEA World Energy Outlook 2007*). In this context, transferring climate-friendly technologies to the developing world appears as an environmental imperative. Of course even though "technology as an effective key to deal with climate change" could be an agreed response, there are several key contentious issues, which still remain unresolved on the technology front in multilateral negotiations. However, all must move on the technological front to initiate early action on climate change.

In 1992, in Rio de Janeiro a historic deal was signed to deal with climate change under the aegis of the United Nations called the United Nations Framework Convention on Climate Change (UNFCCC). This was not only a historic deal but even the event was historic. This was an earth summit in which several heads of states and heads of governments pledged to save the earth and logically they thought the climate deal would help achieve this goal effectively. Four years later, yet another important milestone was reached when world leaders displayed extraordinary leadership by signing the Kyoto Protocol to implement the objectives of the UNFCCC goals. It was decided to reduce emissions over 1990 levels by an agreed load. The industrialized nations (called Annex 1 countries in the Protocol) were obliged to reduce their respective greenhouse gas (GHG) emissions while non-Annex 1 countries (all developing countries) were supposed to receive technological assistance from Annex 1 countries.

Industrialized countries could achieve their targets only through technological inventions because stopping economic activities was never possible. The assistance to be given to developing countries could also come only from technology transfer as was envisaged under the Clean Development Mechanism (CDM) or Joint Implementation (JI). So it is very clear that technology was an important instrument to be used to deal with climate change from very beginning. It is interesting to note that until the recent past, scientists had not agreed that climate change is caused by human action till the 4th assessment report of the Inter-Government Panel on Climate Change (IPCC) was published. Both the UNFCCC and Kyoto Protocol were signed to reduce GHG when skeptics doubted whether climate change is part of a natural phenomenon caused by climatic changes that have occurred for millions of years as part of nature's own cycle. However IPCC's landmark report almost conclusively proved that human action has caused climate change, which essentially began after the industrial revolution. It meant that those technological changes unleashed after the industrial revolution are now responsible for these climatic upheavals.

So technology was the cause and we in the world agreed that technology (of course, of very different types) must be deployed to solve this. All the negotiations conducted after the Kyoto Protocol have invariably centered around two critical issues: one is financing and the other is technology. Without exception, all developing countries are unanimously demanding these two things from industrialized nations. The Committee of Parties (COP as these are now called) discussed these issues several times. In Bali a Bali Action Plan was agreed upon to prepare a regime for a second commitment period under the Kyoto Protocol. Technology again occupies center stage of action. In Copenhagen a lot of euphoria was created, as everyone thought a deal could be reached but unfortunately only a limited accord was agreed on; here again technology figures as a means of achieving the Accord's goals.

Though all have agreed that technology is the key to addressing climate change, many key dimensions of this have remained unresolved. It is perturbing that despite everyone agreeing that technology is the key to this menace, there is still no unanimity on which direction to move. Why? This is because in domestic and international politics we agree on generalities, leaving the specifics unattended, which gives rise to all types of interpretations. We really need to work on narrowing the gap on these contours and only then we may be able to move on unhindered.

Dimensions of Technology-related Issues

There is a strong argument from developing countries that technology transfer from developed countries must be done without attracting Intellectual Property Rights (IPRs). Developed nations claim that in their respective countries the custodian of such technology is the private sector and it could not force them to do this. Rich nations argue that market forces must drive this process and they cite the TRIPS regime as the one that must govern such transfer. Poor nations feel that as climate change is caused by rich nations it is their obligation to give technology support to poor nations to fight it through technology. Another valid argument is that if we fear the imminent dangers of climate change like natural calamities, floods, and water shortages, why not deal with the issue urgently by transferring technology urgently. If we are talking about global public goods why not transfer it for the greater good of saving humanity. Haven't we developed vaccines to fight HIV/AIDS in the public domain, not covered by IPR; why should we not do the same now for the bigger threat of climate change?

The International Energy Agency (IEA) has said: forget developing new technologies. Even if we successfully deploy the known ones, we will be able to reduce the impact of climate change very significantly. We must thus find means of developing new sources of energy and in the meantime ascertain the entry barriers for deployment and diffusion of known technological sources. We must create capacity building in developing countries to effectively use these technologies for the benefit of the poor, who are suffering the ill effects of climate change.

It is desirable that both private money and public money be used to develop new technologies. It is also desirable to have collaborative research with both the private and public sector, within their countries as well as globally. A corpus could be created by rich nations through an initial contribution to be supplemented by a levy on some globally conducted activities that cause GHG (like aviation) to start R&D in the public domain for this.

So far the discussion has focused on technology in relation to mitigation. As rightly noted, we urgently need to reduce the GHG load in the atmosphere to 350 parts per million (PPM) as scientists want or at least to the 450 PPM politicians would like to achieve. To make this happen we need big mitigation strategies. A number of technologies have already been identified to mitigate the effects of global warming. In the absence of a viable long-term alternative (e.g., hydrogen), it appears that a mix of solutions, including energy efficiency, alternative fuels and nuclear power, will be called into play. Some options are already being encouraged by EU policies (e.g., renewable), while others are still subject to further research (e.g. hydrogen, CO_2 sequestration):

- Energy efficiency,
- Renewable energies,
- Alternative fuels for transport,
- Cleaner cars,
- Carbon capture and storage (CCS),
- Hydrogen and fuel cells,
- Nuclear,
- Reducing methane and other dangerous GHGs.

To deal with consequences of climate change that cannot be avoided (floods, heat waves, drought, rising sea levels, etc.), other so-called "adaptation" technologies are envisaged:

- Infrastructure design (of cities, rural areas) such as sea defenses and increased organic surface area in cities to help lower temperatures and reduce surface water flow from rain;
- Early warning and monitoring systems (e.g., earth observation systems such as the EU's Global Monitoring for Environment and Security, or GMES).

But the world needs support even for adaptation. If GHGs remain in the atmosphere for a long time adapting to it is inevitable, necessitating action on adaptation. The world would need technologies to put effective adaptation in place. Poor nations want technologies for both mitigation and adaptation. Rich nations need it mainly for mitigation to meet their legal obligation of reducing emissions.

One major challenge in the fight against global warming is speeding up the roll-out of technologies. But politicians face difficult choices when selecting and deploying them, which relate to:

- The timeframe to implement a given technology (e.g., it will take decades before hydrogen technologies can reach mass-market status, while energy-efficiency technologies are available right away);

- The related short- and long-term choices in R&D priorities (including budgets);
- Introducing fundamental changes to critical infrastructure when the viability of a given technology is still uncertain or resources are subject to other pressures (e.g., fuelling stations for hydrogen cars; shifting land use away from agriculture for large-scale biomass);
- Hesitation from financial markets in supporting heavy, long-term investments in new infrastructure in a fast-moving political and technological environment (e.g., third-generation European pressurized reactor nuclear power stations). This has been exacerbated by the current recession, while support is more urgently needed in efforts to shift to a low-carbon economy and create green jobs;
- How far and for how long to provide financial and regulatory support to the most promising technologies before they are commercially competitive (e.g., CCS, renewables);
- Conveying the technologies to booming economies in the developing world without giving away strategic industrial intelligence (e.g., patent "leakage" in China);
- Public acceptance of or hostility to some energy sources (e.g., hostility to nuclear energy in Germany, though this is changing);
- Resistance from industries and countries to the introduction of new energy production and consumption patterns with the potential to trigger regional political instability (e.g., oil, Saudi Arabia and the US).

So far the discussion on technology has remained only in the political framework, in negotiations and that too at the multilateral level. While we must continue to do this, it is necessary to have another track for bilateral development of technology. There is an interesting model of the Asia-Pacific Partnership on Climate Change. Countries like the US, Japan, China, Australia, South Korea and India have partnered for this laudable objective. We could even develop two-country partnerships do this. I strongly advocate a India-South Korea partnership on the technology front to fight climate change.

Areas of India-South Korea Partnership in Technology

South Korea is a shining example of how to achieve extraordinary success in a short time. Korea is the only country to have joined the OECD having been once an aid-receiving nation. Until 60 years ago Korea and India had the same per capita income. In a short period, Korea has joined an elite club of countries with USD 25,000 per capita income and became an industrially advanced nation. It now can proudly claim to be at the forefront of technology with breakthroughs in several sectors of R&D initiatives. Korea now ranks in the top five countries of the world with such a low population. It has more R&D centers than several developing countries put together.

India has a vast population, with the world's second largest pool of scientists and technologists. Its information technology centers earn in excess of USD 50 billion in foreign exchange for the country. India has a large number of engineering colleges. India has several government-run Science and Technology (S&T) institutes under the S&T Ministry of the central government besides other ministries like Atomic Energy, which conduct research for use in peaceful and development activities like isotopes for water and food irradiation to preserve perishable agriculture produce. India has the world's second largest telecommunications market, and thus good communication technologies. Again India's manpower costs are a fraction of what similar trained human costs would be in Korea.

Thus, Korea's strengths in R&D can be leveraged with India's inherent strengths in these areas. Korean R&D initiatives involving several hundreds of millions of dollars can be used better if collaborative R&D is carried out in India. Again India's 1.2 billion strong population provides a captive market to use such R&D to commercialize such research. India has a Trade-Related Intellectual Property (TRIP) regime which guarantees Intellectual Property Rights (IPR) for innovation in the globally accepted IPR regime. India has already demonstrated its strengths in pharmaceuticals by developing new molecules and drug delivery systems.

So a partnership between Korea and India would certainly benefit both the countries in their respective markets but could also reap huge benefits on a global scale.

India and Korea must enter into a strategic framework umbrella agreement to work in areas of R&D. The agreement could then work on specific areas of mutual interest to actually start operations on sectors. It could earmark resources for this, like human, financial, and physical capital. Some projects could be jointly undertaken and some could be done independently in the respective countries, with complementary roles.

Focus Areas for Korea and India in R&D

Energy

In policy initiatives on climate change , inevitably energy occupies a pivotal role. The type of energy we will use will determine GHG emissions produced. India currently uses almost 2/3rd of its energy requirements from fossil fuels. Coal is the mainstay of India's electricity generation, followed by gas. The main base load power generation comes from coal and gas.

While India strives to diversify its energy portfolio, to bring more renewables into the basket, for a very long time coal and gas will continue to fire India's power. The Planning Commission prepared an Integrated Energy Policy document about three years ago, which estimates that even in the year 2030, India will continue to rely on this fossil fuel stock. As we know coal emits more GHGs than other fuels. If India is required to generate electricity from coal, as it is locally available and cheap, how do we get the GHGs abatement strategies in place? Carbon Capture and Storage (CCS) offers a great opportunity here. If carbon can be sequestrated, then coal is not the bad guy. While we all know about CCS, not much commercialization of this technology has happened, because there are some apprehensions on ecological grounds. We could work on technology deployment to address these concerns.

Nuclear Energy

Nuclear power is certainly not a cause of GHG emission and thus could be called a better option. It is clean power in that sense. However nuclear waste disposal and the safety of nuclear plants from the radiation point of view are matters of concern. If we could focus on R&D in these two areas and address these issues, nuclear power could be the best option. India has developed reactors to generate such electricity and today around 3,000 MWs of electricity are fed into India's grid from this source. India has plans to take this to 20,000 MWs by year 2020.

Renewables

India produces around 24,000 MWs from hydropower. All this is clean power but in the modern world we have certain reservations about large dams for storage to generate electricity. India is the 5th largest producer of wind energy in the world. Suzlon, a company born in India, has already become a world leader in wind turbine manufacture.

Possible areas of cooperation in renewable energy could be as follows.

A. Storage of electricity is the next best thing that is about to happen in the energy sector. This would be the greatest breakthrough, which could herald a sea change in the way we use electricity. Today we need to instantaneously consume electricity the moment it is generated, putting tremendous limitations on the way we use it today. Batteries can store power for a limited period, which provides greater mobility. Cars, mobile phones and a host of similar gadgets work on this today. But imagine if we could store it for a much longer period? It would be a transformational change not just in the energy sector but in the way we live. India and Korea must undertake joint research in this crucial area.

B. Solar power is the oldest form of energy known to mankind. Biological life would never survive without the rays of the sun. In fact all fossil fuel stocks that we are fast depleting were in a way a creation of sun power. The sun comes with all regularity. There is not a day when the sun does not rise. It is a different matter that we do not see it sometimes because clouds hide the sun. But sun is always there. Some countries are more blessed than others in terms of getting more sunshine. There are at least 70 to 80 countries in the world that get at least 300 days of good sunshine and India happens to be one of them. India has 28 states and 7 Union Territories with 600 revenue districts. In almost all the states and in all districts India gets very good radiation from the sun. Thus, India has a huge potential for solar power. India has a huge demand for electricity, being one of the lowest per capita consumers of electricity in the world. Its per capita consumption is near 100 KWH per capita per annum.

India has 6,00,000 villages of which 20,000 or so are very remote and cannot be grid-connected. These are ideal candidates for solar power connected through photo-voltaic (PV) solar power. India is urbanizing very fast. It is estimated that at least 65 percent of India's estimated 1.6 billion population will be living in urban areas by 2050 in apartment buildings and houses that are yet to be constructed. Many office buildings in which these people will work have yet to come up. All these structures are ideally suited for standalone solar PV power. Today's PV solar panels have an efficiency of close to or little above 20 percent. Could India and Korea work on increasing their efficiency? While we could have standalone systems for PV, it is also possible to have a much higher grid-connected solar power from Concentrated Solar Power (CSP) systems. There are some very interesting experiments underway in Europe to generate such power in the deserts of North Africa to power the huge European grid. DESERTEC is one such idea.

India has huge deserts in Gujarat in the west and Rajasthan in the north. Again we have huge potential in several other states where the temperatures are always high due to good quality sunshine. CSP thus could be boon for India as the yearly need of 25,000 MWs of new demand for electricity could easily be met from CSP. The challenge is how to use CSP in less land and almost no water, as both are scarce resources in India. Could our joint collaborative R&D focus on these vital issues?

C. India has a 7,600 kilometer coastline on the west and east coasts. We could harness power from the ocean in many ways. Could we not generate electricity from the power of the ocean waves? It would greatly benefit more than 40 percent of India's population that resides by the sea.

Oceans provide another opportunity. Offshore wind farms could generate electricity. Here land is not required to host a wind turbine. Again all on-shore wind plants are not always aesthetically attractive. Thus, our R&D also must be on this sector.

D. Wind power, on land-mounted turbines, is very successful in India. The 5th largest capacity in the world of such wind power generation comes from India. Due to the velocity of wind most of this capacity operates at less than 20 percent plant load factor (PLF). Increasing the PLF of the existing wind farms is a great challenge for R&D. There is yet another great opportunity. Could we harness wind power at a lower velocity than we currently do? Korea and India could also work on this.

E. Waste to Energy is yet a great promise in store to generate electricity while we address another big challenge before us. 1.6 billion people will generate so much municipal solid waste (MSW) that we could create another big mountain from all this MSW. Disposing MSW itself is a big challenge and if not done well is a huge health hazard. Again huge amounts of land are required for use as landfills, which is already under great stress. Korea has mastered this technology. India's MSW has a very different profile than that of Korea. Thus, R&D must be done after studying the mix of MSW and its calorific value.

F. India does not have much geo-thermal potential. But whatever we have could be used with Korean technology as Korea is in Eastern Asia where such potential has been exploited well like in the Philippines.

Energy Efficiency

India has a huge potential to save energy through efficient management and by resorting to demand-side management (DSM). The Indian Energy Conservation Law has a good legislative framework. Korea is a highly energy-efficient country. We could thus work in this area as well. This could earn carbon credits for Korea. As per one estimate, the potential for energy efficiency in India is 23 percent. It is said that for every unit of electricity saved in India, India need not generate three more units of energy, considering India's transmission and distribution losses and the auxiliary consumption of electricity when it is generated. On this premise, the potential of energy saving could result in three to four times less electricity being generated, resulting in less coal consumption and fewer transmission and distribution networks, which in turn would save land and forests, and thus could have huge ecological benefits.

India has already started working on energy-efficient buildings, and is following LEED ratings of buildings. Korea could develop together with India extremely efficient building standards and in the process could help reduce emissions.

Under the Energy Conservation Act, India has already launched a labeling program for white goods like refrigerators, fans, and air conditioners. The standards for these ratings can constantly be upgraded with the help of Korean regulators in this sector. LG, Samsung and the like are already household names in India and their brand recall value is higher than for other well-known brands in the market. Such companies and the government of Korea with their counterparts could create a longer-term vision to arrive at a high energy efficiency standard. India's publicly owned infrastructure could also be converted into highly energy-efficient entities, with huge spin-off benefits not just for energy savings but also lower cost of delivery as a result of lower energy use. Korea has already demonstrated a very efficient public delivery system in several infrastructure entities and this could be replicated in India.

Public Transport in India

India's headcount as released by the Census Authorities puts India's latest population count at 1.2 billion people, with at least 55 percent of them living in urban areas. Their rising income would mean that many of them opt for privately owned cars. Today we see more cars on Chinese roads than the bicycles of a decade ago. How will India handle the mobility of these 600 to 700 million people in the coming years that will determine the quality of air, the amount of emission and the impact on public health?

Public transport in cities and semi-urban areas is a crucial means of making people mobile without causing any damage to the environment. Korean cities have demonstrated how efficient public transport can be developed and operated. India would need metros, BRTS, fuel-efficient public buses, and in some areas sea transport. A city like Mumbai, Kolkata, Chennai, etc. together would have a population of 70 to 80 million in the next few years. Since all three cities have long coastlines, sea transport is the ideal solution.

There are several Tier 2 and Tier 3 cities where planning and execution of public transport has not been done on a scientific basis. Korea could very effectively participate in both planning and execution of such large urban transportation projects. It is already seen in India that 2/3rd of the deterioration of ambient air quality in the cities is due to emission from vehicles. If both surface as well as underground transportation systems are created in such a manner that they do not damage the ambient air quality, this will go a long way in preparing India for a low carbon growth economy.

R&D in Industrial Sector

How to reduce emissions by bringing in technologies that will not allow emissions to begin with could be an area of our cooperative research. Steel, cement, fertilizers, and ferro-alloys are some segments targeted to make energy more efficient, and this is India's priority now. There are obvious environmental benefits from such an intervention, but there are large economic benefits too. If these industries start using less energy, they would be more economically viable and reduce their cost of production. In the process, these industries would become competitive in global markets and could earn India valuable foreign exchange. In India the lower cost of steel and cement would mean low-cost infrastructure, making India a preferred destination for manufacturing. Korea has the unique distinction of constantly improving energy efficiency and striving for lower cost of production in the manufacturing sector. There is a huge area of cooperation between India and Korea at the level of operating manufacturing facilities.

8 Cooperation between India and Korea in FDI and Services

CHANG HO KWAG

Introduction

After 12 rounds of negotiation, the Comprehensive Economic Partnership Agreement (CEPA) between India and Korea having been concluded in September 2008 has finally come into effect from January 2010. India and Korea were, in the past, not such close partners but now it seems that the CEPA will be able not only to bring them closer but also pave a new path for large-scale cooperation between the two countries. The CEPA should, however, not be seen as the final destination but as a starting point to further strengthen and enhance mutual understanding and cooperation between the two countries. At the same time, it is also too early to say that the CEPA will be able to deliver all the benefits that have been envisaged therein by both countries. The success of the CEPA will largely depend on how sincerely both sides take it forward with win-win strategies.

In a modern international economy, trade liberalization through traditional Free Trade Agreements (FTA) is not the only way of economic cooperation. There are now wider ways of cooperation such as CEPA, which is more comprehensive than an FTA. FTA mainly focuses on trade liberalization between countries, whereas CEPA underlines a wider range of economic engagements in various fields including merchandize trade, service trade, bilateral investments, etc. Several studies have been conducted on economic effects and policy implications of FTA, focusing mainly on merchandise trade but service trade and investment relations have been largely ignored. Now when an increasing number of countries are going in for comprehensive pacts like CEPA, there is a need to study all aspects of CEPA in order to guide policy developments of bilateral cooperation.

The objective of this paper is to contribute to the development of strategies that can enhance bilateral cooperation particularly in the areas of Foreign Direct Investment (FDI) and the service industry. In order to successfully implement partnership between India and Korea, we should first study each other's needs. Section II of this study examines the economic structure and performance of both India and Korea and identifies the underlying economic conditions that can lead to areas of cooperation. Understanding of both economies is essential to draw the outline for mutual benefits. Section III and Section IV attempt to analyze FDI trends and the service trade history. Section V proposes future policy directions to enhance bilateral cooperation between the two countries.

Economic Performance and Structure of Korea and India

There are a number of economic conditions of Korea and India that are favorable for bilateral economic partnership. Firstly, both countries are in need of new catalysts for economic growth. The Korean economy was very strong in the 80s. It then enjoyed an 8.7 percent average growth rate. However, in the 90s its growth rate slowed down to 6.2 percent and further down to 4-5 percent in the 2000s. This slowdown of economic growth is attributed to the weakened growth momentum or vitality of the economy.

On the other hand, the Indian economy has shown strong economic growth in recent years. It has been enjoying an 8.5 percent average growth rate for the past five years. And with its huge domestic market, India has become one of the most attractive FDI destinations for multinational firms. Encouraged by these excellent achievements of high growth rate and huge amounts of inward FDI, India now wants to maintain the current high growth momentum and realize its full growth potential. India has shown a strong commitment in recent years to multilateralism and bilateralism in its trade policy. India has signed a Comprehensive Economic Cooperation Agreement (CECA) with Singapore (2005) and ASEAN (2009), in addition to a CEPA with South Korea.

Table 8.1

Economic Performance of Korea and India from 1981 to 2008

	GDP (million US$)	GDP Growth (annual %)	GDP Per Capita (US$)	Trade (% of GDP)
Korea				
1981~1990	135,504	8.7	3,270	65.8
1991~2000	433,890	6.2	9,574	62.5
2001~2005	658,223	4.5	13,756	71.2
2006	951,773	5.2	19,707	78.0
2007	1,049,236	5.1	21,653	82.3
2008	929,121	2.2	19,115	107.0
India				
1981~1990	246,880	5.6	317	14.0
1991~2000	359,509	5.5	379	22.1
2001~2005	619,114	7.0	580	33.6
2006	914,892	9.7	824	47.4
2007	1,176,890	9.1	1,046	45.9
2008	1,159,171	6.1	1,017	50.7

Source: World Bank.

The second underlying need for cooperation between India and Korea can be found in the complementary industrial structure of two countries. India has a large surplus of underemployed workers in the primary sector. As much as 59 percent of total employees are working in the primary sector, producing only 20 percent of the GDP. The dualist model of Lewis (1954) says that the abundant cheap labor in India can move to the manufacturing sector, which will promote capital accumulation and stimulate economic development. Low wages can be an attraction point for the multinational companies (MNCs). Furthermore, FDI can positively affect the growth and development of the Indian economy by contributing to gross fixed capital formation or by accumulation of human capital and technology.

The third motivating factor for economic cooperation can be found in the current status of the trade balance in both countries. Table 8.3 illustrates Korea and India's deteriorating current account balance. The current account of India and Korea has worsened constantly since 2005 and, in particular, India's current account turned into deficit in 2005.

Table 8.2

Sector Share of GDP and Employment of Korea and India in 2008

	Country/ Sector	*Primary*	*Manufacturing*	*Electricity, Gas and Water Supply*	*Construction*	*Services*
GDP share	Korea	2.6%	25.0%	1.2%	6.3%	64.9%
	India	20.0%	15.8%	1.6%	8.9%	53.7%
Employment share	Korea	0.3%	23.1%	0.4%	4.9%	71.2%
	India	59.0%	11.7%	0.3%	5.6%	23.4%

Source: Bank of Korea, Ministry of Statistics of India.

Table 8.3

Total Reserves and Trade Balance of Korea and India (2001 to 2008)

(Unit: USD million)

	2001	*2002*	*2003*	*2004*	*2005*	*2006*	*2007*	*2008*
Korea								
Current Account	8032.6	5393.9	11949.5	28173.5	14980.9	5385.34	5876	-6406.4
Goods:								
Exports	151478	163414	197289	257710	288971	331842	379045	433427
Imports	-137990	-148637	-175337	-220141	-256288	-303937	-350877	-427433
Services:								
Credit	29055	28388	32957	41882	45129	49891	63349	75990
Debit	-32927	-36585	-40381	-49928	-58788	-68851	-83116	-92723
India								
Current Account	1410.18	7059.5	8772.51	780.196	-10283.5	-9299.06	-11283.9	-36088.3
Goods:								
Exports	44793	51141	60893	77939	102175	123768	149314	187912
Imports	-56828	-60708	-75535	-105975	-149430	-184944	-230977	-315062
Services:								
Credit	17337	19478	23902	38281	52527	69730	86965	102949
Debit	-14483	-15034	-17425	-25205	-32549	-40324	-47592	-56554

Source: International Monetary Fund.

Korea recorded merchandise trade surplus while showing a deficit in the service sectors. This implies that Korea may have a comparative advantage in the manufacturing sector but not in the service sector. In contrast, India has shown a trade surplus in the service sector while showing a deficit in the manufacturing sector. If free trade is allowed between the two countries, there would be large gains from trade. This topic will be discussed later in Section IV.

Investment Relationships between India and Korea

The Role of FDI and its Determinants

Various theories tell us that FDI is an important channel for obtaining resources for economic development of the host country. The three most important channels are capital formation, technology transfer and export promotion.

Firstly, FDI brings capital to the host country and affects the economic growth of it through multiplier effects. But in this case, foreign investments can "crowd in" or "crowd out" the domestic investments depending upon the situations in the host economy. If there is an excess demand and inability of domestic firms to meet such demands, there is a room for foreign investments and, in this way, FDI can "crowd in" domestic investments. However, when the domestic market is very tight and there is no need for further investment, FDI may possibly result into "crowding out" investments from the domestic firms.

Secondly, FDI can bring in modern technology which will increase productivity and which can boost economic growth through spillover effects. Thus, FDI is an important vehicle for transfer of technology. However, it also depends upon the ability of host countries to absorb the technology.

Thirdly, FDI can be a good source of exports because the MNCs, which bring in FDI, have their own very large intra-firm markets, access to which is available only to their own affiliates and, thus, it can provide access to unexplored export markets.

If we look at the empirical research on the effects of FDI on economic growth, the results for a certain country at a certain short-term period are mixed. But many panel data studies across most developing countries in a very long-term period show that FDIs are definitely beneficial to the economic growth of the host country.

The study of Baharumshah and Thanoon (2005) shows: (1) FDI is a growth-enhancing mechanism and its influence on growth is much higher than domestic saving; (2) short-term capital inflow has an adverse effect on short-term as well as long-term growth prospects; and (3) long-term debt has a positive effect on growth but its effect does somewhat disappear in the long-term.

Other studies of the FDI's effects on economic growth also show that FDI inflow has significant positive effects on economic growth. But Borenstein *et al.* (1998) find that the effect of FDI is dependent upon the level of human capital available in the host country. FDI contributes to the economic growth of the host country only when there is sufficient, usually above the threshold level, human capital. The study by Blomstrom *et al.* (1996) shows that FDI has positive effects on economic growth only on the upper class of developing countries with higher educational attainment. Balasubramanyam *et al.* (1996) say that the positive effects are more in export-promoting countries than in import-substitution countries. Olofsdotter (1998) finds that the effect of FDI is stronger in countries with a higher level of institutional capability and bureaucratic efficiency. Bengoa and Sanchez-Robles (2003) find that FDI is growth-enhancing in countries with high levels of human capital, economic stability, and liberalized markets. So to enjoy the full positive effects of FDI, a host country should try to get a high level of human capital, economic and institutional stability, bureaucratic efficiency, etc.

There is also a long history of empirical analyzes of FDI determinants. The host country FDI determinants are classified into three categories: economic determinants, policy framework and business facilitation. The economic determinants are again classified in three sub-groups depending upon the type of FDI: market-seeking, efficiency-seeking and resource-seeking. FDI flows into a host country are determined by the interaction of a variety of the determinants above. Some of them play main roles while others take supporting roles. Over the years, the existing literature on this topic has confirmed that the economic determinants of FDI are the primary factors in influencing FDI flows. UNCTAD (2009) and Nunnenkamp and

Spatz (2002) show that the recent global FDI boom has largely taken place in the non-tradable services sector, which is, by definition, of the market-seeking type. Thus, the host country's market-size variables remain the dominant factors for FDI attractions, and market-seeking FDI has been the

Table 8.4

Host Country Determinants of FDI

I. Economic determinants

A. Market-seeking

- Market size and per capita income
- Market growth
- Access to regional and global markets
- Country-specific consumer preferences
- Structure of market

B. Efficiency-seeking

- Cost difference (of resources and assets, adjusted for productivity for labor resources)
- Quality of infrastructure
- Ease of doing business
- Availability of skill
- Availability of complementary local factors of production

C. Resource-seeking

- Raw materials

II. Policy framework for FDI

- Economic, political and social stability
- Rules regarding entry and operations
- Standards of treatment of foreign affiliates
- Policies on functioning and structure of markets (especially competition and M&A policies)
- International agreements on FDI
- Privatization policy
- Trade policy (tariffs and NTBs) and coherence of FDI and trade policies
- Tax policy

III. Business facilitation

- Investment promotion (including image-building and investment-generating activities and investment-facilitation services)
- Investment incentives
- Hassle costs (related to corruption, administrative efficiency, etc.)
- Social amenities (bilingual schools, quality of life, etc.)
- After-investment services

Source: UNCTAD, 1998.

main type of FDI. The determinants of efficient-seeking FDI constitute the second most important economic determinants of inward FDI, particularly in developing countries.

But for these economic determinants to be fully effective, they should work in various combinations with other policy frameworks or business facilitation measures which are supporting and necessary but not sufficient conditions. Apart from economic determinants, macroeconomic conditions and political stability have been found to be important FDI determinants (UNCTAD, 2007). As for policy framework, UNCTAD (1998) shows that as FDI becomes one of the most important sources of economic growth, most countries try to attract more, and, as a result of which, the general policy frameworks (rules and regulations) are converging. The policy framework, a necessary but not sufficient condition, is taken for granted and becomes a less important determinant. The focus must go to improving business environments such as human resources, infrastructure, market access and created assets (technology etc). The McKinsey Quarterly survey (2004) tells us that regardless of the policy regime, the industry, and the period studied, FDI can bring great benefits to developing nations. So to get the most from FDI, developing countries should abandon their incentives and regulations (local contents, joint-venture requirements) and instead concentrate on strengthening their economic foundations, in particular, to stabilize economy and promote competitive markets.

FDI Trends

Figure 8.1 shows the trend of international FDI flows of the developed, developing and CIS countries. Up to 1997, international FDI flow showed a moderate growth trend. However, from 1998, it has grown very fast and reached the astronomical figure of USD 1,400 billion in 2000. Even though it fell back to USD 600 billion during the recession years in the early 2000s, it went up again to nearly USD 2,000 billion in 2007.

For the developed economies, there was a sudden boom in FDI inflows from 1998. It reached its peak point of USD 1,118 billion in 2000. In the 2nd half of 2000s, there was another boom and the figure reached USD 1,359 billion in 2007. In contrast, FDI flows into the developing world reached only USD 257 billion in 2000, and USD 529 billion in 2007.

Cross-border M&As among developed countries were the main driving force of these booms in recent years. These days, rapid advancement in information technology, knowledge-intensive productions and shrinking economic space due to the progress in transportation and communication technology pose new challenges for the host countries and MNCs, changing their competitive conditions.

The rapid changes in competitive conditions in turn led to the opening of trade, investment and capital markets in the host countries and called for new management paradigms, technical skills and organizational forms of MNCs. And thus FDI came to play a more important role for both MNCs and host countries.

Figure 8.1

FDI Inflows, Global and by Groups of Economies, 1980-2008 (USD million)

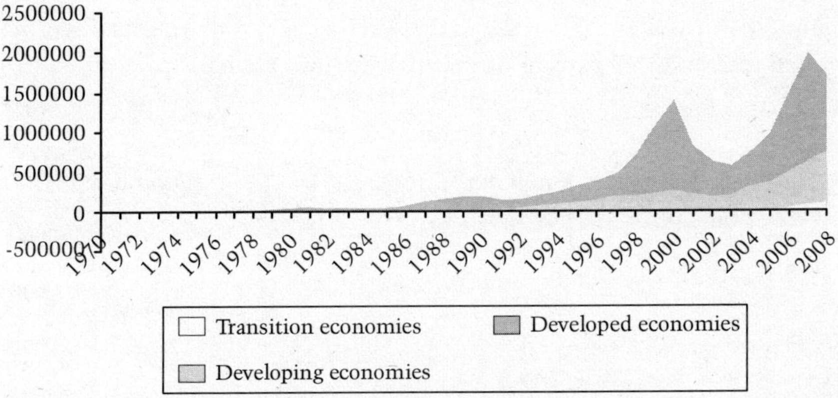

The sector-wise structure of the international FDI flows reveals more information. In 2007, the total inward FDI stocks went up to USD 15.7 trillion, which is 8.1 times bigger than the figure in 1990. During the same period of 1990-2007, FDI stock in the service sector grew 10.6 times while the multiplier was only 5.3 in the manufacturing sector. Given the faster growth, the share of services in total FDI stock rose from 49 percent in 1990 to 64 percent in 2007, while that of manufacturing fell down from 41 percent to 27 percent, and that of the primary sector went down from 9.4 percent to 7.5 percent during the same period.

The increase in the share of the service sector is particularly prominent in the developing world, reflecting their openings of service markets. The share grew from 47 percent in 1990 to 68 percent in 2007. The effect of the service market opening in the developing economies has also been reflected in the figures of regional FDI shares. The share of the developing economies rose from 19 percent to 24 percent in total and from 18 percent to 26 percent in the services sector. However, the share of the developed region in total FDI stock still remains dominant, consisting of 74 percent of world total FDI stock.

Figure 8.2 shows foreign investment flows into Korea and India. China has been included for comparison. In Korea and India, there was no decent level of FDI inflows till 1995. Between 1995 and 2005, on average, around USD 5-6 billion of FDI flowed into Korea and India each year except for the sell-out period (1999-2000) in Korea. However, since 2006, FDI inflow into India has been increasing and reached the USD 40 billion level in 2007 while inflow into Korea remains stagnant at the same level of around USD 5 billion. Nowadays, the level of FDI inflows into India has gone up to around 40 percent of that flowing into China.

Figure 8.2

Comparison: India, Korea and China, 1981-2008, (million dollars)

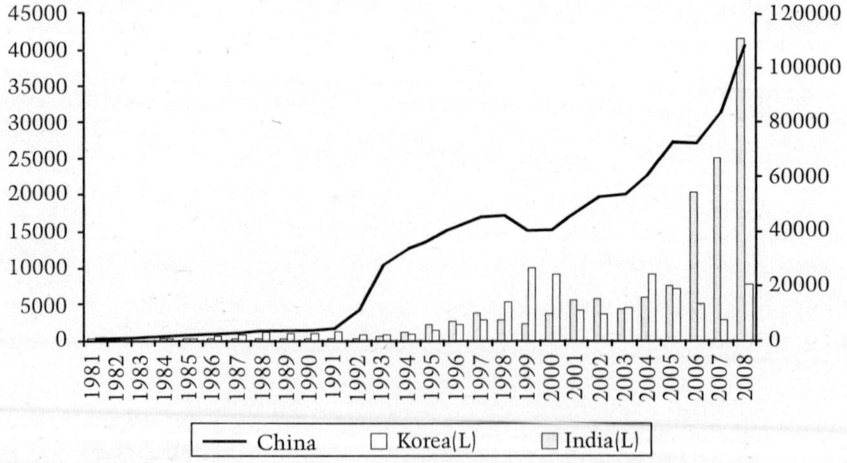

Source: UNCTAD, *World Investment Report 2009*.

If we look at other indicators we can see and evaluate how India has been successful in attracting foreign investment in recent years. The ratio of FDI inflow over gross fixed capital formation shows the contribution and importance of foreign investment to gross fixed capital formation. The ratio of India has been increasing while those of Korea and China have been through their peak levels and are on downward paths. The ratio of India has continuously increased and reached the 7.6 percent level while that of China has been falling down. In China it fell to 6 percent in 2008 after reaching the peak level of 16.8 percent in 1994. In the case of Korea that ratio remains under 5 percent except during the sell-out period.

Another indicator is the ratio of FDI stock over GDP, which explains the role of foreign investment in generating GDP. This indicator tells a similar but slightly different story. In the case of India, the ratio has shown an increasing pattern up to 2005 and then a sharp increase since 2006, reaching 9.8 percent level in 2008, which is higher than the level of China. In the case of China and Korea, the ratios are sliding down from their peak levels. In 2008, the figure for Korea was 10.7 percent and the Chinese figure was 8.7 percent.

The analyses of the two indicators show us that India has been relatively successful in drawing FDI in recent years while Korea has not. However, the figures for both economies still remain far below the world average, indicating that there is still a lot of room for both countries to make more efforts to draw bigger amounts of FDI for their economic development.

UNCTAD developed two very interesting indices regarding FDI flows: the FDI performance index and the FDI potential index. The FDI performance index is constructed as a ratio of a country's share in global FDI inflows to its share in global GDP.

$$IND_i = \frac{FDI_i / FDI_W}{GDP_i / GDP_W} \qquad (1)$$

where, IND_i = the Inward FDI Performance Index of the ith country, FDI_i = FDI inflows in the ith country, FDI_w = World FDI inflows, GDP_i = GDP in the ith country, GDP_w = World GDP.

Countries with an index value of 1 receive FDI exactly in line with the relative size of their economy. Countries with an index value greater than 1 attract more FDI than may be expected on the basis of relative GDP.

The FDI potential index is the average of the scores of 12 economic and structural variables. The score for each variable is derived as follows:

$$\text{Score}_i = \frac{V_i / V_{min}}{V_{max} - V_{min}} \qquad (2)$$

where V_i = the value of a variable for the country i, V_{min} = the lowest value of the variable among the countries, V_{max} = the highest value of the variable among the countries.

In contrast to the performance index, the potential index is based largely on key measurable factors that tend to change fairly slowly over time. The variables included in constructing the index are the rate of growth of GDP, per capita GDP, share of exports in GDP, telephone lines per 1,000 inhabitants, commercial energy use per capita, share of R&D expenditures in gross national income, share of tertiary students in the population, country risk, etc. The country with the lowest value is given a score of zero and the country with the highest value a score of one.

Figure 8.3 summarizes the findings of the two indices calculated as the averages of three years' ranks in two periods (1988-1990, 2005-2007). During the past two decades India has made non-negligible progress in both indices. The performance index improved from rank 121 to rank 112 and the potential index from 96 to 85. However, even with all these improvements, India still remains in the "Under Performer" category, implying that it has big challenges to improve both FDI performance and potential.

In the case of Korea, the performance index has deteriorated from rank 93 to rank 124 during the same period, while the potential index has remained at the rank of 19. Thus, it remains in the "Below Potential" category along with Japan. This result shows us that Korea did not make much effort to improve the potential index nor was it successful in attracting more FDI. However, the fact that Korea ranked 19 in the potential index means that it is already equipped with fairly good environments for FDI inflows and, thus, by improving some key factors it can attract a lot more FDI inflows.

Figure 8.3

FDI Performance & Potential Indexes of Concerned Countries (UNCTAD)

Country, year (performance index/potential index)

In the case of China and the US, included just for comparison, both countries moved from "Front Runner" to "Below Potential". Against this backdrop, the reasons of their downgrades are that both economies are so big that they have to attract fairly large amounts of FDI and also that their economies have grown faster than they have drawn FDI inflows.

The sector-wise break-up of FDI stock in India shows that the service sector received 61 percent of total FDI stock, while the manufacturing sector got 31 percent and the primary sector 3.2 percent. Even though it is a natural consequence of recent market openings in the service sector in most developing countries, it is not a desirable development for a country like India, which needs fast development of the manufacturing sector as we discussed in the previous section.

In the case of Korea, the sector-wise structure of FDI flows tells us that about 41 percent of the total FDI inflow comes to the manufacturing sector. That is not desirable either since it is in the service sector that Korea needs more inward FDI with advanced knowledge.

Bilateral FDI Relationship between India and Korea

The analysis of the FDI stock in India according to the countries of origin indicates that Korea ranks at 8 sharing only 1 percent of total stock. A big bunch of FDI, 37.5 percent of the total, came through Mauritius, a tax haven. FDIs from the US consist of 9.1 percent and that from Japan 3.4 percent. During the past four years, a big amount of FDI came through Singapore after India concluded the CECA with Singapore.

The total FDI stock during the period of 1991–November 2009 is USD 125.9 billion and, out of the total, only USD 1.3 billion has originated from Korea (according to Korean data, the figure is USD 1.6 billion). A big bunch of Korean FDI came in during the mid-90s when LG Electronics, Samsung Electronics and Hyundai Motors put their first step in India and then another wave came in during the period of 2006–2009 when three big Korean players set up their second plants. Thus, naturally most of Korean FDI came into the manufacturing sector. The figure is USD 1.34 billion, 84 percent of total Korean FDI.

On the other hand, FDI inflow of Indian origin into Korea is almost negligible. The figure of FDI stock of Indian origin is only USD 82 million (only 0.1 percent of total FDI stock in Korea, which is worth USD 152.5 billion). One big investment was Tata Motors' acquisition of Daewoo Motors' Commercial Vehicle part in 2004 worth USD 52.6 million.

With these FDI relations between the two economies, we can analyze bilateral FDI intensities. The bilateral intensity is a ratio that compares the actual value of the FDI stock of country 'i' in country 'j' with what might be expected given the world position of each of them as home and host economies, respectively. Thus, the bilateral FDI intensity from country 'i' to country 'j' can be denoted as:

FDI intensity ratio(R) = FDI_{ij} / $ExpFDI_{ij}$

FDI_{ij} = Actual amount of FDI stock from country i to country j.

$ExpFDI_{ij}$ = Expected value of FDI stock from country i to country j.

$$= \frac{FDI_{wj}}{FDI_{ww}} \star \frac{FDI_{iw}}{FDI_{ww}} \star FDI_{ww} \qquad (3)$$

where FDI_{wj} = Total inward stock in the j country; FDI_{iw} = Total outward FDI stock of country *i* in the world; and FDI_{ww} = Worldwide inward or outward FDI stock.

If the intensity ratio is greater than 1, the FDI relationship is stronger than would be expected based on the relative importance of the two economies as home and host; if it is less than 1, it is weaker than expected. The results of the bilateral FDI intensity are unfortunately very unsatisfactory. The intensity of FDI from India to Korea is 0.01 and that from Korea to India is 0.38. Both are well below the value 1, meaning thereby that the relationships are far weaker than expected based on the relative importance of the two economies as home and host. This can also mean that both economies have opportunities as well as challenges to further expand bilateral investment relationships.

Service Trades of Korea and India

In this section, how India and Korea can cooperate in the service sector will be analyzed. One well-known quantitative method to measure the relative competitiveness is the Revealed Comparative Advantage (RCA) index which indicates how competitive a sector of a certain country is in the world market. RCA measures the share of one particular commodity in a certain country's total exports divided by the share of world exports of the same sector or commodity in total world exports. This can be mathematically denoted as follows:

$$RCA_{ij} = (X_{ij} / X_{it})/(X_{wj} / X_{wt}) \tag{4}$$

where x_{ij} and x_{wj} are the values of country *i*'s exports of product *j* and world's exports of product *j* and where X_{it} and X_{wt} refer to country *i*'s total exports and world's total exports.

The higher the index is above the value 1 in a particular commodity market, the stronger the comparative advantage the economy exhibits in that commodity. Likewise, the lower the index is below the value of 1 in a commodity, the weaker the comparative advantage the economy exhibits in that commodity. If the RCA equals 1, that means the country is neutral in comparative advantage in the world market of that commodity. The bilateral RCA between Korea and India in a particular sector can also be calculated in the same manner. The practice of using the RCA index can be easily extended to measure the revealed competitiveness in the service sector and several empirical studies have already analyzed the relative competitiveness of service sectors using RCA indices.

During the past decade, Korea achieved current account surplus for most of the years while India showed current account deficits for most of the years and what is worse, the deficit has been increasing in recent years. However, in service trade we see different pictures. Korea has been a net service importer since 1999 and the amount of net import has been increasing, reaching USD 19.6 billion in 2006. In the sharp contrast, India turned into a net service exporter in 2004 and its amount has increased USD 12 billion in 2006.

Figure 8.4 shows the overall RCAs of Korea and India. In the case of Korea, RCA of merchandise exports remains above 1, revealing that Korean goods are somewhat competitive in the world markets. However, RCA of service exports remains below 1, implying that Korean service exports are not so competitive in the world markets.

The RCA indices of India tell us a different story. RCA of merchandise exports has been continuously below 1, revealing the lack of competitiveness of Indian products in world markets. But the RCA of Indian service exports remains above 1 and has been increasing in recent years, denoting the strong competitiveness of Indian services in world markets.

Even though Korean service exports are not so competitive in the world market, RCA analyses on sub-sectors of services tell us that the transport service is the one (and the only) sub-sector that is competitive in the world market. In contrast, in the case of India, many sub-sectors are revealing comparative advantages. Computer and information has been shown to be very competitive and communication also has been proved to be relatively competitive in the world markets. The RCA values of computer and information have been around 17, which indirectly indicates the level of competitiveness even though the RCA value does not exactly mean the level of competitiveness. The bilateral competitiveness between India and Korea cannot be analyzed since there are no detailed data on merchandizes and service trades between the two economies. Thus, we have to draw policy implications based on the analyses of RCA of both economies' service sectors in the world markets.

Figure 8.4

Overall RCA of Korea and India from 1998 to 2006 (Unit: USD million)

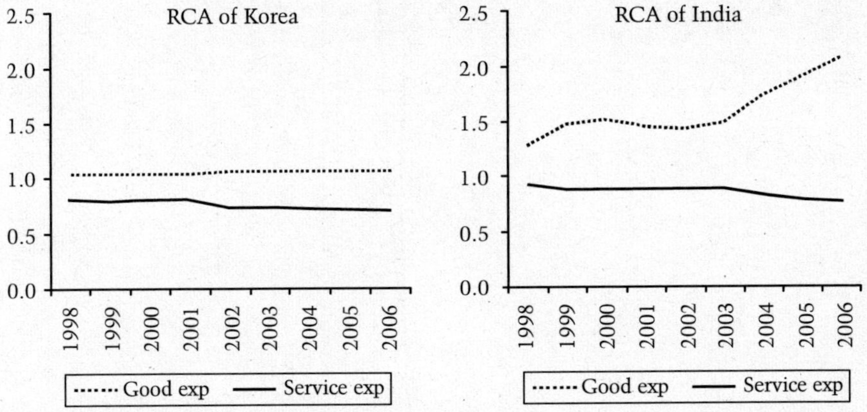

Source: UNCTAD *Statistical Database Online/Handbook of Statistics.*

What the results of the above RCA analyses on Korean and Indian economies tell us is that the two countries have industrial structures that are complementary in promoting competitiveness in the world markets. Korea is competitive in the merchandise (manufacturing) sector while India in the service sector. And within the service sector, Korea is exhibited to be competitive in transport service while India in computer and information, and communication.

Thus, India, being a labor-surplus economy, can contribute to the development of the Korean service sector by providing engineers with a high level of knowledge in the computer and information sector (movement of natural persons, Mode 4, in the definition of service supply in GATS). On the other hand, Korea, having become capital-intensive economy, can contribute to the fast development of the Indian manufacturing sector by setting up many green field or brown field plants in India (FDI in the manufacturing sector).

Figure 8.5

RCAs of Korean Service Sectors

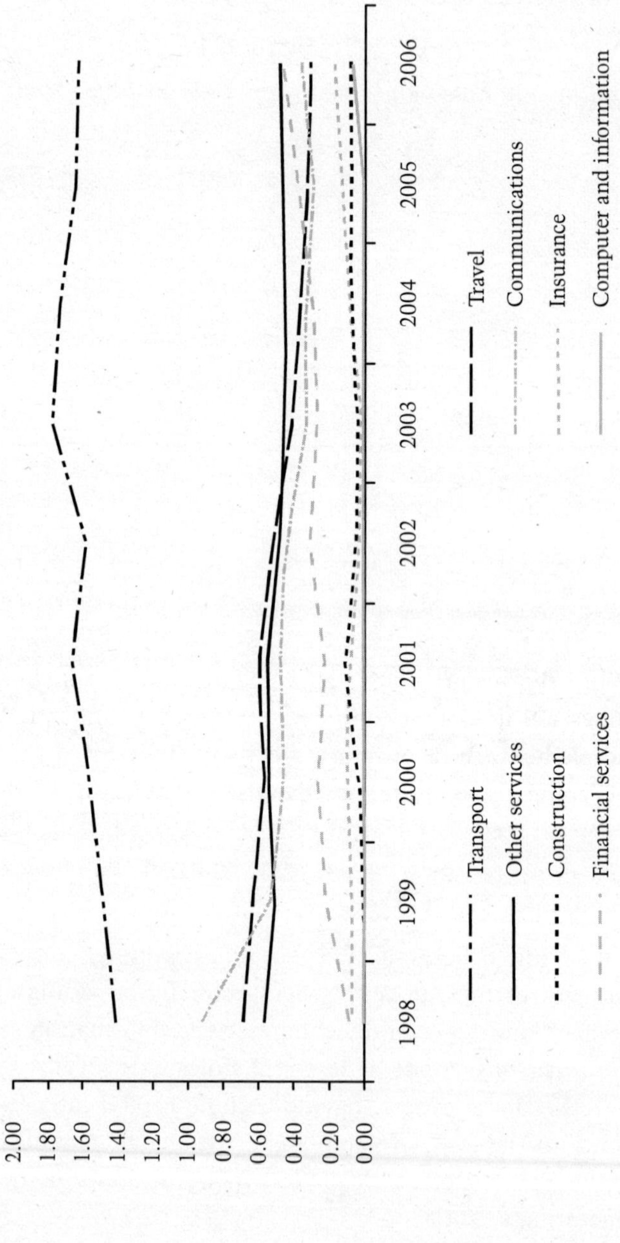

Figure 8.6

RCAs of Indian Service Sectors

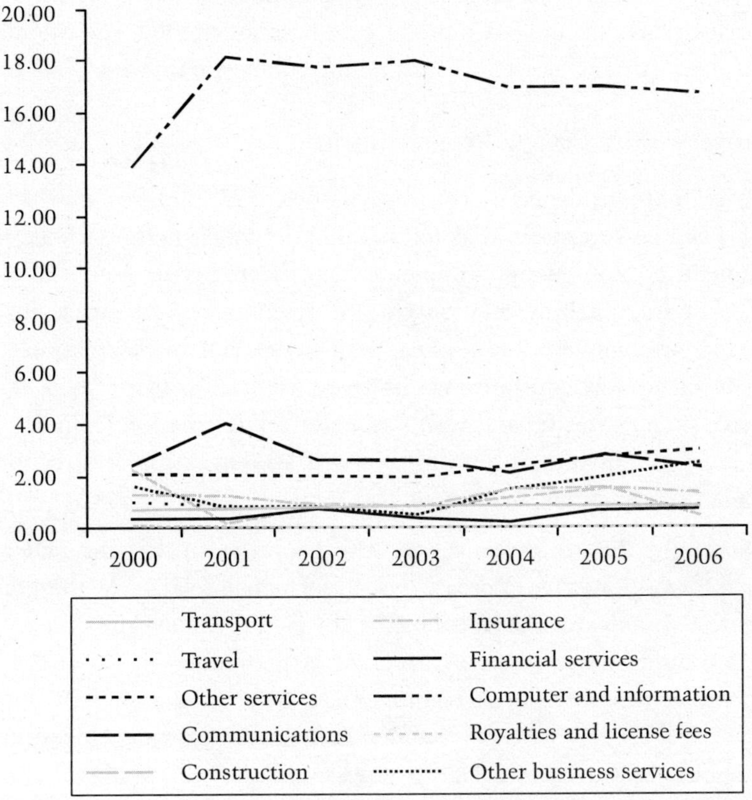

India needs to develop its manufacturing sector in a short period of time because it needs to generate more job opportunities and improve trade balances. Germany, Japan and Korea have been much talked about as the top three countries that are very good at manufacturing activities. And among those three, Japan and Korea are often referred to as good at mass productions. And of the final two, Korea can be selected to remain good at the labor-intensive manufacturing sector, generating a huge number of job opportunities that will be badly needed in India in the years to come since a bigger number of young people will come into the job market.

On the other hand, Korea needs to go to the Indian market since its own domestic market is almost saturated and it should not miss the opportunity to enter and capture a promising market with very high future potential. India can serve as a production base for the EU, the Middle East and African markets as well as for the huge domestic market.

Summary and Policy Implications

The main findings of the discussions and analyses in the above sections can be summarized as follows. Firstly, the structures of the Indian and Korean economies are complementary, having great potential to help each other in attacking challenges and utilizing opportunities for their economic development. India is eager to invite FDI in the manufacturing sector to create jobs and improve its trade balance. Korea is good at labor-intensive manufacturing and wants to enter a huge market in India. Thus, there are great opportunities for win-win strategies for both economies particularly in bilateral investment and service trade.

Secondly, the performances of both countries in drawing FDI are far below the world average. Korea's low performance relative to the potential in Figure 8.3 indicates that a couple of key factors among the determinants of FDI should be improved in order to attract more FDI. On the other hand, India, despite overall improvement of performance and potential indexes, still remains in the "Under Performer" category, meaning that India should improve the overall business climate.

Fortunately, we have the "doing business index" released each year by the World Bank on this matter. This index surveys 183 countries and ranks them accordingly based on the measures on 10 regulatory areas. Singapore ranks 1st, providing the most favorable business environments to FDI. Korea, China, and India ranked 19th, 89th and 133rd, respectively. One of the notable features of Korea's business climate is that it ranked 150th in the "hires and fires" category, showing the rigidity of the Korean job market. The survey shows that when a company wants to lay off a worker in Korea, it has to pay on average 91 weeks of salary.

In the case of India, the categories in which India ranks at a low level are "starting a business", "dealing with licenses", "paying taxes", and "enforcing contracts". There are too many procedures and it costs too

Table 8.5

Ease of Doing Business Index in 2009

Economy	Rank	Start Business	Deal License	Hires Fires	Property	Get Credit	Protect Invest	Paying Taxes	Export Imports	Contracts	Close Business
Singapore	1	4	2	1	16	4	2	5	1	13	2
Thailand	12	55	13	52	6	71	12	88	12	24	48
Japan	15	91	45	40	54	15	16	123	17	20	1
Korea	19	53	23	150	71	15	73	49	8	5	12
Malaysia	23	88	109	61	86	1	4	24	35	59	57
China	89	151	180	140	32	61	93	125	44	18	65
Vietnam	93	116	69	103	40	30	172	147	74	32	127
Bangladesh	119	98	118	124	176	71	20	89	107	180	108
Indonesia	122	161	61	149	95	113	41	127	45	146	142
India	133	169	175	104	93	30	41	169	94	182	138

Source: World Bank (2009). *Doing Business 2010*.

much to get a license from the Indian government. It takes on average around five years to resolve a business conflict through the courts, implying that India needs to reform its legal system to make it more business-friendly.

Thirdly, mutual benefits can be obtained through services trade. Some Indian service sectors are found to be competitive in the world market: computer and information, and communication sectors are very competitive. In contrast, Korean service sectors are in general not so competitive except for transportation service. Thus, India can contribute to the development of Korean service sectors by providing highly enabled engineers, particularly in computer and information, communication sectors.

Finally, for an action plan to enhance mutual cooperation in bilateral investment and service trade, both economies need to exchange government persons who are taking care of FDI and service trade. By doing so, they can share information, increase understanding and help more Korean manufacturing firms invest in India and more Indian professionals, particularly engineers, come to Korea, resulting in greater mutual benefits.

References

Baharumshah, A.Z. and M.V. Thanoon (2005). "Foreign Capital Flows and Economic Growth in East Asian Countries", *China Economic Review*.

Balasubramanyam, V.N., M. Saliu and D. Sapsford (1996). "Foreign Direct Investment and Growth in EP and IS Countries", *Economic Journal* 106(1): 92–105.

Bengoa, M. and B. Sanchez-Robles (2003). "Foreign Direct Investment, Economic Freedom and Growth: New Evidence from Latin America", *European Journal of Political Economy* 19(3): 529–45.

Blomstrom, M., R. Lipsey and M. Zwjan (1996). "Is Fixed Investment the key to Economic Growth?", *Quarterly Journal of Economics* 111(1): 269–76.

Borenstein, E., J. De Gregorio and J.W. Lee (1998). "How does Foreign Direct Investment Affect Economic Growth?", *Journal of International Economics* 45(1): 115–35.

Lewis, Arthur W. (1954). "Economic Development with Unlimited Supplies of Labor", *Manchester School of Economics and Social Studies* 22: 139–191.

Mckinsey (2004). *Quarterly Survey*.

Nunnenkamp, P. and J. Spatz (2002). "Determinants of FDI in Developing Countries: Has Globalization Changed the Rules of the Game?", *Transnational Corporations* 11(2): 1–34, (August).

Olofsdotter, K. (1998). "Foreign Direct Investment, Country Capabilities and Economic Growth", *Weltwirtschaftliches Archiv* 134(3): 534–47.

Government of India (2005). *Economic Survey* 2004–05.

———. (n.d.). *Fact Sheet of FDI*. Department of Commerce.

UNCTAD (1998). *World Investment Report 1998: Trends and Determinants*.

———. (2007). "Worldwide Survey of Foreign Affiliates", *Occasional Note*. Geneva.

———. (2009). *The Role of International Investment Agreements in Attracting Foreign Direct Investment to Developing Countries*. pp.11-12.

———. *Handbook of Statistics*. Statistical Database Online. *www.unctad.org*

World Bank (2009). *Doing Business 2010*.

World Economic Forum (2007). *Global Competitiveness Report 2007–2008*.

Websites:

World Bank, *www.WorldBank.org/*

International Monetary Fund, *www.imf.org/*

The Bank of Korea, *www.bok.or.kr/*

Ministry of Knowledge of Economic, *www.mke.go.kr*

Korea Eximbank, *www.koreaexim.go.kr*

9 Trade Promotion after the Korea-India CEPA

CHOONGJAE CHO

Introduction

The history of trade between Korea and India is nearly 15 centuries old. During that time, trade had taken place through the Silk Road and by maritime routes. History books state that textiles, herbs and spices, incense, glass products, peacock feathers and jewelry were imported to Silla and these goods were luxury items sought by the kingdom's nobles. Before this period, Korea imported Buddhist culture from India by the efforts of a number of eminent priests.

In the modern era, Korea was a colony of Japan, while India was a crown colony of Britain. Sharing a common yet painful experience, Korea and India were able to console and encourage each other. The 1919 Independence Movement of Korea and "The lamp of the East", a poem by the great poet, Rabindranath Tagore, gave hope to both countries. Relations between Korea and India became stronger after the Korean War, when India offered humanitarian aid to Korea.

Such history served as the background when Korea and India finally established diplomatic relations in December 1973, and a trade agreement was signed and entered into force on August 1974. Following the introduction of the reform policy in 1991 in India, Korea-India trade had been gradually increased; and from 2000 to 2009, trade between the two countries increased rapidly, by a factor of 15. On January 2010, the Korea-India Comprehensive Economic Partnership Agreement (CEPA),[1] signed by the two countries, also went into effect. At the same time, the two countries promoted the relationship as a strategic partnership.

---

1. Just CEPA hereafter.

The essential task from now on would be to deepen and expand relations between Korea and India. It is in this context that this article will state the measures for promotion of bilateral trade.

The analysis of the content and implications of the Korea-India CEPA and the economic impact on the two countries will be explained first. In addition, the current status of the bilateral trade, along with its features and challenges, will be analyzed by way of trade index analysis. Lastly, the necessary policy advices and strategy will be suggested to improve the long-term health of trade relations between the two countries.

Korea-India CEPA

The Korea-India CEPA went into force on January 2010, after four years from the first official negotiation. The CEPA negotiation was initiated by the declaration at the Korea-India Summit in March 2006. Since then, 12 rounds of negotiations have taken place in Seoul or Delhi in turn. Prior to India's general election in February 2009, Korea and India signed the Interim Agreement in Delhi. And then on August 7, 2009, Korea and India signed the agreement in Seoul. India had already completed all formalities for implementation of the agreement at the time. After that, the National Assembly of Korea passed the ratification of agreement by unanimous vote in November 2009.

The CEPA is significant in that Korea established an institutional framework for bilateral relations in the economic field with India, the first country that comprises the so-called BRICs countries. India has a nominal GDP that stands at USD 1.2 trillion and ranks as the 12th largest economy in the world. Also, India is the world's second largest in the world in terms of population (1.2 billion). Before the Lehman Brothers' bankruptcy, India recorded an annual average economic growth of 8.4 percent for five years. In 2009, in the midst of global recession, India was still able to maintain its rate of GDP growth at 7 percent. And the CEPA is significant in that Korea took a position of advantage over the Indian market, which was not as developed as those in China, Japan and EU. Those countries are in the process of negotiating FTAs with India but are yet to reach a conclusion of the FTA.

Table 9.1

Korea-India CEPA Progress and Timetable

Date	*Contents*	*Note*
May 2004	Korea designates India as Short-term FTA Partner	FTA Promotion Roadmap
Jan. 2005–Jan. 2006	Korea and India holds four consecutive meetings of Joint Study Group (JSG) CEPA 2005	Public hearing on the Korea-India CEPA in Dec.
Jan. 26, 2006	Both parties agree to launch the CEPA negotiations	At the Ministerial Meeting for External Economic Affairs
Mar. 2006–Sep. 2008	Korea and India holds 12 rounds of official negotiations	De facto conclusion in Sep. 2008
Oct–Nov. 2008	Korea and India convene two rounds of CEPA legal scrubbing meeting	Stipulation/modification of legal text
Feb. 2009	Korea and India initial the Korea-India CEPA	The general election in India, Apr.–May 2009
Aug. 7, 2009	Korea and India sign the Korea-India CEPA	Approval by Indian Cabinet in July 2009
Aug. 26, 2009	The Korean government submits the ratification agreement bill and obtains approval	
Nov. 6, 2009	Korea proceeds with ratification from the National Assembly	
Jan. 1, 2010	Korea-India CEPA enters into force	

Source: Ministry of Foreign Affairs and Trade (synthesis of reports released).

From the Indian perspective, Korea is the first OECD country it concluded an FTA with. So far, India had concluded an FTA with Maldives, Sri Lanka, Singapore, Mauritius and Bhutan. Additionally, India has concluded FTAs with economic blocs like SAFTA and ASEAN. An FTA with India is especially significant in that Korea has the largest economy among India's FTA partners.

Contents of Korea-India CEPA and Economic Impacts

Goods, Origin and Trade Remedies

The tariff concession rate is relatively low. As an alternative to low concession rate, the agreement includes effective and future-oriented contents in the sector of trade in goods. The origin rules are accepted by both countries at normal levels. According to the CEPA, about 85 percent of tariffs on the trading items will be eliminated or decreased within 10 years at the most. Korea's tariff elimination rate is at 84.7 percent and

Table 9.2

Conclusion of India's Key FTAs and Progress

Major FTAs Concluded

Year	*Contents*	*Note*
1981	Conclusion of the India-Maldives FTA	-
1998	Conclusion of the India-Sri Lanka FTA	Under consultation in progress to expand to CEPA (2008)
2003	Conclusion of India-Singapore FTA	Entry into force in 2005
2004	Conclusion of India-MERCOSUR FTA	Not yet in effect because of ratification issues in Brazil and the Argentine Republic
2004	Conclusion of India-SAFTA* FTA	Consent to the expansion into Service sectors (2008)
2006	Conclusion of FTA between India and The Kingdom of Bhutan	Entry into force in 2006
2008	Completion of negotiations	Entry into force in Jan. 2010 (Malaysia, Singapore for India-ASEAN FTA and Thailand). Scheduled to come into force later for other countries. Under consultation toward completion of discussion on service and investment sectors
2009	Conclusion of CEPA between India and The Republic of Korea	Entry into force in Jan. 2010

Major FTAs under Negotiation and Consultation

Partner	*Recent Progress*
China	The Joint Study between two economies completed in Oct. 10, 2008.
Japan	The 12th meeting of the JTF held September 29–October 1, 2009 in Tokyo.
EU	The 8th Round held during January 25–29, 2010.
GCC**	The 2nd round of negotiations held in Riyadh on September 9–10, 2008.
Malaysia	The 2nd India-Malaysia CEPA held in June 2008.
BIMSTEC***	The 2nd BIMSTEC Summit held on November 13, 2008.
Thailand	• The India-Thailand FTA expected to be concluded in 2010. • 17 Rounds of negotiations held so far.
Singapore	• The 1st round of review concluded on October 1, 2007. • Both sides agreed to launch a 2nd review in early 2010.
Canada	Both sides agreed to launch preliminary negotiations for CEPA in January 2009.
Australia	Two economies held Joint Study in May and August, 2008.

Note: * Bangladesh, The Kingdom of Bhutan, India, Maldives, Nepal, Pakistan, Sri Lanka (seven nations).

** GCC (Gulf Cooperation Council): the United Arab Emirates, Saudi Arabia, Kuwait, Qatar, Oman, Bahrain.

*** BIMSTEC: (Bay of Bengal Initiative for Multi-Sectoral Technical and Economic Cooperation): Bangladesh, The Kingdom of Bhutan, India, Myanmar, Nepal, Sri Lanka, and Thailand).

Source: Synthesis of reports released.

India's is at 74.5 percent. If we include the items on which tariffs will be decreased, Korea's rate will be 89.7 percent and India's will be 85.4 percent, making Korea's tariff concession rate a relatively high one.

Table 9.3

Details of Tariff Concession Rate

Staging Category	*India's Schedule of Tariff Concessions*			
	Number of Items	*Share (%)*	*Amount of Imports (US$ million)*	*Share (%)*
Category	3,739	71.5	2,984	74.5
E-0*	202	3.9	1,538	38.4
E-5**	180	3.4	560	14
E-8***	3,357	64.2	886	22.1
RED****	459	8.8	342	8.5
SEN*****	261	5.0	96	2.4
EXC******	768	14.7	580	14.5
Total	5,227	100	4,001	100
Staging Category	*Korea's Schedule of Tariff Concessions*			
	Number of Items	*Share (%)*	*Amount of Imports (US$ million)*	*Share (%)*
Category	9,984	88.6	1,679	84.7
E-0*	6,824	60.6	1,148	63
E-5**	2,310	20.5	205	10.3
E-8***	850	7.5	226	11.4
RED****	34	0.3	3	0.2
SEN*****	478	4.2	94	4.8
EXC******	765	6.8	205	10.3
Total	11,261	100	1,981	100

Note: * Duties on entire elimination of the tariff of the item in staging category E-0 on the date of the entry into force.

** Duties on removal of the tariff of the item in staging category E-5 in five equal annual stages beginning on the date of the entry into force.

*** Duties on removal of the tariff of the item in staging category E-8 in eight equal annual stages beginning on the date of the entry into force.

**** Duties on reduction of the tariff of the item in staging category RED to one to five percent from the base rate in eight equal annual stages beginning on the date of the entry into force.

***** For India, duties on the reduction of the tariff of the item in staging category SEN by 50 percent of the base rate in ten equal annual stages; for Korea, by 50 percent of the base rate in eight equal annual stages beginning on the date this Agreement enters into force.

****** Exemption from the obligation of tariff reduction or elimination.

Source: Ministry of Foreign Affairs and Trade.

India's tariff rate, however, remains relatively high. A detailed observation reveals the average tariff on non-agricultural products of India to be 11.5 percent. This is higher in comparison with other countries—China (9.0%), Indonesia (6.7%) and the Philippines (5.8%). As a result, although the eliminating and decreasing tariffs will take some time, the impact is expected to be more significant, with the impact growing larger with the passage of time.

India's tariff concession rate is the lowest compared to countries which Korea has concluded FTAs with. The allowed period for tariff elimination is the longest, ranging from 5 to 8 years or up to 10 years. India's tariff concession rates are not as significant compared to Korea's FTAs with other FTA partners. In the case of the Korea-USA FTA, the tariff concession rate in the US is 91.4 percent and in the case of the Korea-EU FTA, the EU shows a tariff concession rate of 99 percent. The concession is over 90 percent even for emerging economies in ASEAN.

Figure 9.1

Non-Agricultural Products' Tariff Rate

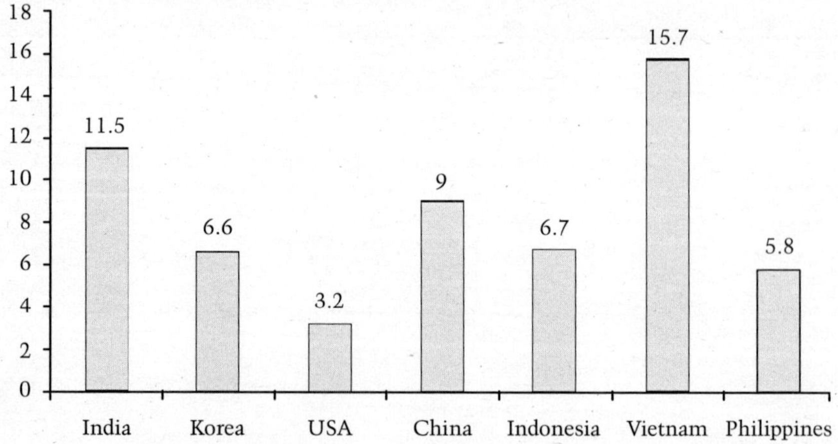

Source: WTO tariff data (2007).

The agricultural items considered too sensitive have been excluded from the articles of the tariff concession, with most other products being included in the concession. Korea's top 10 export products to India include machinery, steel, automobile components, etc. The items due for immediate abolition of tariff concession rate are corded or cordless phones and home electronics. Automobile components, oil and steels will be eliminated or decrease to 1-5 percent in 5 to 8 years. Those top 10 export items occupy 40 percent of exports to India.

Additionally, diesel engines, rail locomotives and elevators, all of which have a potential impact on trading, are included in the concession items. The concession levels, in detail, is for lowering of those rates on diesel engines from 12.5 percent by 1-5 percent within eight years. The rates for rail locomotives and elevators will be eliminated from the current level of 10 percent and 12.5 percent, respectively, to 0 percent within five years.

Table 9.4

Concession on Major 10 Items Exported to India

Rank	*Major Exports to India*				
	Items (HS 6-digit)	*Base Rate of India*	*Staging Category*	*Amount of Exports in 2008*	
				USD million	*Share*
1	Auto parts	12.5	RED	1,131	12.6
2	Gas oil (jet)	10	SEN	769	8.6
3	Radio-telephony apparatus	0	E-0	499	5.6
4	Ships (tankers)	12.5	E-8	430	4.8
5	Parts of line telephone sets	0	E-0	248	2.8
6	Hot-rolled sheet and strip of iron or non-alloyed steel	5	E-5	208	2.3
7	Newsprint	12.5	E-5	172	1.9
8	Cold-rolled sheet and strip of iron or non-alloyed steel	5	E-5	165	1.8
9	Other consumer electronics	12.5	E-0	150	1.7
10	Ships (vessels for the transport of goods)	12.5	E-8	133	1.5
	Sub-total: Major export items			3,780	42.1
	Total: Total export			8,977	100

Source: Ministry of Foreign Affairs and Trade, Korea.

Additional concession review will remain a possibility two years later as the CEPA comes into force. In practical terms, as in the case of the FTA between India and Singapore, after going into effect in 2005 through the additional review, India's tariff concession was concluded with concessions on 275 items in 2007. Henceforth if a wide gap is found between the Korea-India CEPA concession level and concession levels of Japan or the EU-India FTA, Korea and India could re-negotiate to improve their level of concession.

The rules of origin are set in accordance with existing standards. In the case of some products that are considered sensitive, specific rules apply. The standards are that the regional value content[2] will not be less than 35 percent and the goods will have undergone a change in tariff classifications in a subheading, at the 6-digit level of the HS. And goods that undergo working or processing in Kaesong Industrial Complex should be applied to preferential tariff treatment[3] as an exemption from the Principle of Territoriality.

In the sector of trading remedies, more improved articles are introduced. Lesser Duty Rule (LDR), a duty less than the margin of dumping where such lesser duty would be adequate to remove the injury to the domestic industry; Prohibition of Zeroing, in which all individual margins, whether positive or negative, should be counted toward the average; and Exemption from investigation after termination on Review are included in the CEPA.

Service and Investment

Both Korea and India agreed on liberalization on service items, for which a high level of liberalization is demanded by DDA negotiation. This indicates that Korea gains opportunities to open up the Indian market on medical, telecommunication, energy distribution, transport service, construction, advertisement and entertainment and distribution excluding retail. In particular, India could give favorable consideration to application for establishment of branches of Korean banks, which were given to 10 applications over four years after the implementation of CEPA.

The movement of independent professionals[4] between the two countries is introduced. This is the very first bilateral agreement where Korea would allow entry of professionals from India. As a result of this

2. RVC = (FOB-VNM)/FOB *100 (where, RVC is the regional value content, FOB is the value of FOB [Free On Board], VNM is the CIF value of non-originating materials).
3. All FTAs (Singapore, EFTA, ASEAN, USA) include the preferential tariff on Gaesung products in agreement articles.
4. Defined as a self-employed person possessing appropriate educational and other qualifications relevant to the service to be provided, and engaged in the supply of a contracted service, where the professional has a service contract from a person of the other Party.

agreement, the movement of professionals, which covered 163 sectors like computer engineers, business consultants, machinery and telecommunications researchers and assistant English teachers for primary and secondary schools, will be actively promoted.

In the investment sector, investor protection is strengthened overall. The articles related to National Treatment and protection of investors are applied at the level before and after establishment of business activities. These articles include the protection system for investors from government policy changes (ISD). And steps for restrictions and compensation are also included in the CEPA when expropriation, direct or indirect, has occurred. Any requirements or commitments such as export or domestic resource level, transfer of technology, etc. are prohibited in CEPA.

Economic Cooperation

Both Korea and India accepted that economic cooperation would take place in various sectors. The cooperation will cover 13 sectors, which include trading, investment, information and communications, energy, textiles, etc.

The Economic Impacts

Macroeconomic Impacts

According to Computable General Equilibrium (CGE) analysis, Korea's real GDP will be expected to grow 0.18 percent in the long term[5] after implementation of the CEPA. 0.18 percent growth of nominal GDP will be generated in India as well. Meanwhile, the level of welfare in both countries will be boosted, making a wide range of goods and services available at cheaper prices. The welfare value for Korea will increase by about USD 926 million, while the increase will amount to about USD 520 million for India.

The volume of industry products for both countries will increase but growth will be relatively greater for Korea. Production in Korea is

---

5. Within 10 years of elimination and invocation of the decrease of custom tariffs.

estimated to increase by about USD 3.9 billion over the long term. India's production will increase by about USD 150 million.

Industry-wise, the impact of CEPA on the service sector is likely to be greater than that on the manufacturing sector in Korea. The reason for greater growth in Korea is that Korea's service sector is bigger than its manufacturing sector. Also, the impact of the service sector includes not only growth of its exports and imports from better market access, but also demand for new services which is related to production and exports in manufacturing.

Meanwhile, the real impact will be greater than the figure estimated here, because the data utilized are based on those for 2001, and the volume of the economy and trade have increased rapidly since then. So if new data are used, the estimated impact will be greater.

Table 9.5

Economic Cooperation in CEPA

Energy	Strengthening cooperation in such fields as exploration of oil/minerals, development of alternative/renewable energies.
IT	Strengthening mutual cooperation for active utilization of Korea's "hardware" and India's "software".
SMEs	Strengthening cooperation for development/transfer and improvement in quality of managerial skills.
Textiles	Strengthening mutual cooperation for technical development and training of personnel in the textiles industry.
Others	Visual-audio content, tourism, government procurement, science & technology.

Source: Korea-India CEPA.

Table 9.6

Macroeconomic Effects of CEPA (Long-Term)

		Korea	*India*
GDP	Increase by (%)	0.18	0.18
	Amount (US$ million)	778.4	868.0
Contribution to welfare (US$ million)		925.5	519.9

Source: KIEP analysis (based on data 2001).

Table 9.7

Impact on Korea-India CEPA Industrial Products

(Unit: USD million)

	Korea	*India*
Agriculture	168	181
Fisheries	9	0
Manufacture	1,730	–187
Service	2,030	153
Total	3,938	148

Source: KIEP analysis (based on data 2001).

Impact on Each Industry

Manufacturing[6]

The degree of opening of the India market is insufficient but the impact on manufacturing export would be greater than expected due to the fact that India has high tariffs and import elasticity.

After the implementation of CEPA, Korea's exports to India will increase by USD 177 million trade annually in response to the decrease and elimination of tariffs. That growth rate is estimated at 3.9 percent compared to average exports in 2004-2006. Imports from India to Korea are expected to grow by about USD 37 million (1.6%) on average annually. Also it will result in a trade surplus for Korea of about USD 140 million annually.

The impacts on export growth are expected to be in the manufacturing sector in the following order: machinery industry (USD 42 million), automobiles (USD 30 million), and chemicals (USD 23 million). In the case of a formal FTA, the automobile industries will be affected the most, whereas the CEPA has not exhibited a secondary "great" impact on exports, since the complete automobile industry is not included in tariff concession and Korean automobile companies like Hyundai Automobile India have engaged in production and sales to maintain 20 percent market share in India.

6. This chapter is a summary of Korea Institute for Industrial Economics and Trade (KIET) report on the analysis of the impact of manufacturing export.

In examining the impact on growth of imports, the following industries—chemicals (USD 8 million), textiles (USD 6 million), machinery (USD 4 million)—will increase in the order written. From the analysis, total trade surplus is expected to accrue to the following industries—machinery (USD 38 million), automobiles (USD 28 million), chemicals (16 million), and electricity and electronics (UDS 14 million) in the order written. The only industry where trade deficit is expected will be textiles: about USD 3 million.

As far as the growth rate of imports and exports is concerned, the automobile and machinery industries are expected to be the highest trading sectors.

Service

Regarding expanding service market access and the agreement on national treatment, Korea will seize the opportunity to boost competitiveness in the service industry and facilitate exports as well.

Favorable consideration for launching Korean bank branches in India will contribute to enhancement of operating competitiveness and effectiveness in the banking sector. Currently, India's government has only given permission for foreign banks to establish two branches or less annually. Also, most foreign banks have less than 10 branches in India. This being the case, there is still promise for entry into India's financing market. Two Korean bank branches are currently in operation in India, and many other Korean banks have a keen interest in locating branches in India.

Table 9.8

Established Branches of Foreign Banks in India

Bank	*No. of Branches*	*Bank*	*No. of Branches*
Standard Chartered	90	Bank of America	5
HSBC	47	Ceylon Bank	5
Citibank	39	Barclays Bank	5
ABN-Amro Bank	28	Bank of Tokyo Mitsubishi	3
Deutsche Bank	11	Shinhan Bank	2
BNP Paribas	8	Others	25
Bank of Nova Scotia	5	Total	273

Note: Based on March 2008.
Source: Reserve Bank of India.

Figure 9.2

Rate of Annual Increase in Trade by Industry in 10-year Period after CEPA

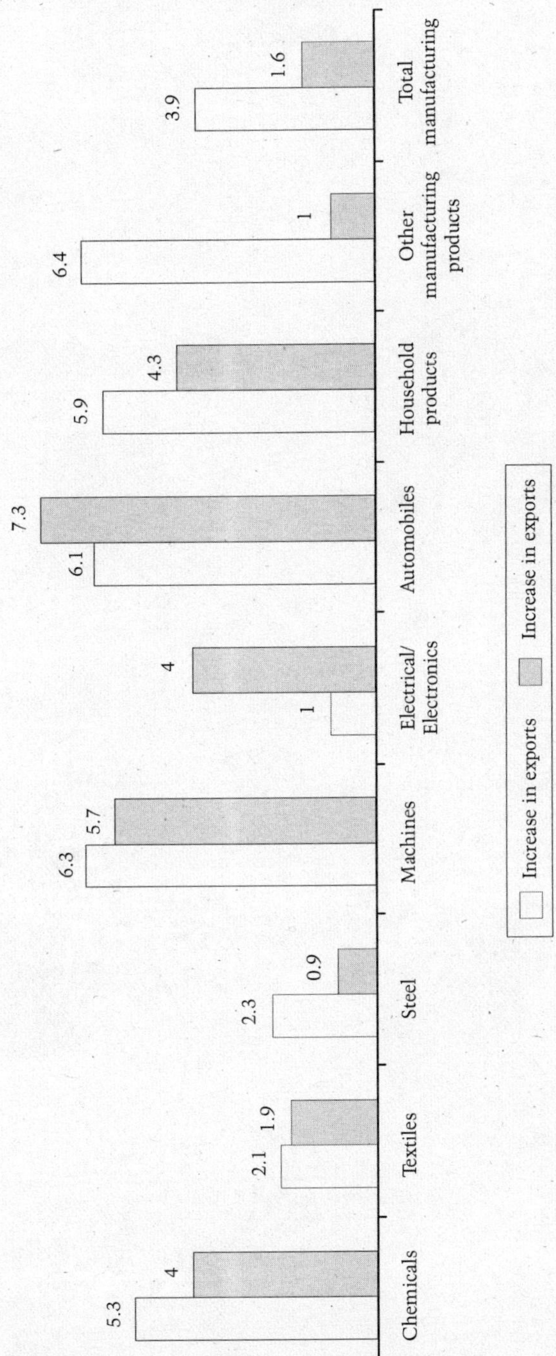

Source: KIET analysis (based on data 2004-2006 average).

Figure 9.3

Survey Results on Utilization of Professional IT Workers among Korean Small/Medium Venture Firms

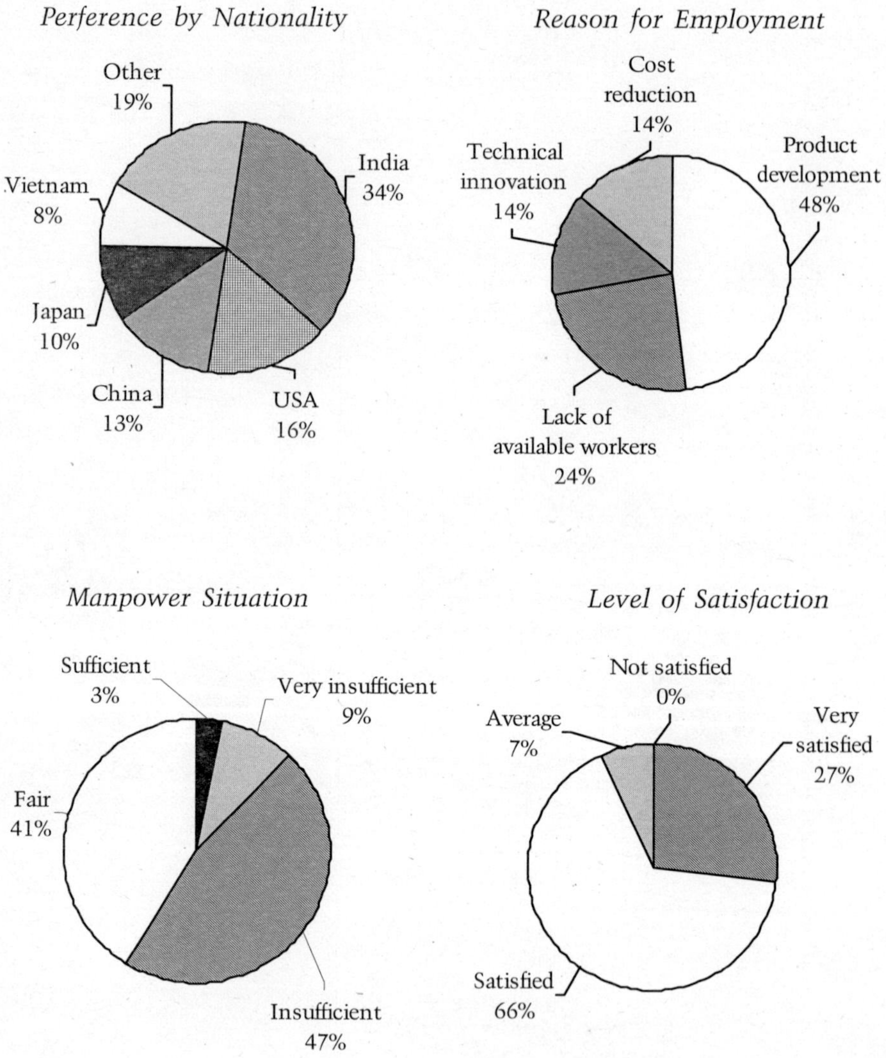

Source: Korea Venture Business Association surveyed in 2007.

The business environment has improved in telecommunications and the impact on this sector is being generated for the short and long term. In particular, there is an agreement related to telecommunications standards that encourages competition, and securing international contracts. It will generate transparency in terms of restrictions and allow improved forecasts.

As a result of the movement of natural persons, skilled and independent workers may fill the workforce gap in Korea where many businesses suffer from an apparent lack of skilled labor, and will contribute to the improved growth of the said industries. Moreover, IT software specialists from India will most likely boost the Korean software industry by developing software products and its quality. Also, there will be a positive impact on globalization of domestic companies and enhancing price competitiveness. According to the survey for middle and small IT companies, employers prefer Indian specialists and are mostly satisfied after hiring them.[7] That also contributes to the diversification of overseas expansion of Indian IT engineers and to the increase of service exports to Korea[8].

Features and Challenges of Trade between Korea and India

Trade Status

Trade between Korea and India has been rapidly increasing since 2000. As statistics show, in 2002, the total amount of trade was USD 2.6 billion. But the amount increased to over USD 10 billion in 2007 and became USD 15.6 billion in 2008. In 2009 the amount had fallen to USD 12.2 billion, due to the global economic recession.

---

7. The total number of Indian IT specialists was about 1,400 by 2007.
8. In the author's opinion, the growing influx of specialists from India will not likely lead to chaos in the Korean labor market. The institutional framework has included in the CEPA articles on illegal residency issues. The articles included are concerned with controlling the influx by tightening qualifications, quota and modification of visas. A sudden and temporary surge in specialists is expected as a result of the CEPA. However, social problems are unlikely since domestic companies' hiring requirement for hiring high-skilled specialists include at least a university degree.

On other hand, the growth rate of trade between Korea and India is greater than the growth of total trade conducted by Korea. From 2004 to 2008, the compound annual growth rate (CAGR) of Korea's total trade was 16 percent. Meanwhile during the same period, the CAGR for both countries was 30 percent. Even when taking year 2009, the peak year of global recession, into account, the former recorded growth of 7 percent, and the latter 18 percent. The rate of growth of bilateral trade between Korea and India has been two times the speed of Korea's trade growth.[9]

Table 9.9

Korea-India Trade (Unit: USD billion)

	2002	2003	2004	2005	2006	2007	2008	2009
Export	1.38	2.85	3.63	4.55	5.53	6.6	8.98	8.01
Import	1.25	1.23	1.85	2.31	3.64	4.62	6.58	4.14
Balance	0.14	1.62	1.78	2.24	1.89	1.98	2.40	3.87
Amount	2.63	4.09	5.48	6.86	9.17	11.22	15.56	12.15

Source: *KITA.net.*

Table 9.10

Korea's Total Trade and Korea-India Trade (Unit: USD billion)

	2004	2005	2006	2007	2008	2009	CAGR(%)	
							2004-2008	2004-2009
Total trade	478.3	545.6	634.8	728.3	857.3	686.6	16.0	7.0
Korea-India trade	5.5	6.9	9.2	11.2	15.6	12.5	30.0	18.0

Source: *KITA.net.*

Features and Challenges of Trade between Korea and India

Trade imbalance has been the major feature and challenge of trade between Korea and India. Korea has hitherto recorded only surpluses in its trade with India. As the amount of trade become larger, the gap of the imbalance becomes wider. The value of trading surplus went from

9. The growth rate of imports from India has increased 40 percent. This stems from improved capability for naphtha production on the part of India, thus leading to increased import by Korea of naphtha from India.

USD 140 million in 2002 to USD 2.4 billion. The amount of trade shrank in 2009, yet the surplus for Korea has actually increased to USD 3.9 billion.

Figure 9.4

Trend of the Growth Rate of Korea's Total Trade and Korea-India Trade

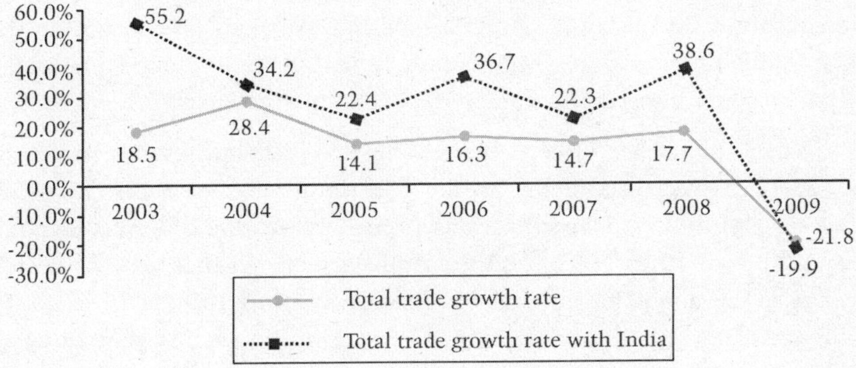

Source: *KITA.net*.

Figure 9.5

Korea's Trade Balance with India

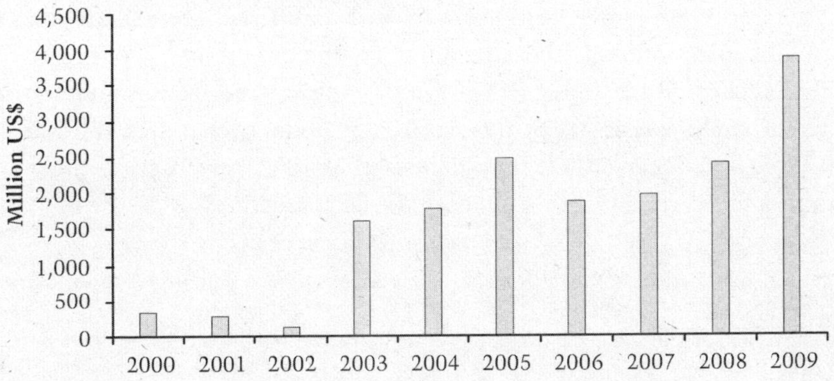

Source: *KITA.net*.

The second feature and challenge has been that the trade structure between both countries is not competitive but is more likely to be fixed.

When one looks at the Trade Specification Index,[10] there are many trade items that in the Trade Specification Index are shown to be near 1 or –1. And this will be clearly demonstrated with the passage of time. In 2004, the number of items showing a TSI range between –0.5 and 0.5 (HS 2-digit) was 21, which decreased to 18 in 2007.

In addition, there have been not much changes in export and import specification items. Korea's import specification items are concentrated on agriculture and fisheries, groceries and mining goods (HS code from 01 to 27) and Korea export specification items are tools, metal products, electronics and transport machinery (HS code from 81 to 99).

Third, the degree of dependence upon specification items is rising, as is trading in specialized items. In the TSI, the number of items that were close to perfect export specifications from Korea to India decreased from 14 in 2004 to 10 in 2007. And the number of items that were of nearly perfect specifications for imports decreased from 19 in 2004 to 14 in 2007. This indicates that the concentration of specification items on trading is higher, given the doubling of trade volume during the same period.

Fourth, the trade structure between Korea and India is not competitive, yet it is difficult to see it as complementary. Certainly, there are trade major items that consist of finished goods and intermediate products for trading.[11] However, it still cannot be considered complementary, because both countries are insufficient in terms of intra-industry specialization. In practical terms, looking at the Intra-Industry Trade Index (IIT)[12] which indicates horizontal and vertical international specialization, the number of items over 0.5 in IIT was 17 in 2004 and 15 in 2007. This shows that relatively high numbers of intra-industry specialization items have decreased.

10. The TSI is close to 1, which means export specialization. Figures close to –1 mean import specialization.

11. The list of the main export goods from Korea to India includes components of automobiles, lubricating base oil, tankers, cellular trunked radio system, steel, metal, paper and cargo ships. The list of the main import goods from India includes light oils and preparations, ferrochromium, oil-cake and residues, non-alloy pig iron, rape, feed and sesame seeds are mostly raw or intermediate goods.

12. The Grubel-Lloyd (GL) Index is utilized. The GL Index has a figure between from 0 to 1.0 means export or import specialization; figures close to 1 mean more depth in intra-industry trade.

Figure 9.6

Change in Korea's Trade Specification Index over India

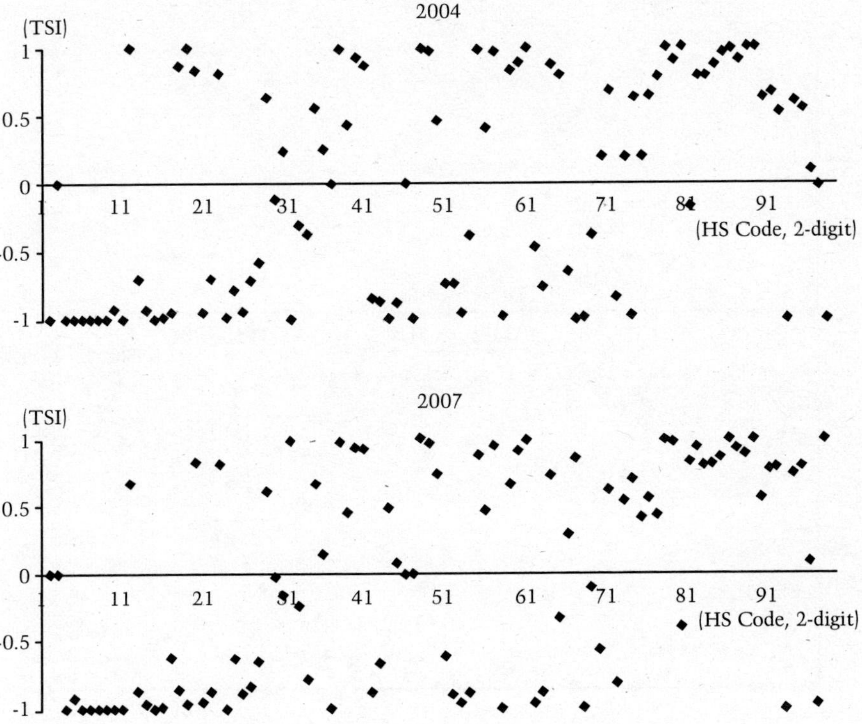

Source: KIEP DB.

Lastly, the share of exports and imports for both countries has been asymmetrical. The ratio of export and import volumes with India in Korea has increased rapidly with active trade, but in India the ratio has remained stagnant. The percentage of trade with India in Korea's total trade was 0.7 percent in 2002 and increased to 1.8 percent in 2009, or more than twice the previous figure. During the same period, the ratio of Korea's exports to India accounted for went from 0.8 percent to 2.2 percent and the ratio of imports accounted for went from 0.6 percent to 1.3 percent. As these statistics show, it is possible that for Korea growth

Figure 9.7

Changes in Korea's Intra-Industry Trade Index over India

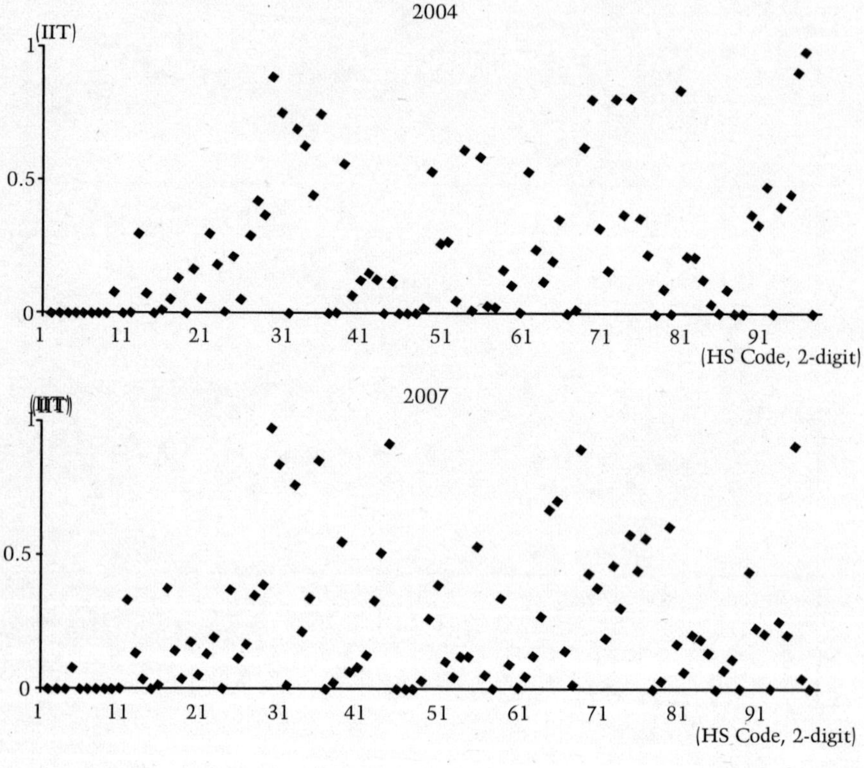

Source: KIEP DB.

of trade rate with India is increasing twice as fast as its growth rate for total trade.

Meanwhile, India's imports from Korea accounted for 2.2 percent of its total trade in 2001, 3.6 percent in 2003 and 2.4 percent in 2007. From 2007 to 2008, it stayed at 2.7-2.8 percent, which is lower than in 2003. As for trade with China, India's imports from China accounted for 11 percent of its total imports in 2007 and after. It can be seen that the scale of importing by India from China has been too huge and has increased too rapidly for Korean exports to India to catch up.

Figure 9.8

Shares of Trade to India in Korea's Overall Trade

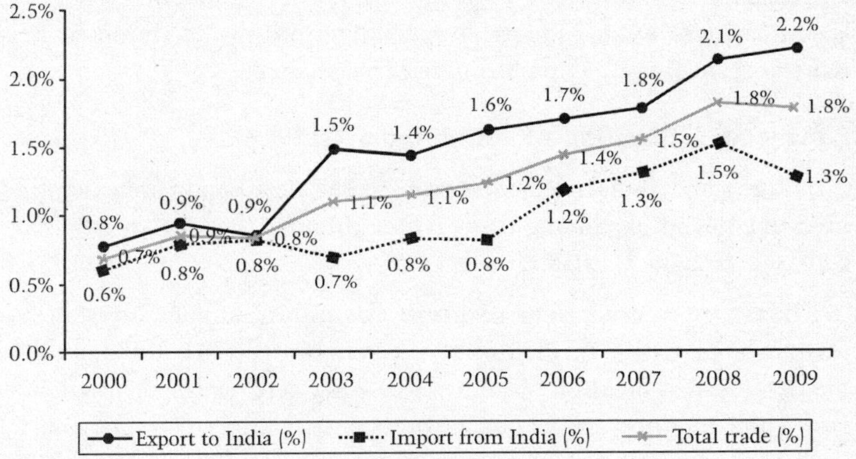

Source: *KITA.net.*

Figure 9.9

Shares of Key Countries in India's Total Imports

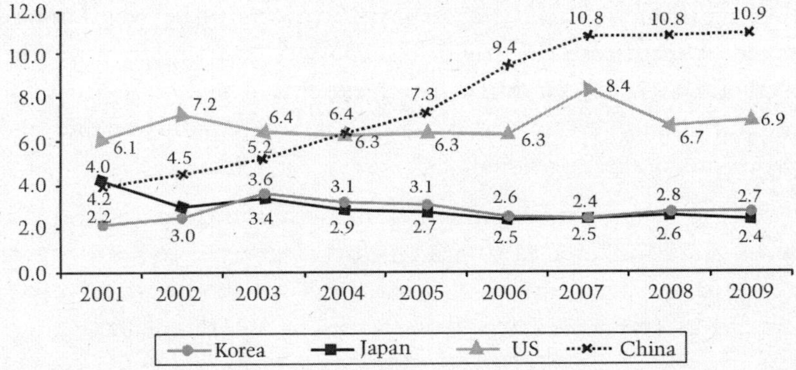

Source: *KITA.net.*

The Way to Expand and Deepen Trade between Korea and India

Trade between Korea and India has increased rapidly since 2000. In doing so, the challenges that the imbalance, concentrated on the specifications, weak industrial specialization and asymmetric trade structures, identified as problems need resolving.

Enhancing Utilization of Korea-India CEPA

Korea and India need to maximize the new opportunity for trade, investment and expanding cooperation through the implementation of CEPA on January 1, 2010.

First, it is crucial to reassure the public and businessmen in utilizing the CEPA to maximize its benefits. Both countries should make efforts to create a system for issuing certificates of origin more easily and monitor application of preferential tariff treatment and take immediate action on existing documents as well. Plus, under the joint committee for fulfillment of articles on review, it is essential to continue efforts to improve conditions for concessions.

Apart from that, the further proceedings agreed at the CEPA should be allowed to move forward soon. Details of further proceedings include the recognition for licensing or certifications of service suppliers, issuance of certificates of origin by exporters and suppliers instead of official authorities, simplified and expedited customs procedures, Internet customs, establishment of a customs committee and audio-visual co-production agreement.

On the other hand, companies in both countries recognize that active utilization of CEPA is an issue of greater importance after negotiation and ratification. And attempts will be necessary to reach benefits to its companies as well as to nations and the public.

To Achieve Excess Target of Trade

Both countries agreed to a target of USD 30 billion by 2014 at the Korea-India Summit on January 2010. The target was adjusted downward because of the sudden outbreak of global recession and a sharp decrease of trade by 24 percent in 2009. But considering the impact of CEPA and the growing trend of trade, it is likely that the target will be reached earlier.

During the last period from 2004 to 2008, the annual growth rate of exports and imports of the two countries was 26 percent and 41 percent, respectively. When we apply the past growth rate to the future (2014), the figure stands at USD 40 billion. In January and February of 2010, the growth rate for trade was 121 percent. This explains that the target has underestimated the potential power of the Agreement. In 2006, Korea-India summit talks set the trade value at USD 10 billion in 2008, but the actual figure was USD 15.6 billion. Therefore, it will be necessary to hit the target of USD 30 billion early and adjust the figures to set a higher target value.

To Improve the Imbalance Expanding Trade in Service

The biggest challenge, trade imbalance, will prove difficult to solve in a short time. The imbalance appears concentrated in the commodity sector, meaning the differences of competitiveness in both manufacturing sectors. It is a difficult issue that will take a long time to improve.

As one of the solutions, more active trade in services is needed. Particularly, expanding IT service imports from India to Korea will contribute to easing the trade imbalance and will also boost both countries' industries and economy. In the CEPA both Korea and India have already agreed on the movement of professionals in 163 professional fields, of which about 90 lists are related to IT specialists.

Korean IT industries tend to focus on hardware, whereas India's is on software, which forms a complementary relationship. From the Korean perspective, the software sector is gaining importance since the recent launching of Smart Phone. The development of the software industry and the inflow of highly skilled IT software professionals from India have become necessary. In order for that to happen, it is essential for the Korean government to support small and medium-sized companies, providing them with a database containing the list of IT professionals. Needless to say, support from the Indian government will also be necessary.

Figure 9.10

Future of Korea-India Trade

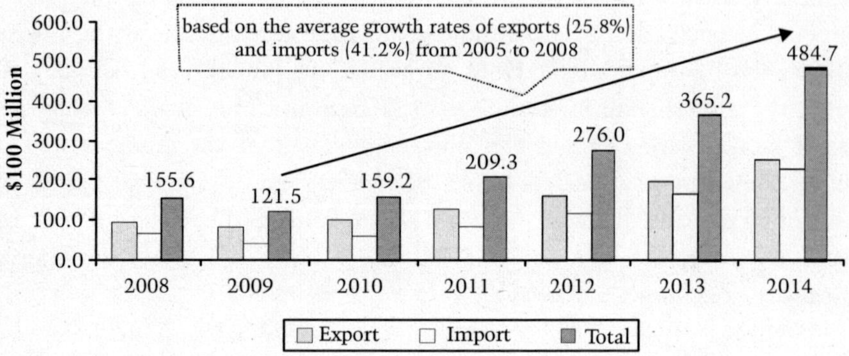

Source: Author.

Expanding Investment

Vertical and horizontal specialization in both industries are needed to ease the trade imbalance and weighting for item specification. The efficient way to promote the better trade structure is to expand investment. In the case of Korea, expanding investment to India and expanding trade dovetail neatly with each other. In CEPA there are statements which are included that are provisions salient to investment protection. To accelerate investment between Korea and India, a proactive attitude is required.

Channels of collaboration such as the Korea-India Association of Investment Promotion and the Korea-India Economy Collaborations Committee are important in reinforcing mutual cooperation. Both governments must also provide more support and information on trade and investment, to the general public and businessmen in both countries.

The Korean Company Industrial Cluster in India requires completion much earlier than initially planned. Korean companies, especially small and medium companies, have faced difficulties in gaining access to the Indian market without factory sites, which urgently needs resolving. Both countries must expend greater effort and support for completing the Cluster.

Indian companies also should lend weight to promoting investment in Korea. There are already special economic zones in many areas in Korea and some of its companies may be available for M&A. One of the successful examples of an M&A is TATA Motors' takeover of Daewoo's commercial automobile line.[13]

Korea-South Asia FTA Joint Negotiation

Korea is ranked at no. 4 and India is ranked at no. 3 in the Asian economic scale. And both countries are politically open countries, sharing core values of democracy and market economy. Korea and India can take the lead in economic integration in Northeast Asia and South Asia. Korea had entered into an FTA that went into force or is being negotiating with many countries and economic blocs. India has driven the creation of the South Asia Free Trade Agreements (SAFTA) and implemented an FTA with Sri Lanka, Thailand, Singapore and ASEAN.

Korea and India have similar diplomatic philosophies, represented in Korea's New Asia Initiative and India's "Look-East Policy", which acknowledge the need to expand diplomatic relations with Asian countries. Toeing the same diplomatic line, Korea and India need to pull together to realize an FTA with South Asia. This will be helpful in developing the Korea-India CEPA further.

The economy of South Asia and its growth rate are going beyond ASEAN's. Based on population and demographic stability, South Asia will be considered one of the largest consumption markets along with India. According to the UN, in 2020 the list of 10 most populous countries in the world will include India (1.37 billion), Pakistan (230 million) and Bangladesh (190 million), which will be ranked 2, 5 and 8, respectively.

---

13. Recently Mahindra & Mahindra, well known in India's automobile and machinery sector, has become known as one of the contenders for takeover in the bidding for Ssangyong Automobile.

For South Asia, the benefit of an FTA and cooperation with Korea will show up in the form of rapid economic growth and industries development, which has the experience of a developing country.

References

Comprehensive Economic Partnership Agreement between the Republic of Korea and the Republic of India, August 2009.

Korea International Economic Policy DB and released materials.

Korea Institute for Industrial Economics and Trade, released materials.

Korea International Trade Association DB.

Korea Venture Business Association surveyed materials in 2007.

Ministry of Foreign Affairs and Trade Korea, released materials.

Reserve Bank of India (various issues). *Bulletins*.

Sahoo, P., D.K. Rai and R. Kumar (2009). "India-Korea Trade and Investment Relations", *Working Paper* No. 242. ICRIER.

WTO (2007). WTO Tariff Data.

www.fta.go.kr

www.commerce.nic.in

Appendix A-9.1

1. Korea's Trade Specialization Index over India (HS 2-digit)

HS	*HS Description*	*2004*	*2005*	*2006*	*2007*
01	Live animals	-1.000	-	-1.000	-
02	Meat and edible meat offal	-	-	-	-
03	Fish and crustaceans, molluscs and other aquatic invertebrates	-0.996	-0.998	-0.989	-1.000
04	Dairy produce; birds eggs; natural honey;	-1.000	-0.998	-1.000	-0.922
05	Products of animal origin, not elsewhere specified	-1.000	-0.976	-1.000	-1.000
06	Live trees and other plants	-1.000	-1.000	-0.824	-0.996
07	Edible vegetables and certain roots and tubers	-1.000	-1.000	-1.000	-1.000
08	Edible fruit and nuts; peel of citrus fruit or melons	-1.000	-1.000	-1.000	-1.000
09	Coffee, tea, mate and spices	-0.920	-0.997	-0.995	-0.995
10	Cereals	-1.000	-0.846	-1.000	-1.000
11	Products of the milling industry; malt; starches; inulin	0.997	0.867	0.450	0.668
12	Oil seeds and oleaginous fruits	-0.702	-0.653	-0.867	-0.867
13	Lac; gums, resins and other vegetable saps and extracts	-0.927	-0.950	-0.976	-0.965
14	Vegetable plaiting materials; vegetable products nes	-1.000	-1.000	-1.000	-1.000
15	Animal or vegetable fats and oils	-0.987	-0.999	-0.984	-0.985
16	Preparations of meat, of fish or of crustaceans	-0.947	-0.824	-0.809	-0.624
17	Sugars and sugar confectionery	0.868	-0.268	0.334	-0.858
18	Cocoa and cocoa preparations	1.000	0.985	0.998	-0.961
19	Preparations of cereals, flour, starch or milk; bakers' wares	0.835	0.194	0.802	0.826
20	Preparations of vegetables, fruit or nuts	-0.943	-0.917	-1.000	-0.947
21	Miscellaneous edible preparations	-0.701	-0.792	-0.900	-0.870
22	Beverages, spirits and vinegar	0.817	0.813	0.881	0.808
23	Residues and waste from the food industries	-0.993	-0.985	-0.990	-0.996
24	Tobacco and manufactured tobacco substitutes	-0.786	-0.576	-0.657	-0.630
25	Salt; sulfur; earths and stone; plastering materials	-0.946	-0.925	-0.902	-0.886
26	Ores, slag and ash	-0.711	-0.557	-0.933	-0.831
27	Mineral fuels, mineral oils and products of their distillation	-0.581	-0.575	-0.609	-0.652
28	Inorganic chemicals	0.633	0.466	0.634	0.610
29	Organic chemicals	-0.116	-0.022	-0.230	-0.025
30	Pharmaceutical products	0.247	0.038	0.017	-0.162
31	Fertilizers	-1.000	0.647	-0.221	0.987
32	Tanning or dyeing extracts	-0.308	-0.274	-0.337	-0.240
33	Essential oils and resinoids; perfumery, cosmetic or toilet preparations	-0.371	-0.768	-0.736	-0.782
34	Soap, organic surface-active agents	0.557	0.337	0.270	0.665

contd...

...contd...

HS	*HS Description*	*2004*	*2005*	*2006*	*2007*
35	Albuminoidal substances; modified starches; glues; enzymes	0.252	0.338	0.578	0.147
36	Explosives; pyrotechnic products; matches	-	-	-	-1.000
37	Photographic or cinematographic goods	0.995	0.951	0.958	0.976
38	Miscellaneous chemical products	0.437	0.355	0.463	0.450
39	Plastics and articles thereof	0.931	0.927	0.920	0.932
40	Rubber and articles thereof	0.872	0.858	0.866	0.918
41	Raw hides and skins (other than fur skins) and leather	-0.846	-0.913	-0.946	-0.875
42	Articles of leather; saddlery and harness	-0.871	-0.910	-0.662	-0.669
43	Fur skins and artificial fur; manufactures thereof	-1.000	-1.000	0.847	0.488
44	Wood and articles of wood; wood charcoal	-0.876	-0.951	-0.315	0.081
45	Cork and articles of cork	-	-	-	-
46	Manufactures of straw, of esparto or of other plaiting materials	-1.000	-1.000	-	-!
47	Pulp of wood or of other fibrous cellulose material	1.000	1.000	-0.996	1.000
48	Paper and paperboard; articles of paper pulp, of paper or of paperboard	0.981	0.989	0.989	0.969
49	Printed books, newspapers, pictures and other products of the printing indu ...	0.467	0.583	0.810	0.736
50	Silk	-0.739	-0.721	-0.768	-0.610
51	Wool, fine or coarse animal hair; horsehair yarn and woven fabric	-0.731	-0.661	-0.803	-0.896
52	Cotton	-0.952	-0.943	-0.964	-0.958
53	Other vegetable textile fibers; paper yarn and woven fabric of paper yarn	-0.383	-0.101	-0.912	-0.879
54	Man-made filaments	0.987	0.974	0.969	0.879
55	Man-made staple fibers	0.413	0.399	0.286	0.466
56	Wadding, felt and non-wovens; special yarns, twine, cordage, ropes and cabl ...	0.970	0.958	0.937	0.947
57	Carpets and other textile floor coverings	-0.979	-0.995	-0.985	-0.999
58	Special woven fabrics; tufted textile fabrics; lace, tapestries; trimmings; ...	0.836	0.734	0.668	0.661
59	Impregnated, coated, covered or laminated textile fabrics	0.893	0.854	0.850	0.907
60	Knitted or crocheted fabrics	0.997	0.998	0.990	0.993
61	Articles of apparel and clothing accessories, knitted or crocheted	-0.465	-0.751	-0.817	-0.953
62	Articles of apparel and clothing accessories, not knitted or crocheted	-0.758	-0.725	-0.837	-0.877
63	Other made up textile articles; sets; worn clothing and worn textile articles ...	0.879	0.751	0.781	0.727
64	Footwear, gaiters and the like; parts of such articles	0.803	-0.258	-0.555	-0.329
65	Headgear and parts thereof	-0.648	0.342	-0.318	0.295

contd...

...contd...

HS	*HS Description*	*2004*	*2005*	*2006*	*2007*
66	Umbrellas, sun umbrellas, walking sticks, seat sticks, whips, riding-crops	-1.000	-1.000	0.877	0.855
67	Prepared feathers and down and articles made of feathers or of down	-0.985	-0.973	-0.850	-0.988
68	Articles of stone, plaster, cement, asbestos, mica or similar materials	-0.377	-0.134	-0.043	-0.102
69	Ceramic products	0.200	0.118	-0.406	-0.568
70	Glass and glassware	0.681	0.810	0.756	0.619
71	Natural or cultured pearls, precious or semi-precious stones	-0.839	-0.857	-0.666	-0.807
72	Iron and steel	0.195	0.353	0.535	0.540
73	Articles of iron or steel	0.631	0.642	0.490	0.699
74	Copper and articles thereof	0.196	0.043	0.213	0.421
75	Nickel and articles thereof	0.641	0.478	0.981	0.555
76	Aluminum and articles thereof	0.778	0.879	-0.032	0.436
78	Lead and articles thereof	1.000	0.855	1.000	1.000
79	Zinc and articles thereof	0.905	0.839	0.716	0.976
80	Tin and articles thereof	1.000	-0.616	1.000	-0.392
81	Other base metals; cermets; articles thereof	-0.164	0.349	0.305	0.829
82	Tools, implements, cutlery, spoons and forks, of base metal	0.786	0.917	0.821	0.937
83	Miscellaneous articles of base metal	0.791	0.843	0.763	0.797
84	Machinery and mechanical appliances; parts thereof	0.874	0.783	0.805	0.815
85	Electrical machinery and equipment and parts thereof; sound recorders and r ...	0.964	0.962	0.958	0.865
86	Railway or tramway locomotives, rolling-stock and parts thereof	0.998	1.000	1.000	1.000
87	Vehicles other than railway or tramway rolling stock	0.911	0.919	0.932	0.931
88	Aircraft, spacecraft, and parts thereof	1.000	0.914	0.855	0.889
89	Ships, boats and floating structures	1.000	1.000	-0.057	1.000
90	Optical, photographic, cinematographic, measuring, checking, precision, med ...	0.631	0.580	0.546	0.558
91	Clocks and watches and parts thereof	0.669	0.840	0.692	0.774
92	Musical instruments; parts and accessories of such articles	0.525	0.433	0.456	0.791
93	Arms and ammunition; parts and accessories thereof	-1.000	-1.000	1.000	-1.000
94	Furniture; bedding, mattresses, cushions and similar stuffed furnishing	0.600	0.598	0.729	0.746
95	Toys, games and sports requisites; parts and accessories thereof	0.552	0.291	0.649	0.796
96	Miscellaneous manufactured articles	0.099	0.152	0.198	0.088
97	Works of art, collectors' pieces and antiques	-0.018	-	0.973	-0.959
99	Commodities not specified according to kind	-1.000	-1.000	-1.000	0.998

2. Korea's Intra-Industry Trade Index over India (HS 2-digit)

HS	*HS Description*	*2004*	*2005*	*2006*	*2007*
01	Live animals	0.000	-	0.000	-
02	Meat and edible meat offal	-	-	-	-
03	Fish and crustaceans, molluscs and other aquatic invertebrates	0.004	0.002	0.011	0.000
04	Dairy produce; birds eggs; natural honey;	0.000	0.002	0.000	0.078
05	Products of animal origin, not elsewhere specified	0.000	0.024	0.000	0.000
06	Live trees and other plants	0.000	0.000	0.176	0.004
07	Edible vegetables and certain roots and tubers	0.000	0.000	0.000	0.000
08	Edible fruit and nuts; peel of citrus fruit or melons	0.000	0.000	0.000	0.000
09	Coffee, tea, mate and spices	0.080	0.003	0.005	0.005
10	Cereals	0.000	0.154	0.000	0.000
11	Products of the milling industry; malt; starches; inulin	0.003	0.133	0.550	0.332
12	Oil seeds and oleaginous fruits	0.298	0.347	0.133	0.133
13	Lac; gums, resins and other vegetable saps and extracts	0.073	0.050	0.024	0.035
14	Vegetable plaiting materials; vegetable products nes	0.000	0.000	0.000	0.000
15	Animal or vegetable fats and oils	0.013	0.001	0.016	0.015
16	Preparations of meat, of fish or of crustaceans	0.053	0.176	0.191	0.376
17	Sugars and sugar confectionery	0.132	0.732	0.666	0.142
18	Cocoa and cocoa preparations	0.000	0.015	0.002	0.039
19	Preparations of cereals, flour, starch or milk; bakers' wares	0.165	0.806	0.198	0.174
20	Preparations of vegetables, fruit or nuts	0.057	0.083	0.000	0.053
21	Miscellaneous edible preparations	0.299	0.208	0.100	0.130
22	Beverages, spirits and vinegar	0.183	0.187	0.119	0.192
23	Residues and waste from the food industries	0.007	0.015	0.010	0.004
24	Tobacco and manufactured tobacco substitutes	0.214	0.424	0.343	0.370
25	Salt; sulfur; earths and stone; plastering materials	0.054	0.075	0.098	0.114
26	Ores, slag and ash	0.289	0.443	0.067	0.169
27	Mineral fuels, mineral oils and products of their distillation	0.419	0.425	0.391	0.348
28	Inorganic chemicals	0.367	0.534	0.366	0.390
29	Organic chemicals	0.884	0.978	0.770	0.975
30	Pharmaceutical products	0.753	0.962	0.983	0.838
31	Fertilizers	0.000	0.353	0.779	0.013
32	Tanning or dyeing extracts	0.692	0.726	0.663	0.760
33	Essential oils and resinoids; perfumery, cosmetic or toilet preparations	0.629	0.232	0.264	0.218
34	Soap, organic surface-active agents	0.443	0.663	0.730	0.335
35	Albuminoidal substances; modified starches; glues; enzymes	0.748	0.662	0.422	0.853
36	Explosives; pyrotechnic products; matches	-	-	-	0.000

contd...

...*contd...*

HS	*HS Description*	*2004*	*2005*	*2006*	*2007*
37	Photographic or cinematographic goods	0.005	0.049	0.042	0.024
38	Miscellaneous chemical products	0.563	0.645	0.537	0.550
39	Plastics and articles thereof	0.069	0.073	0.080	0.068
40	Rubber and articles thereof	0.128	0.142	0.134	0.082
41	Raw hides and skins (other than fur skins) and leather	0.154	0.087	0.054	0.125
42	Articles of leather; saddlery and harness	0.129	0.090	0.338	0.331
43	Fur skins and artificial fur; manufactures thereof	0.000	0.000	0.153	0.512
44	Wood and articles of wood; wood charcoal	0.124	0.049	0.685	0.919
45	Cork and articles of cork	-	-	-	-
46	Manufactures of straw, of esparto or of other plaiting materials	0.000	0.000	-	-
47	Pulp of wood or of other fibrous cellulose material	0.000	0.000	0.004	0.000
48	Paper and paperboard; articles of paper pulp, of paper or of paperboard	0.019	0.011	0.011	0.031
49	Printed books, newspapers, pictures and other products of the printing indu ...	0.533	0.417	0.190	0.264
50	Silk	0.261	0.279	0.232	0.390
51	Wool, fine or coarse animal hair; horsehair yarn and woven fabric	0.269	0.339	0.197	0.104
52	Cotton	0.048	0.057	0.036	0.042
53	Other vegetable textile fibers; paper yarn and woven fabric of paper yarn	0.617	0.899	0.088	0.121
54	Man-made filaments	0.013	0.026	0.031	0.121
55	Man-made staple fibers	0.587	0.601	0.714	0.534
56	Wadding, felt and non-wovens; special yarns, twine, cordage, ropes and cabl ...	0.030	0.042	0.063	0.053
57	Carpets and other textile floor coverings	0.021	0.005	0.015	0.001
58	Special woven fabrics; tufted textile fabrics; lace, tapestries; trimmings; ...	0.164	0.266	0.332	0.339
59	Impregnated, coated, covered or laminated textile fabrics	0.107	0.146	0.150	0.093
60	Knitted or crocheted fabrics	0.003	0.002	0.010	0.007
61	Articles of apparel and clothing accessories, knitted or crocheted	0.535	0.249	0.183	0.047
62	Articles of apparel and clothing accessories, not knitted or crocheted	0.242	0.275	0.163	0.123
63	Other made up textile articles; sets; worn clothing and worn textile articles ...	0.121	0.249	0.219	0.273
64	Footwear, gaiters and the like; parts of such articles	0.197	0.742	0.445	0.671
65	Headgear and parts thereof	0.352	0.658	0.682	0.705
66	Umbrellas, sun umbrellas, walking sticks, seat sticks, whips, riding-crops	0.000	0.000	0.123	0.145
67	Prepared feathers and down and articles made of feathers or of down	0.015	0.027	0.150	0.012

contd...

...contd...

HS	*HS Description*	*2004*	*2005*	*2006*	*2007*
68	Articles of stone, plaster, cement, asbestos, mica or similar materials	0.623	0.866	0.957	0.898
69	Ceramic products	0.800	0.882	0.594	0.432
70	Glass and glassware	0.319	0.190	0.244	0.381
71	Natural or cultured pearls, precious or semi-precious stones	0.161	0.143	0.334	0.193
72	Iron and steel	0.805	0.647	0.465	0.460
73	Articles of iron or steel	0.369	0.358	0.510	0.301
74	Copper and articles thereof	0.804	0.957	0.787	0.579
75	Nickel and articles thereof	0.359	0.522	0.019	0.445
76	Aluminum and articles thereof	0.222	0.121	0.968	0.564
78	Lead and articles thereof	0.000	0.145	0.000	0.000
79	Zinc and articles thereof	0.095	0.161	0.284	0.024
80	Tin and articles thereof	0.000	0.384	0.000	0.608
81	Other base metals; cermets; articles thereof	0.836	0.651	0.695	0.171
82	Tools, implements, cutlery, spoons and forks, of base metal	0.214	0.083	0.179	0.063
83	Miscellaneous articles of base metal	0.209	0.157	0.237	0.203
84	Machinery and mechanical appliances; parts thereof	0.126	0.217	0.195	0.185
85	Electrical machinery and equipment and parts thereof; sound recorders and r ...	0.036	0.038	0.042	0.135
86	Railway or tramway locomotives, rolling-stock and parts thereof	0.002	0.000	0.000	0.000
87	Vehicles other than railway or tramway rolling stock	0.089	0.081	0.068	0.069
88	Aircraft, spacecraft, and parts thereof	0.000	0.086	0.145	0.111
89	Ships, boats and floating structures	0.000	0.000	0.943	0.000
90	Optical, photographic, cinematographic, measuring, checking, precision, med ...	0.369	0.420	0.454	0.442
91	Clocks and watches and parts thereof	0.331	0.160	0.308	0.226
92	Musical instruments; parts and accessories of such articles	0.475	0.567	0.544	0.209
93	Arms and ammunition; parts and accessories thereof	0.000	0.000	0.000	0.000
94	Furniture; bedding, mattresses, cushions and similar stuffed furnishing	0.400	0.402	0.271	0.254
95	Toys, games and sports requisites; parts and accessories thereof	0.448	0.709	0.351	0.204
96	Miscellaneous manufactured articles	0.901	0.848	0.802	0.912
97	Works of art, collectors' pieces and antiques	0.982	-	0.027	0.041
99	Commodities not specified according to kind	0.000	0.000	0.000	0.002

3. Korea's Share of Import from India (HS 2-digit)

HS	*HS Description*	*2004*	*2005*	*2006*	*2007*
01	Live animals	0.003	0.000	0.000	0.000
02	Meat and edible meat offal	0.000	0.000	0.000	0.000
03	Fish and crustaceans, molluscs and other aquatic invertebrates	0.010	0.009	0.011	0.008
04	Dairy produce; birds eggs; natural honey;	0.004	0.003	0.000	0.002
05	Products of animal origin, not elsewhere specified	0.005	0.007	0.004	0.003
06	Live trees and other plants;	0.003	0.003	0.004	0.005
07	Edible vegetables and certain roots and tubers	0.001	0.001	0.001	0.001
08	Edible fruit and nuts; peel of citrus fruit or melons	0.003	0.003	0.003	0.005
09	Coffee, tea, mate and spices	0.005	0.009	0.006	0.008
10	Cereals	0.034	0.000	0.000	0.000
11	Products of the milling industry; malt; starches; inulin	0.000	0.000	0.000	0.000
12	Oil seeds and oleaginous fruits	0.017	0.013	0.041	0.030
13	Lac; gums, resins and other vegetable saps and extracts	0.045	0.055	0.055	0.048
14	Vegetable plaiting materials; vegetable products nes	0.056	0.159	0.192	0.234
15	Animal or vegetable fats and oils	0.009	0.009	0.007	0.008
16	Preparations of meat, of fish or of crustaceans	0.013	0.005	0.002	0.001
17	Sugars and sugar confectionery	0.000	0.003	0.001	0.010
18	Cocoa and cocoa preparations	0.000	0.000	0.000	0.001
19	Preparations of cereals, flour, starch or milk; bakers' wares	0.000	0.001	0.000	0.000
20	Preparations of vegetables, fruit or nuts	0.004	0.002	0.003	0.004
21	Miscellaneous edible preparations	0.003	0.006	0.007	0.007
22	Beverages, spirits and vinegar	0.000	0.000	0.000	0.000
23	Residues and waste from the food industries	0.323	0.119	0.192	0.178
24	Tobacco and manufactured tobacco substitutes	0.016	0.012	0.033	0.062
25	Salt; sulfur; earths and stone; plastering materials	0.011	0.010	0.008	0.008
26	Ores, slag and ash	0.033	0.018	0.039	0.021
27	Mineral fuels, mineral oils and products of their distillation	0.009	0.012	0.020	0.027
28	Inorganic chemicals	0.003	0.003	0.003	0.003
29	Organic chemicals	0.016	0.015	0.025	0.022
30	Pharmaceutical products	0.002	0.003	0.004	0.004
31	Fertilizers	0.000	0.001	0.002	0.000
32	Tanning or dyeing extracts	0.015	0.016	0.020	0.023
33	Essential oils and resinoids; perfumery, cosmetic or toilet preparations	0.007	0.007	0.007	0.007
34	Soap, organic surface-active agents	0.002	0.002	0.002	0.001
35	Albuminoidal substances; modified starches; glues; enzymes	0.005	0.005	0.003	0.008

contd...

...contd...

HS	*HS Description*	*2004*	*2005*	*2006*	*2007*
36	Explosives; pyrotechnic products; matches	0.000	0.000	0.000	0.002
37	Photographic or cinematographic goods	0.000	0.000	0.000	0.000
38	Miscellaneous chemical products	0.003	0.004	0.003	0.003
39	Plastics and articles thereof	0.001	0.002	0.002	0.002
40	Rubber and articles thereof	0.002	0.003	0.003	0.003
41	Raw hides and skins (other than fur skins) and leather	0.035	0.042	0.051	0.042
42	Articles of leather; saddlery and harness	0.006	0.006	0.005	0.003
43	Fur skins and artificial fur; manufactures thereof	0.000	0.000	0.000	0.000
44	Wood and articles of wood; wood charcoal	0.001	0.001	0.001	0.000
45	Cork and articles of cork	0.000	0.000	0.000	0.000
46	Manufactures of straw, of esparto or of other plaiting materials	0.001	0.000	0.000	0.000
47	Pulp of wood or of other fibrous cellulose material	0.000	0.000	0.000	0.000
48	Paper and paperboard; articles of paper pulp, of paper or of paperboard	0.000	0.000	0.001	0.001
49	Printed books, newspapers, pictures and other products of the printing indu ...	0.001	0.002	0.001	0.001
50	Silk	0.040	0.037	0.026	0.015
51	Wool, fine or coarse animal hair; horsehair yarn and woven fabric	0.015	0.017	0.029	0.043
52	Cotton	0.213	0.178	0.196	0.175
53	Other vegetable textile fibers; paper yarn and woven fabric of paper yarn	0.011	0.014	0.013	0.013
54	Man-made filaments	0.001	0.001	0.001	0.004
55	Man-made staple fibers	0.007	0.005	0.006	0.004
56	Wadding, felt and non-wovens; special yarns, twine, cordage, ropes and cabl ...	0.001	0.001	0.001	0.001
57	Carpets and other textile floor coverings	0.082	0.086	0.085	0.067
58	Special woven fabrics; tufted textile fabrics; lace, tapestries; trimmings; ...	0.004	0.005	0.007	0.008
59	Impregnated, coated, covered or laminated textile fabrics	0.004	0.004	0.003	0.002
60	Knitted or crocheted fabrics	0.000	0.000	0.001	0.001
61	Articles of apparel and clothing accessories, knitted or crocheted	0.001	0.002	0.003	0.004
62	Articles of apparel and clothing accessories, not knitted or crocheted	0.005	0.005	0.005	0.004
63	Other made up textile articles; sets; worn clothing and worn textile articles ...	0.007	0.008	0.006	0.008
64	Footwear, gaiters and the like; parts of such articles	0.000	0.001	0.001	0.002
65	Headgear and parts thereof	0.001	0.001	0.001	0.001
66	Umbrellas, sun umbrellas, walking sticks, seat sticks, whips, riding-crops	0.000	0.000	0.000	0.000

contd...

...contd...

HS	*HS Description*	*2004*	*2005*	*2006*	*2007*
67	Prepared feathers and down and articles made of feathers or of down	0.021	0.007	0.005	0.006
68	Articles of stone, plaster, cement, asbestos, mica or similar materials	0.007	0.006	0.005	0.005
69	Ceramic products	0.001	0.001	0.001	0.003
70	Glass and glassware	0.001	0.001	0.001	0.001
71	Natural or cultured pearls, precious or semi-precious stones	0.010	0.046	0.049	0.073
72	Iron and steel	0.012	0.013	0.010	0.011
73	Articles of iron or steel	0.009	0.008	0.009	0.012
74	Copper and articles thereof	0.009	0.012	0.007	0.004
75	Nickel and articles thereof	0.001	0.000	0.000	0.001
76	Aluminum and articles thereof	0.001	0.000	0.006	0.003
78	Lead and articles thereof	0.000	0.009	0.000	0.000
79	Zinc and articles thereof	0.029	0.052	0.048	0.005
80	Tin and articles thereof	0.000	0.001	0.000	0.001
81	Other base metals; cermets; articles thereof	0.006	0.002	0.002	0.001
82	Tools, implements, cutlery, spoons and forks, of base metal	0.006	0.003	0.004	0.004
83	Miscellaneous articles of base metal	0.003	0.002	0.003	0.004
84	Machinery and mechanical appliances; parts thereof	0.001	0.003	0.003	0.003
85	Electrical machinery and equipment and parts thereof; sound recorders and r ...	0.000	0.001	0.001	0.001
86	Railway or tramway locomotives, rolling-stock and parts thereof	0.000	0.000	0.000	0.000
87	Vehicles other than railway or tramway rolling stock	0.005	0.005	0.004	0.005
88	Aircraft, spacecraft, and parts thereof	0.000	0.000	0.000	0.000
89	Ships, boats and floating structures	0.000	0.000	0.041	0.000
90	Optical, photographic, cinematographic, measuring, checking, precision, med ...	0.001	0.001	0.001	0.002
91	Clocks and watches and parts thereof	0.001	0.000	0.000	0.000
92	Musical instruments; parts and accessories of such articles	0.475	0.567	0.544	0.209
93	Arms and ammunition; parts and accessories thereof	0.000	0.000	0.000	0.000
94	Furniture; bedding, mattresses, cushions and similar stuffed furnishing	0.001	0.001	0.001	0.001
95	Toys, games and sports requisites; parts and accessories thereof	0.000	0.001	0.000	0.000
96	Miscellaneous manufactured articles	0.012	0.010	0.007	0.009
97	Works of art, collectors' pieces and antiques	0.001	0.000	0.000	0.000
99	Commodities not specified according to kind	0.003	0.004	0.002	0.000

Section III

Global Security Challenges: Role for India-Korea Cooperation

10 Strategic Challenges and Risks in a Globalizing World

An Indian Perspective

N.S. SISODIA

The world is undergoing a major power shift, raising fears about its destabilizing impact. The global financial crisis, from which China and India have emerged relatively unscathed, has accelerated this transition. Multilateral institutions, particularly the United Nations, are not sufficiently effective in dealing with global crises. Despite the prospects of a full-scale inter-state war receding, global military expenditures continue to remain high and are in fact rising. Violence in the 21st century is accounted for more by intra-state conflicts, civil strife and terrorism rather than inter-state wars. The emerging challenges to security include proliferation of weapons of mass destruction, growing uncertainties about energy supplies, climate change, conflicts in cyberspace and pandemics. In this era of transnational security threats India's security policies are focusing on securing its core interests through cooperative relations with the key powers in the world. This essay argues how the changing security environment and India's policy have made a strong relationship between the RoK and India both likely and mutually beneficial.

Introduction

The global security environment is undergoing rapid transformation. The euphoria that prevailed after the Cold War about the onset of an era of peace has gradually dissipated. While the probability of classical, inter-state conflicts or a "great war" like the Second World War appears low, intra-state warfare and tensions continue to abound. Many historical disputes persist, while new strategic challenges and risks are emerging.

This article surveys the strategic challenges and risks confronting the world and discusses the prospects of India-RoK relations. Divided into five sections, Section I provides an overview of the key features of the prevailing strategic environment; Section II focuses on the regional security environment; Section III analyzes the emerging strategic risks; Section IV briefly discusses India's security policies and Section V assesses the progress and prospects of India-South Korea bilateral relations. The essay concludes with a rationale for India-South Korea cooperation in the changing strategic environment.

Global Security Environment

For some years, power balance has been shifting to Asia and scholars have been describing the present century as the Asian century. The shift is occurring mainly due to the rise of China both as a dynamic, high-growth economy and as a potent military power. This trend has gained further momentum with the continued growth or rise of other powers like the Republic of South Korea, Singapore, Malaysia, Taiwan, Indonesia and India. Despite its stagnation in the past two decades, Japan remained a key economic player in the global economy. Its economic strength translates into a substantial defense budget. However, the earthquake and tsunami of March 2011 will result in a grave setback to its economy. Under Putin's rule Russia has witnessed rapid resurgence, mainly due to rise in hydrocarbon and commodity prices but also due to the reassertion of national will. In Africa and Latin America, the growth of South Africa and Brazil, respectively, has been noteworthy. Thus, the world is rapidly moving from a unipolar phase to what has been variously described as a multipolar, non-polar or a polycentric era. However, in terms of military strength, the US will continue to maintain its edge for many years to come. The world is also witnessing the diffusion of power among non-state actors like the media, multinational corporations, civil society groups and terrorist organizations who are challenging state sovereignty.

The global financial crisis accompanied by an unprecedented recession has weakened the economic clout of the United States and accelerated the rise of China, which has since overtaken Japan as the world's second largest economy, with around 10 percent growth in the year

2010. In 2009, the US budget deficit was estimated at $1 trillion, which amounted to 7.5 percent of its GDP. According to the International Monetary Fund global loan losses were estimated at US$ 3.5 trillion. Several reputed companies based in the West collapsed as a result of the financial crisis and many managed to survive only as a result of massive doses of financial stimulus. The financial crisis soon spread to real sectors, dried up liquidity, dampened manufacturing and led to huge job losses. This crisis, and by far the gravest recession since the Great Depression, has come at a time when the US and NATO forces are overextended in Iraq, Afghanistan and more recently in Libya. The crisis has also jolted the European Union and countries like Greece, Ireland, Portugal and Spain, saddled with heavy debts and deficits, face grim economic prospects.

Great power transitions in history have often been associated with disastrous conflicts. In the prevailing scenario, the world can no longer rely on the stabilizing influence of a hegemon. Given the decline of the US, its allies face some loss of confidence in its ability to deliver on its security commitments. American unilateralism and economic decline have tarnished its standing and diluted its soft power to a considerable extent. A sense that the US, pre-occupied as it is in Iraq, the Af-Pak region and lately Libya, may not have the capacity to intervene elsewhere has led to increasingly assertive behavior among other states.

Rise of China

Above all, China's inexorable rise to great power status is becoming a source of concern among many nations. Countries in Asia and elsewhere are looking anxiously to see if China will be a status quo or a revisionist power. According to those subscribing to the "realist" school in international relations, great power rise in history has often led to conflicts, given the inherent nature of such a rise which seeks to challenge the previously established order. Most powers are wary about China's rise—Russia about its growing clout in Central Asia and North-East Asia, Japan about its vulnerability to a powerful China, and India about its growing assertion and continuing support to Pakistan. China asserts that its "peaceful rise" will be unique in world history. This is a premise that will be watched closely, especially in light of such analyses as by Alastair Iain Johnston who has argued that the Chinese have historically favored a muscular/"parabellum" strategic culture that has privileged the instruments of force in their diplomatic engagements.[1]

The Chinese economy has grown at an impressive pace during the past three decades. While this has provided enormous prosperity overall, the export-driven growth concentrated mainly in coastal areas has led to stark disparities and societal tensions. Chinese cities for instance are among the most polluted in the world. The series of attacks on schoolchildren are also being seen as signs of social tensions due to various factors. The Chinese will have to tackle these and related socio-political instabilities under a "closed" political system that does not tolerate much public dissent.

Adding to the uncertainties is increasing Chinese military expenditures, coupled with lack of transparency regarding those figures, as well as a lack of clarity regarding Chinese strategic goals. According to SIPRI Year Book 2010, China's military expenditure in 2009 was estimated at $100 billion, next only to that of the US. From 2000 to 2009, it grew by a phenomenal 217 percent, compared to the global average of 49.2 percent.[2] The Chinese defense expenditure has thus grown by more than 10 percent each year for the past 10 years.[3] These Chinese imponderables will determine the nature of its rise and as one of China's biggest neighbors with unresolved border disputes, India will be affected profoundly by these developments.

Weak Multilateral Institutions

The global power transition has eroded the relative stability of the Cold War era. The bipolarity of that era often influenced the course of inter-state tensions. During that period, State behavior could often be predicted and in any case was often controlled by the existential concerns of the two super powers. Unfortunately, the UN system erected by the

1. Johnston (1998).
2. SIPRI (2010).
3. "China's Defence Spending to Rise at Decade-Low Pace", March 3, 2010 at *http://www.businessweek.com/news/2010-03-03/china-s-defense-spending-to-rise-at-decade-low-pace-update1-.html*; See also Chen and Feffer (2009).

victors of the Cold War and the United Nations Security Council (UNSC) also remained ineffective as its members tended to judge issues based on their own narrow national interests. The UN system's effectiveness will be further constrained due to its inability to reform and reflect contemporary realities. Other regional structures like NATO, SCO, ASEAN, and the ASEAN Regional Forum also face severe limitations in managing inter-state tensions.

The present-day security challenges need to be viewed in the above geo-political context. Some of these challenges are traditional, others are non-traditional, and yet others are emerging on the horizon. While inter-state wars are much less likely, they cannot be entirely ruled out. In many parts of Asia, territorial and historical disputes remain unresolved. Historical differences tend to get accentuated by new tensions and circumstances. Thus, conventional wars are still a possibility in hot spots of Middle East, Africa, East Asia and South Asia.

Growing Militaries

Despite prospects of inter-state conflicts receding, global defense expenditure has been rising. According to SIPRI data, between 2000 and 2009 it has grown from $1053 billion to $1572 billion, an increase of 49 percent. In East, South and West Asia, it has grown during this period by 71 percent, 57 percent and 40 percent, respectively.[4] This is indicative of the persisting mistrust and apprehensions among major powers, adding to risks of conflicts.

However, asymmetric warfare and intra-state conflicts are more often the cause of violence today. In fact, for the sixth year running, no active inter-state conflict was recorded by SIPRI in its annual review.[5] During the entire period 2000–2009 only three conflicts were fought between states, the remaining being intra-state. These are being caused due to issues of identity, ethnicity, religion, minority rights, sectarianism, economic disparities and criminal networks.

4. SIPRI (2010).
5. Ibid.

Regional Security Environment in Southern Asia

Southern Asia, in particular, has been facing the scourge of religious extremism, terrorism and civil strife. The present problems can be partly attributed to the multi-dimensional plurality of Southern Asia. The region was economically, culturally and politically closely interconnected. These connectivities have been disrupted with the decolonization of the region. The new states are in the process of national consolidation which remains a work in progress in many parts. But the region has been profoundly affected by religious extremism and terrorism. India is situated in a difficult neighborhood and faces the complex task of managing its security situation so that the primary objective of its own "inclusive" economic development is not hampered.

Afghanistan-Pakistan Region: The Epicenter of Terrorism

The Afghanistan-Pakistan corridor has been described as the "epicenter" of global terrorism. The former British Prime Minister Gordon Brown observed that Pakistan was linked to 75 percent of all terror plots affecting the United Kingdom.[6] Tacit support for terror activities directed against India by state or quasi-state agencies is a matter of deep concern for India. The world has been witness to the terror attacks inflicted on Mumbai on November 26, 2008, when nearly 170 people of different nationalities perished, but the conspirators are roaming freely in Pakistan.

Pakistan has become a "rentier" state as it sustains itself on the massive amounts of aid that the US and the West have been providing it—more than $12 billion since the September 11, 2001 terror strikes in New York.[7] While the restoration of electoral democracy in Pakistan raised some hopes initially, its polity continues to be dominated by the Army. There are growing fears about the talibanisation of the Pakistani State, which has been rocked by increasing violence. Al-Qaeda leaders including Ayman Zawahiri are reported to be hiding in the FATA region of Pakistan. The Pakistani Army has been involved in a major conflict with the Taliban in the Swat Valley. The long-drawn strife has displaced half a million civilians. However, given the previous history of close links of the Pakistan Army and

6. CNN World (2008).

7. Hodge (2009); See also Fox News (2009).

intelligence agencies with the Taliban and other Jihadi outfits, the sincerity of their resolve in fighting them has become questionable. The Pakistan Army seeks strategic depth in Afghanistan and views Jihadi outfits like Lashkar-i-Taiba as strategic assets *vis-à-vis* India. Hence, its approach toward fighting Jihadi groups has remained ambivalent. The Government in Pakistan has not shown any willingness to prosecute the conspirators and perpetrators of terror attacks in India and the dialogue revived between India and Pakistan at the level of Prime Ministers has been stalled due to what is widely believed in India to be pressure from the Pakistan Army. India may find it difficult to engage in a dialogue with Pakistan on other substantial issues, unless Pakistan desists from supporting terror groups against India. Despite this dilemma, the dialogue process between the two countries was initiated again after the April 2010 SAARC Summit at Thimphu. Senior Indian Ministers, including those from Foreign Affairs and Home Affairs (Interior Ministry), travelled to Islamabad to carry forward the process. However, the dialogue process has failed to make much progress due to the continued inability and disinterest of the Pakistani leadership to address core Indian concerns regarding cross-border terrorism. In March 2011, India's Prime Minister once again invited Pakistan's Prime Minister to witness a cricket match between Pakistan and India, as a gesture of goodwill and a signal that India desires peaceful relations with Pakistan.

In Afghanistan, a member of SAARC, President Obama's Af-Pak strategy is increasingly being seen as "kowtowing" to Pakistani demands, on the issue of Indian "presence" in the country and on drone strikes inside Pakistan, among others. The surge announced by President Obama in December 2009 has added another 30,000 troops to the 70,000 already present in the country. The US President has promised Americans that he will start withdrawing these troops by the summer of 2011, when greater responsibilities are intended to be given to the Afghan security forces.[8] There are many imponderables regarding the post-July 2011 situation in Afghanistan. A precipitate exit would seem unlikely given the enormous

8. See "Remarks by the President in Address to the Nation on the Way Forward in Afghanistan and Pakistan", December 1, 2009. At *http://www.whitehouse.gov/the-press-office/remarks-president-address-nation-way-forward-afghanistan-and-pakistan*

stakes involved. However, the Pakistan Army and the Taliban are biding their time in the hopes of filling the vacuum. This would undoubtedly lead to negative security implications for India and the region as a whole, given Pakistan's own political instabilities and connivance in fostering trouble inside Afghanistan. It remains doubtful that the troop surge and anti-Taliban offensives can help bring about a measure of stability so that an Iraq-type "success" can be claimed in Afghanistan. Continued instability in the Af-Pak region is likely to remain a matter of grave security concern for the region and other parts of the world.

India has been specifically targeted for attacks in Afghanistan. The July 7, 2008 and October 8, 2009 Indian Embassy attacks are a case in point, as was the March 2010 attack on a hotel housing Indian nationals. India however has been committed to helping build a stable Afghanistan and assisting its development, as was conveyed to President Karzai during his visit to New Delhi in April 2010.[9] India's nation-building activities have come in for appreciation from varied quarters, including from the Afghans themselves. New Delhi has invested around US$ 1.2 billion in developmental assistance and is involved in constructing the Afghan national parliament building as well. It has also completed the Zaranj-Delaram highway. The US Af-Pak strategy has so far not shown very encouraging results. There is a perception in Afghanistan that the NATO forces would be leaving Afghanistan well before the American Presidential election in 2012. This has emboldened both Taliban and its supporters in Pakistan. The continued criticism of President Karzai by Western powers has only served to further undermine his government's legitimacy. Afghan civilian institutions and security forces remain weak. Poppy cultivation continues to flourish and finance the Taliban and warlordism in Afghanistan.

India's Unstable Periphery

Intra-state conflict had badly affected Sri Lanka, which is emerging from the long-drawn civil war with the Liberation Tigers of Tamil Eelam. However, in the absence of a political solution to the problem, the strife

9. "Fight against terror dominates Manmohan, Karzai Delhi talks", April 26, 2010. At *http://www.hindustantimes.com/Fight-against-terror-dominates-Manmohan-Karzai-Delhi-talks/Article1-535887.aspx*

could resurface. Nepal has been suffering for years due to the armed struggle of Maoists. In an extraordinary event the monarchy in Nepal was overthrown peacefully and the country was declared a republic. However, the effort of political parties including the Maoists to write a new Constitution has yet to bear fruit, while peoples' problems, which had caused the strife in the first place continue to remain neglected. Bangladesh succeeded in restoring electoral democracy but it is not yet clear whether the political divisiveness, underdevelopment and religious extremism which have led to violence in the past would be effectively tackled in the foreseeable future.

India is thus surrounded by states affected by instability and intra-state violence until the recent past. These conditions had adversely impacted growth and delivery of public services. India cannot remain insulated from the negative security implications of instability in its neighborhood, particularly in its northwestern region.

Threat of Proliferation and Terrorism

The proliferation of Weapons of Mass Destruction (WMD) continues to be a source of concern. As President Obama observed, while there is hardly any prospect of inter-state nuclear confrontation, the risks of nuclear strike have increased. In a speech delivered at Prague, President Obama had advocated nuclear disarmament but also expressed doubts about being able to achieve it during his lifetime. Unfortunately, these encouraging pronouncements have not been resolutely followed up in practice. So long as some powers retain nuclear weapons, others will seek them. The Nuclear Non-Proliferation Treaty (NPT) has worked to some extent because most aspiring powers were part of an alliance system and beneficiaries of deterrence. Despite the treaty, the proliferation of nuclear technology and materials has taken place. Its principal architect, Pakistan's A.Q. Khan who had operated his vast proliferation network, with its reach to Libya, Iran and North Korea, was released without being subjected to any penalties. Given the predominant role of the military in Pakistan, this network could not have functioned without the Pakistan Army's tacit support. The security of nuclear weapons and materials in Pakistan has been a source of anxiety given the strong "jihadi" culture permeating that country and documented efforts of groups like Al-Qaeda to obtain and use nuclear weapons/materials.[10] India has been an active participant in efforts to ensure nuclear security, including at last year's Nuclear Security Summit (NSS) called by President Obama in April 2010. India also enacted the Weapons of Mass Destruction (WMD) and their Delivery Systems (Prohibition of Unlawful Activities) Act, 2005, which entered into force on June 6, 2005, in line with the provisions of the UN Security Council Resolution 1540 of 2004 that requires member states to enact domestic legislation to secure nuclear materials and their transfer.

The proliferation of WMD and related technologies continues to be a matter of concern. The role played by China and North Korea in Pakistan's nuclear weapons pursuit is well documented.[11] China also allegedly gave 50 kilograms of highly enriched uranium (HEU) to Pakistan in 1982.[12]

While firmly opposed to Iran acquiring nuclear weapon capability, India supports its nuclear energy program to which it is entitled as a member of the NPT. Due to growing apprehensions about the availability of hydrocarbons and concerns about climate change, there is increasing interest in nuclear energy and some analysts are already referring to a "Nuclear Renaissance". The development of nuclear energy in a large number of countries is also likely to lead to worries about the security of nuclear technology and materials. Easy access to technological information has today greatly empowered non-state actors. Not deterred by international treaties and driven by irrational ideological considerations, they may employ chemical or biological weapons. Such attempts have been made in the past and evidence of terror groups' interest in such technologies has also come to the notice of intelligence agencies.

Emerging Strategic Risks

Apart from the "real and present" challenges mentioned above, the global community faces many emerging "strategic risks". These may become vital concerns in the years to come.

10. See for instance Mowatt-Larssen (2010).
11. See "China's Nuclear Exports and Assistance to Pakistan". At *http://www.nti.org/db/china/npakpos.htm*
12. Smith and Warrick (2009).

Maritime Security

In this era of growing interconnectedness, ensuring maritime security has become vital. Nearly 90 percent of global trade and 65 percent of hydrocarbons are transported on sea routes. Apart from this, nearly 95 percent of the Internet traffic is managed through undersea cables. Any disruption of this traffic through the actions of hostile state or non-state actors can seriously hamper the flow of information, energy or commerce. The growing incidence of piracy by countries like Somalia has adversely affected shipping. Over 100,000 ships travel through the Indian Ocean each year. Thus, the region extending from the Suez and Hormuz to the Malacca Straits remains vulnerable.

Energy Security

Depleting hydrocarbon resources and instability in regions which are the principal sources of hydrocarbon energy have increased concerns about energy security. Conflict and instability in West Asia and Africa have impeded fresh investment and the induction of technology that would help meet the growing global demand. Pipelines, which can establish economically efficient connectivities, cannot be laid in disturbed regions. Worries about global warming and peak oil also add to concerns about energy security. Countries like China with a large demand have tended to acquire ownership of hydrocarbon resources in various countries, and others have followed suit. The Russian government has used its hydrocarbon resources as an instrument of geo-political power. There is growing anxiety about the rise of resource nationalism in the future, particularly if the global community fails to find alternative sources of energy.

Climate Change

Climate change is another emerging "strategic risk". The negative effects of climate change could include the submergence of coastal communities and an exacerbation of existing problems like poverty, food and water shortages. It could hasten the spread of diseases and increase the potential for distress and conflict. Huge water deficits exist in countries located in India's neighborhood, including China, Iran, and Pakistan. With the melting of glaciers and inefficient use of water, the problem of water deficits is likely to become more acute. These have the potential of accentuating existing tensions and conflicts. Water concerns can however be managed if the necessary political will exists. Internationally, over 150 bilateral treaties have been signed in the past five decades. In the India-Pakistan context, the US-brokered Indus Waters Treaty is a good example of water sharing.

Pandemics

Pandemics and virulent infectious diseases like HIV/AIDS, influenza, and the 2003 SARS virus are also a growing concern. The World Bank predicts that the next pandemic, could match the magnitude of the 1918 influenza flu, and could kill more than 70 million people, causing a major recession that exceeds $3 trillion.[13]

Cybersecurity

Information and Communications Technologies (ICT) have played a key role in globalization, but at the same time, they have greatly increased mankind's dependence on ICT, making several systems like transport, banking and finance, and telecommunications vulnerable to cyber attacks which should now be factored in by national security planners. India could also face the prospects of disruptive cyber activities in conflicts, like that faced by Estonia in 2007 and Georgia in 2008. The irregular warfare capabilities of non-state actors will only increase in the coming decades.[14] Terror groups are also increasingly using the Internet to spread their ideology, seek funds, or network better. The Pentagon's *Global Trends 2025: A Transformed World* indicates that future radicalism could be fuelled by global communications and mass media.[15] The UK Ministry of Defence Development, Concepts and Doctrine Centre (DCDC) in its report predicting scenarios for 2007-2036 also notes that the explosion of ICT not only leads to greater prosperity but also heightens grievances.

13. Lyn (2009); See also Barry (2010).
14. Davar (2010).
15. NIC (2008).

India's Defense and Security Policies

In the context of this survey of strategic challenges and risks, this section briefly discusses the security policies of India, focusing specially on their recent reorientation.

India's defense and security policies have focused on the core national security objectives which are enduring. These are founded on India's core values of democracy, secularism, pluralism and peaceful coexistence. Since its independence, India has been engaged in socio-economic development of its people. India's national security objectives can be summarized as follows:

- Defending the country's borders as defined by law and enshrined in the Constitution;
- Protecting the lives and property of its citizens against war, terrorism and militant activities;
- Protecting the country from instability and religious and other forms of radicalism and extremism emanating from neighboring states;
- Securing the country against the use or the threat of use of weapons of mass destruction;
- Development of materials, equipment and technologies that have a bearing on India's security, particularly its defense preparedness through indigenous research, development and production, *inter alia* to overcome restrictions on the transfer of such items;
- Promoting further cooperation and understanding with neighboring countries and implementing mutually agreed confidence-building measures; and
- Pursuing security and strategic dialogues with major powers and key partners.

During the Cold War, India pursued a policy of non-alignment, essentially to avoid being a member of either of the power blocs. The basic objective was to ensure strategic autonomy and avoid any entanglements. In 1971, India signed an agreement with the Soviet Union but never became a part of the Soviet bloc. This agreement enabled India to secure defense equipment and aid for economic development from the Soviet Union when such assistance was not forthcoming from other sources. During this period, India also attempted to achieve self-reliance and rapid economic growth with equity. But given the inefficiencies of a centrally planned, public sector-dominated and highly regulated economy, its growth rate remained low. India had to also fight wars with two of its largest neighbors—with Pakistan in 1947-48, 1965 and 1971; and with China in 1962. While India won the 1971 war against Pakistan, which was bifurcated decisively, in an act of generosity it did not press Pakistan for a conclusive settlement, with the result that Pakistan continues to harbor hostility against India. Expecting friendship and cooperation from China, India was caught unawares in Sino-Indian war of 1962. It was this defeat in the border war with China that jolted India into a more realistic approach toward its defense preparedness.

During the mid-80s, policy makers in India began to revisit their approach to economic development. A modest attempt was made to liberalize the economy and bring about deregulation. However, it was the grave foreign exchange crisis of 1991 which precipitated fundamental changes in India's economic policies. The comprehensive reforms introduced in the 1990s included delicensing of industry, liberalization of trade, deregulation of the financial sector and positive measures to promote the private sector. Economic reforms and the consequent opening of India's economy accelerated economic growth and led to an outward orientation of India's foreign and defense policies.

The collapse of the Soviet Union which demonstrated to Indian planners the limitations of a centralized economy and the need to connect with other parts of the world had a profound impact on India's economic and foreign policies. A natural corollary of India's economic reforms was the liberalization of its foreign policy. India established diplomatic relations with Israel and soon a vigorous cooperation in defense ensued. Despite its centuries-old trade and maritime linkages India had neglected its links with countries of East and Southeast Asia. A conscious policy decision was taken to restore these linkages through India's "Look-East Policy". This led to rapid growth in trade with countries of the region.

India had to develop its own nuclear deterrence as the nuclear weapon powers failed to heed its calls for disarmament. The Peoples' Republic of China with whom India has an unresolved boundary dispute had developed its own arsenal and Pakistan was pursuing a covert program. In the absence of the cover of a nuclear umbrella, India had to perforce develop its own nuclear weapons. These are meant for a credible minimum deterrence. India's nuclear doctrine has committed to a policy of no-first use and non-use against non-nuclear weapon states. Its nuclear posture is thus entirely for defensive purposes.

India-Korea Relations: Retrospect and Prospect

For nearly five decades after attaining their freedom, the Republic of South Korea (RoK) and India remained in a state of "strategic disconnect".[16] The main reasons for this were India's policy of non-alignment and economic autarky. Despite its non-alignment, due to its proximity with the Soviet Union, India was perceived by the US and its allies including the RoK, as a part of the Soviet bloc. India's limited trading relations also prevented the growth of economic ties with South Korea.

Common strategic interests, experience and beliefs underpin the relationships between the RoK and India. Both countries share a somewhat similar historical experience of national partition, followed by the need to face hostile counterparts in Pakistan and North Korea, respectively. Both countires also share an uneasy relationship with their powerful neighbor, China. Following economic reforms in the 90s, India began to look outwards and forged economic and trading links with countries in Southeast and Northeast Asia. With the end of the Cold War, India was no longer seen as a member of the "other" bloc and its relations with the United States and its allies began to improve significantly. India made a conscious effort to develop economic ties with the Asian tigers and other countries of Southeast Asia under its "Look-East Policy" launched during Prime Minister Narasimha Rao's regime. As this policy matured, it began to cover the countries of Northeast Asia especially Japan and the Republic of Korea and a strategic dimension also began to be added.[17] It was during

16. Brewster (n.d.).
17. *Ibid.*

the visit of President Roh-Myun-Hwan to India in 2004 that the "long-term cooperative partnership" was established between the RoK and India, which now serves as the bedrock of bilateral relations between the two countries. This relationship was elevated to the level of "Strategic Partnership" during the visit of RoK President, Lee Myung-bak to India in January 2010.

There are three important pillars on which India-RoK bilateral relations can be developed. The first is the potential of economic ties through comprehensive economic partnership agreement and the creation of new multilateral economic groupings in Asia; the second is a bilateral security relationship including supply of defense equipment and joint R&D programs; and the third is energy security and civilian nuclear cooperation.

Economic Cooperation

India and Korea have entered into a comprehensive economic partnership agreement effective from January 2010, which lays the basis for a new chapter in their commercial and economic cooperation.[18] This is complemented by the existing Bilateral Investment Promotion and Protection Agreement (BIPPA) between the two countries. As a consequence of this institutional framework, bilateral trade in 2010 increased impressively by 45 percent over 2009, reaching a figure of $17 billion. Investments both ways are around $4 billion.[19] The main South Korean investors in India have been the LG, Samsung, Hyundai and Daewoo, operating mainly in the consumer electronic and automotive sectors. As a natural corollary to growing links, the number of business visas issued by the Indian Embassy in Seoul is increasing. The bilateral trade target for 2014 has been pegged at US$ 30 billion. With comprehensive economic partnership, India offers RoK a low-cost manufacturing base for exports to third-country markets. This agreement also signals greater integration among Asian markets and offers South Korean companies a competitive edge *vis-à-vis* those from Japan and China.

18. *Ibid.*
19. Message from H.E. Skand R. Tayal, Ambassador of India to the Republic of Korea, on the occasion of the 62nd Republic Day, Embassy of India, Seoul, South Korea.

Defense and Security Cooperation

The foundation for India-South Korea defense relations was laid in 2005 when the two countries signed a Memorandum of Understanding (MoU) on cooperation in the defense industry and logistics. This facilitated defense industry cooperation and the joint development of self-propelled artillery and mine-countermeasures vessels. Yet another MoU on cooperation between the coast guards of the two countries was signed in March 2006, followed by a joint coast guard exercise in July 2006. Later the two countries agreed to conduct joint naval exercises and regular service-to-service consultations. Initially, the focus of naval cooperation is to be on search-and-rescue and antipiracy operations. India can provide security to South Korea's sea-lanes of communications in the Indian Ocean through to the Straits of Malacca.[20]

In May 2007, the defense ministers of India and Korea held their first dialogue. Defense relations between the RoK and India received a substantial impetus during Indian Defense Minister A.K Antony's visit to South Korea in September 2010, when two MoUs were signed. The first MoU envisaged the exchange of defense-related experience and information, exchange of visits by military personnel and experts, military education and training and the conduct of military exercises. This MoU also visualized the exchange of ship and aircraft visits as jointly decided between the two countries. The second MoU signed between India's Defence Research and Development Organisation (DRDO) and South Korea's Defense Acquisition and Procurement Agency (DAPA) seeks to identify future defense technology areas of mutual interest and the pursuit of research and development work in both countries. Co-development and co-production of defense products with Indian industry through DRDO is also envisaged.[21]

Security, Civil Nuclear Cooperation and Space

Since India and the RoK are both heavily dependent on imported energy, energy security is likely to impinge on their bilateral relations. The two countries entered into a number of agreements for cooperation in the

20. Brewster. (n.d.)

21. Panda (2010).

energy sector in November 2005. These included South Korea's assistance in building strategic underground storage facilities in India. Cooperation in the sector also envisages swap deals of energy supplies from different sources.[22]

Since the mid-90s India and South Korea have had modest cooperation in the sphere of civilian nuclear technology and an agreement for cooperation in this area was announced in January 2010. This will provide a significant opportunity to South Korea's large nuclear industry to participate in India's nuclear power sector.[23]

Following an agreement on cooperation in the peaceful uses of outer space between the Indian Space Research Organisation (ISRO) and the Korea Aerospace Research Institute, an ISRO team visited RoK in January 2011 to explore bilateral cooperation in this sector.

Conclusion

The contemporary and emerging security challenges call for much greater cooperation amongst nation states than has been possible in the past. The cooperation is vital not only because of the prohibitive direct and indirect costs of modern wars but also because many challenges are transnational and no nation can meet them alone. In recent years, efforts made to tackle transnational terrorism, piracy, global financial crisis and pandemics are examples of how cooperative action alone can help achieve success.[24] Such cooperative frameworks and action will be needed to deal with climate change, proliferation of weapons of mass destruction, and protection of the global commons like the oceans, outer space and also the cyber space. The challenge of depleting resources, particularly energy resources, also calls for a cooperative approach and action.

In the coming years, this approach will also open up an opportunity for close defense cooperation between India and the Republic of Korea. As mentioned above, India has forged strategic partnerships with the US, Japan, Russia, and the European Union. A strategic partnership and a comprehensive

22. Brewster (n.d.).
23. *Ibid*.
24. Möcli *et al.* (2011).

economic partnership agreement have also been established with the Republic of Korea. Both India and the RoK enjoy a vibrant relationship in the economic sphere with many Korean companies in the auto and white goods sectors doing flourishing business in India. A good understanding between the two countries, of each other's security concerns will be conducive to deeper cooperation. The Indian policy of diversifying defense acquisitions and encouraging the private sector offers opportunities for substantive cooperation in research and development, joint production and other collaborative ventures.

Both countries depend on open trade and energy imports. The security of sea lanes of communication is therefore of vital importance to both. This offers yet another opportunity for maritime cooperation. Finally, given the vital need for cooperative efforts amongst nation states to fight transnational security challenges, both the RoK and India can greatly benefit from mutual defense cooperation.[25]

We live in an uncertain and insecure world. While there are many positive trends which offer hope for more rational action by nation states, history is replete with examples of violent conflicts, even when peace and stability was expected. There are emerging challenges and security risks coupled with the potential role of non-state actors. In this uncertain world, all nation states need to adopt a common approach in facing common challenges. There is an opportunity for South Korea and India, with many commonalities and complimentaries, to join hands in this process.

25. Panda (2011).

References

Barry, John M. (2010). "The Next Pandemic", *World Policy Journal,* August 11. At *http://www.worldpolicy.org/blog/next-pandemic*

Brewster, David (n.d.). "India's Developing Relationship with South Korea: A Useful Friend in East Asia", *Asian Survey* 50(2): 402-25.

Chen, Sean and John Feffer (2009). "China's Military Spending: Soft Rise or Hard Threat?", *Asian Perspective* 33(4): 47-67. Available at *http://www.asianperspective.org/articles/v33n4-c.pdf*

CNNWorld (2008). "Brown: Pakistan Linked to most UK Terror Plots", December 14.

Davar, Kamaleshwar (2010). "Changing Face of Modern Conflicts: Shaping the Indian Response", *Journal of the United Service Institution of India* CXL(580): 189-97, April-June.

Dittmer, Lowell (n.d.). *Asian Survey* 51(I): 1–4.

Fox News (2009). "Billions in US aid never reached Pakistan Army", *Fox News*, October 4. At *http://www.foxnews.com/world/2009/10/04/billions-aid-reached-pakistan-army*

Hodge, Nathan (2009). "Surprise! Pakistan Siphoned off billions in US Military Aid", October 5. At *http://www.wired.com/dangerroom/2009/10/surprise-pakistan-siphoned-off-billions-in-us-military-aid/#ixzz0ws21IT6Xhttp://www.wired.com/dangerroom/2009/10/surprise-pakistan-siphoned-off-billions-in-us-military-aid*

Johnston, Alastair Iain (1998). *Cultural Realism: Strategic Culture and Grand Strategy in Chinese History.* Princeton: Princeton University Press.

Lyn, Tan Ee (2009). "Economic Costs of a Flu Pandemic", *Reuters*, April 25. At *http://www.reuters.com/article/idUSTRES53O0WO20090425*

Mowatt-Larssen, Rolf (2010). "Al Qaeda Weapons of Mass Destruction: Threat, Hype or Reality? A Timeline of Terrorists' Efforts to Acquire WMD", *Belfer Center for Science and International Affairs Paper*, January. Available at *http://belfercenter.ksg.harvard.edu/files/al-qaeda-wmd-threat.pdf*; See also "The Threat: The Demand for Black Market fissile material". At *http://www.nti.org/e_research/cnwm/threat/demand.asp*

Möcli, D., A. Wenger and V. Mauer (eds.) (2011). *Strategic Trends 2011: Key Developments in Global Affairs.* Zurich: Center for Security Studies.

NIC (2008). *Global Trends 2025: The National Intelligence Council's 2025 Project.* Available at *www.dni.gov/nic/NIC_2025_project.html*

Panda, Rajaram (2010). "Fruits of Antony's visit to South Korea: Defence Ties Strengthen further", *IDSA Comment*, September 7. Available at *http://www.idsa.in/idsacomments/FruitsofAntonysvisittoSouthKoreaDefenceTiesStrengthenfurther_rpanda_070910*

———. (2010). "India-Republic of Korea: Past and Future Projections", *Journal of Defence Studies* 5(1): 16-38, January.

SIPRI (2010). *SIPRI Yearbook 2010: Armaments, Disarmaments and International Security.* Oxford University Press.

Smith, R. Jeffrey and Joby Warrick (2009). "A Nuclear Power's Act of Proliferation", *Washington Post*, November 13. At *http://www.washington post.com/wp-dyn/content/article/2009/11/12/AR2009111211060.html*

11 The Korea-India Strategic Partnership for the 21st Century

Visions for Security and Military Cooperation

CHANGSU KIM

Introduction: Where we stand Today and where we are Heading

In the East Asian security environment, characterized by increasing complexity, uncertainty and unpredictability, security cooperation among the United States and its allies and friends and emerging powerhouses such as China and India will continue to be important for the peace, stability and prosperity of the region and beyond. This is particularly true at a time of global changes and surprises, or tectonic shifts, as we have over the last several years witnessed a barrage of articles and books portending an overly simplified "gradual global redistribution of economic power from the West to 'the Rest'"[1] or the so-called decline of American power, or the emerging post-American world, or an equally overly simplified "rise of the new Asian Hemisphere" proclaiming an Asian Century.[2]

In the foreseeable future the so-called North Korea problem, proliferation of weapons of mass destruction and ballistic missiles, and the so-called China factor with far-reaching implications for regional security as a whole, on the other hand, will almost certainly continue to be major sources of regional security conflict and cooperation in East Asia and

1. Cronin (2008).
2. For an insightful analysis of changing American power in international affairs, especially on whether the balance of power is shifting from the United States to Asia and on convincing rebuttals to these scholarly claims, see Harding (2008).

beyond. Added to these, other non-traditional and transnational security threats and challenges, such as terrorism, natural and man-made disasters, pandemic diseases, climate change, energy, water and food shortages, piracy and others, are increasingly gaining weight and prominence in the making of security strategies and defense policies and the implementation of concrete, detailed plans for each of the countries in the region. These rapidly changing security environments are bound to entail multiple sets of security arrangements and mechanisms in the beginning decades of the 21st century in order to enable effective responses and promotion of common interests of all the countries involved.

It is against this backdrop that the current and future security cooperation among the allies of the United States, most notably Japan, South Korea, and Australia, and other friends like India, is vital to maintaining security and prosperity in East Asia and the Asia-Pacific region. From a South Korean perspective, the existing US-Japan-South Korea security cooperation can be the prime mover and shaker of a new emerging multilateral security regime, as it pertains to the Six-Party Talks in Beijing, WMD non-proliferation and counter-proliferation, cooperative threat reduction, regional peace mechanisms, and various non-traditional security challenges. Then, what is the role of India in this emerging multilateral security mechanism? And where does India fit in, with its tremendous potential to be a strategic partner for all major regional powers?

A "strategic partnership" was proclaimed by South Korean President Lee Myung-bak and Indian Prime Minister Manmohan Singh at their summit on January 25, 2010. The two leaders agreed to upgrade their relations to a "strategic partnership" and expand mutual trade volume to USD 30 billion by 2014. They also agreed to expand their countries' cooperation to cover diplomacy, security, global issues, and culture based on their existing economic ties and agreed to the need for a pact on the civilian use of nuclear energy, a prerequisite for South Korea's participation in India's atomic power plant construction.

The overall Korea-India relationship started primarily from trade and investment and has moved toward a more comprehensive economic partnership. And in the near future, our relationship will head toward the end-state of a comprehensive security partnership which encompasses all aspects of national security—political, economic, energy and strategic security concerns— of our two nations. On August 7, 2009 the two nations signed the Comprehensive Economic Partnership Agreement (CEPA) and it came into effect as of January 11, 2010.

Economic performance and outlook in the Asia-Pacific region will remain an important factor in creating a vision for our bilateral security and military cooperation over the long term. As two IMF economists pointed out recently,[3] "Asia's growth remains heavily dependent on external demand and this means an unbalanced production structure, heavily tilted toward industry. A successful rebalancing will require reforms in many Asian economies." Any well-constructed plan or program in the security and defense realm can hardly be implemented without the support of proper budgets. Here at the Dialogue, therefore, it is very opportune for us to explore the scope of our future bilateral security cooperation after discussions on our economic and trade relations in the previous sessions.

This paper will deal with some major security issues facing our two nations and will explore the potential for cooperation in the security, defense, and military fields in the coming years. As two promising members of the G-20, our two nations do possess new-found layers of a mutually beneficial and reinforcing strategic partnership, which includes defense, economic and security dimensions. Korea maintains different levels of partnerships with many major powers,[4] such as a comprehensive strategic alliance with the United States, a strategic cooperative partnership with the People's Republic of China, a "future-oriented mature relationship" with Japan, a strategic partnership with the Russian Federation, and a strategic partnership with India. On the other hand, India maintains a "strategic economic partnership" with the US, a "strategic and global partnership" with Japan, and strategic partnerships with the EU, France, Australia, Russia, Indonesia, Israel, Turkey, Vietnam, etc.

Because US relations with China, Japan, Korea, Australia, and India are seen as the prime movers in what might be called the era of Asian regional integration, the Indo-Korean relationship will likely unravel

3. Pradhan and Unteroberdoerster (2010).

4. For a useful introduction, see Kim (2008).

around this US nexus. A multitude of multilateral cooperative relations will continue to thrive in the Asia-Pacific, as we face, for example, a potential US-Japan-India-Australia coalition *vis-à-vis* China, an emerging economic powerhouse with rapidly modernizing naval forces. To give another example, increasingly closer India-Australia relations also merit our special attention, as members of the British Commonwealth. Most countries have their own allies, friends, and strategic partners in this era of globalization and networking, along with their own versions of a hedging strategy against other powers. South Korea and India are no exception to this prevailing mood.

The next chapter will look at the vision and implementation of South Korea's strategic alliance with the United States and then draw lessons to apply them to its strategic partnership with India in the following chapters.

The RoK-US Strategic Alliance for the 21st Century

A Joint Vision Statement (JVS) issued at the Lee-Obama Summit of June 16, 2009 set the tone for the comprehensive security alliance for the 21st century. The JVS envisions an "alliance to ensure a peaceful, secure and prosperous future for the Korean Peninsula, the Asia-Pacific region and the world; a comprehensive strategic alliance of bilateral, regional and global scope, based on common values and mutual trust; a better future for all people on the Korean Peninsula, establishing a durable peace on the Peninsula and leading to peaceful reunification on the principles of free democracy and a market economy." The following bullets elaborate how the Republic of Korea and the United States of America perceive the major security concerns facing them:

- *Maintaining a Robust Defense Posture:* continuing commitment to extended deterrence, including the US nuclear umbrella.
- *Restructuring the Alliance:* RoK taking the lead role in the combined defense of Korea, supported by an enduring and capable US military force presence.
- *Deepening Bilateral Relations:* further strengthening economic, trade and investment relations through KORUS FTA; green growth as a new engine for sustainable economic prosperity; civil space

cooperation; clean energy research and peaceful use of nuclear energy.

- *Achieving a Complete and Verifiable Elimination:* North Korea's nuclear weapons and existing nuclear programs as well as ballistic missile programs.
- *Promoting Respect for Human Rights:* protect the fundamental human rights of the North Korean people.
- *Cooperating in the Asia-Pacific Region:* foster prosperity, keep the peace, and improve standards of living through open societies and open markets; enhance security through effective cooperative regional efforts.
- *Coordinating at the Global Level:* address the various global security challenges of terrorism, proliferation of WMDs, piracy, organized crimes and narcotics, climate change, poverty, infringement on human rights, energy security, and epidemic diseases; enhance coordination on peacekeeping, post-conflict stabilization and development assistance; strengthen coordination at multilateral mechanisms such as the G-20.
- *Achieving Common Alliance Goals at Every Level:* utilize proven bilateral mechanisms such as the annual Security Consultative Meeting (SCM) and "2+2" meetings.

Implementing the Strategic Alliance for the 21st Century:[5]

- *Deterring North Korea's Nuclear Weapons Threat:* provision of continued extended deterrence, including the US nuclear umbrella; roles and utility of the Six-Party Talks as compared with those of the bilateral and five-party talks; discussions on responding to North Korean contingencies; role of other regional powers and multilateral mechanisms; South Korea's peaceful use of nuclear energy.

5. A similar presentation was made at the 12th INSS-KIDA Workshop, co-sponsored by The Korea Institute for Defense Analyses and The Institute for National Strategic Studies, Washington, DC, July 13, 2009.

- *Countering North Korea's Missile Threat:* extension of South Korean missile ranges for defensive purposes; utility of the PAC-3 or its equivalents; relationship with Missile Defense; responses of regional powers and their reactions to our enhanced bilateral, trilateral and multilateral cooperation.
- *Proliferation Security Initiative (PSI) Cooperation:* extended efforts to engage regional friends and allies in security cooperation; invitation extended to China and North Korea to observe training exercises; linkage with development of a Northeast Asia missile defense architecture; relations with and implications for the North-South Korean maritime transport agreement.
- *Effective Reponses to Non-traditional, Transnational Threats:* alliance-based efforts to deal with non-traditional security threats at the regional and global levels; positive signs from regional powers; combined operations of many navies off Somalia.
- *Stabilization and Reconstruction Activities in Afghanistan:* enlargement of RoK civilian medical and vocational training teams in Afghanistan; political decision to send RoK special operations forces; expansion of engagement by the international community; new Central Asia Diplomacy of Japan, China and South Korea.

The current Lee Myung-bak government in Seoul has consistently implemented its "Policy of Mutual Benefits and Common Prosperity" (*sangsaeng gwua gongyeong)* with a launch of what is known as the "Denuclearization, Opening-up, 3000 Policy Initiative" (*bihaek, gaebang, samcheon jeongchaek gusang*). The national security strategy of this conservative government supports the Six-Party Talks and the US-DPRK dialogue within its framework, in order to solve the North Korean nuclear problem as a prerequisite for building a new peace regime on the Korean peninsula. While maintaining a pragmatic policy toward the North, the South also prepares against contingencies involving a massive influx of North Korean refugees and the loss of control of North Korean nuclear weapons and materials and boosts its efforts to increase information-sharing with the US, Japan, PRC and Russia, and potentially with India.

India's National Security Strategy and Defense Policy

It goes without saying that India's security policy is focused on shaping an international security environment conducive for its continued economic growth and political, social stability and the territorial integrity and pursuit of sovereignty and autonomy. In recent years, as China has emerged as the No. 2 economic powerhouse with a concomitant showing of its military presence and modernization and other signs of more assertive diplomacy in the international arena, India has rekindled its interest in forming a security policy that can guarantee a uniquely stronger and more influential India. Its engagement with the US, China, Japan, Russia, Australia, and other major powers in addressing new security challenges deserves our renewed interest here in South Korea. As a "comprehensive strategic ally" of the US and a "strategic cooperative partner" of China, South Korea today finds itself increasingly caught between the traditional ally and the emerging power over many security issues. This is why Seoul finds it to be in its best interest to develop good security relations with other regional powers as well, including India. In the years ahead, when South Korea can successfully manage its armistice and build a new peace regime on the Korean peninsula, its primary security concern would be more centered on how to deal with the changing US-China relations.

PM Manmohan Singh announced, "India will establish a Global Centre for Nuclear Energy Partnership. This will be owned and managed by the Government, but will be open to international participation in terms of academic exchanges and R&D efforts... I feel a sense of vindication of India's position. The intersection of international terrorism and clandestine proliferation affects our security directly. The concerns that we have been expressing for decades on the dangers of proliferation and risk of nuclear materials finding their way into the wrong hands are today finding widespread acceptance."[6]

On the challenges facing India, the Prime Minister goes on to say that "the first challenge before us is to quickly revert to the high GDP growth path of 9 percent and then find the means to cross the 'double-digit growth barrier'. This calls for imparting a fresh momentum to the impressive

---

6. Prime Minister Manmohan Singh's Press Conference at Washington DC, April 13, 2010.

recovery in growth witnessed in the past few months. Therefore, the second challenge is to harness economic growth to consolidate the recent gains in making development more inclusive. The thrust imparted to the development of infrastructure in rural areas has to be pursued to achieve the desired objectives within a fixed time frame. The third challenge relates to the weaknesses in government systems, structures and institutions at different levels of governance. Indeed, in the coming years, if there is one factor that can hold us back in realizing our potential as a modern nation, it is the bottleneck of our public delivery mechanisms."[7]

"Foreign Direct Investment (FDI) inflows during the year have been steady in spite of the decline in global capital flows. India received FDI equity inflows of US$ 20.9 billion during April-December, 2009 compared to US$ 21.1 billion during the same period last year." And "As far as India's relations with China are concerned, the economic content of the relationship has increased very significantly. China is today probably India's largest trading partner. There are large Chinese investments in our country. There are large investments in China. On the economic front the relationships are moving in the right direction and at the Copenhagen conference India and China worked very closely to organize their position and there is now a recognition in China that in multilateral issues there is a similarity of approach between India and China and that both countries can gain by working together."[8]

India's National Security Policy (NSP) states that its goal is not self-sufficiency in the traditional autarkical sense, which is viewed to be unattainable, but self-reliance.[9] To Indian leaders, the most important aspects of self-reliance are the ability of India to field weapons manufactured locally, and to provide for security of supply of spare parts and components. India must also be prepared to defend against land-, air-, and sea-based missile attacks. The NSP report also states that the Indian Navy must execute both sea denial and sea control missions against Chinese and Pakistani incursions. Indian nuclear forces must be ready to

---

7. Minister of Finance (2010). *Budget 2010-11.* Speech of Pranab Mukherjee. February 26.
8. Prime Minister Manmohan Singh's Press Conference at Washington DC, April 13, 2010.
9. India's National Security Policy, *dni.gov/nic.*

conduct timely counter-strikes against enemy targets, as well as employ such weapons in single or numerically limited demonstrative strikes against battlefield targets or targets deep within the enemy territory.

According to the report, India is debating the direction of its future defense products. Some argue that India should develop the eventual capability to fully design, develop, and produce completed major armament systems. Others argue that India's considerable scientific and technical talent should be focused more efficiently on component design in conjunction with foreign partners to produce armament systems focused on competitive niche areas.

The report also states that under the national self-reliance program, *India 2020*, strategic objectives have been set to reach high levels, if not complete self–reliance, in national production, including defense production over the next 20 years. Historically, India has tried to achieve self-reliance by a combination of diversification of sources of supply, licensed manufacture of armaments, and indigenous design, development, and production. However the decade of wars starting with the Sino-Indian conflict of 1962 caused India to forgo extensive indigenous developments in favor of rapidly acquiring Soviet equipment on long-term credits at low interest rates. At that point, licensed manufacture of Soviet systems became the primary vehicle for self-reliance.

Now let us turn to how US-Indian relations have developed in the past several years and how they will evolve in the next decade. As far as US policy toward South Asia is concerned, Washington has undergone a major policy shift.[10] For the first time in its history, the US was committing itself to expanding civil nuclear cooperation with India at the expense of a strained international non-proliferation system. A major driver in the Bush administration's radical overtures to New Delhi was China. India's burgeoning economy, democratic ideals, and second largest standing army in the world caught the Bush administration's eye as it looked to preserve US pre-eminence in Asia by balancing China with India. This ambition partly underpinned the US decision to make India a "major world power".[11]

10. Singh and Kim (2005).

11. See Subrahmanyam (2005).

Despite the US' newfound interest in India, however, India has its own calculations toward China. There is a limit to how the US can use India against China. While India has a pressing stake in curbing China's rise with US assistance, there seems to be limited awareness in the US of shared Sino-Indian interests that may produce friction in the US-Indian relationship. Three areas come to mind: economics and energy; domestic politics; and geo-politics.

Even as the US agrees to assist India in generating nuclear energy, it is unlikely to wean India from Iran or Iranian energy. Tehran is an invaluable friend to New Delhi in a tough neighborhood and energy security is a critical priority for India. Keeping its options open may put it at odds with the US even as it competes and cooperates with China.

New Delhi launched a potentially revolutionary "strategic partnership for peace and prosperity" with China on April 11, 2005.[12] The move was aimed at ending the Sino-Indian border dispute on Aksai-Chin (existing since 1962), and at boosting mutual trade and economic ties. Prospects for a more cooperative relationship between the two Asian giants are to be read in light of regional powers' ambitions to reshape the world order along the guidelines of a balanced multipolarity—a goal already expressed by China, France, and Russia, among other states.

However, to rise as a great power, India appears to need more than economic assets and a strong military. These Indian needs—along with concerns over the Indian Ocean's security—form the context that led New Delhi to sign a 10-year defense agreement with Washington. Strategic partnerships are not intended to directly challenge the US, but rather to rapidly obtain economic, technological and military power. Interestingly, the US was involved in helping India "become a world power", which could be a sign of Washington's gradual acceptance of an embryonic multipolarity in Asia. However, US' fundamental interests in developing better relations with India are the necessary containment of China and New Delhi's help in the war against militant Islamic groups—a need that is growing stronger due to the unstable political landscape in Pakistan.

---

12. For the full text of the agreement, see "China, India to Build Strategic Partnership", at *china.org.cn* for April 11, 2005.

The slowly escalating competition between the US and China has helped to create a fertile environment for India's ambition to gain status as a great regional power. Cooperation with China has become one of the most discussed issues in India's business community for a number of reasons, but the loudest talk has been the opportunities based on combining India's "software" economy with China's "hardware" economy. There are also geo-political motivations for India to align itself with China. Both countries favor multipolarity: for Beijing, this trend will help to weaken US influence in its sphere of influence; for New Delhi, this shift creates an environment for it to gain influence over its near-abroad.

However, India has also seen gains from advancing its relationship with the US. Washington has often touted the "natural alliance" between the two expansive, multiethnic democracies, but it is on military issues that India would most like to develop its relationship with the US. During the tsunami relief effort of 2005, the two states' navies worked together, which helped to cement their budding military-to-military ties. It appears that the US would like India's navy to serve as a bulwark against China as Beijing becomes more active in the Indian Ocean. Also, there are some areas where the US Navy cannot operate, such as the Malacca Straits, where India's presence might be seen as less threatening than that of the US.

In this environment, India has been very successful in using strategic partnerships with both Washington and Beijing to further its interests on the Indian subcontinent and the Indian Ocean. For the near term, New Delhi can be expected to emphasize points of agreement with China and the US, while looking to gain better positioning for itself in the region.

Visions for Security and Military Cooperation between India and RoK

Naval and maritime security cooperation would be the most visible and certain means of expanding security and military cooperation between our two nations. As India has "initiated a series of initiatives to cater for the Chinese challenge,"[13] and as "the Indian navy has stepped up its

13. Kalyanaraman (2010).

deployments throughout the Asia-Pacific and been regularly participating in bilateral and multilateral exercises," South Korea also needs to take into consideration these new developments in a broader security context:

- Operationalization of the MOU on Defense Industry and Logistics Cooperation including cooperation in defense manufacturing industries;
- Coast Guard cooperation and Quality Assurance of Defense Material and Services;
- Regular Service-to-Service exchanges at the senior and middle level to generate confidence between the two sides;
- Regular ship exchanges and conduct of joint exercises as also cooperation in areas like anti-piracy and search and rescue operations to provide visibility and generate goodwill. This could be done through port visits by ships followed by PASSEX as well as basic-level joint exercises. Operational Turn Around (OTR) facilities at RoK ports for Indian Naval Ships may also be considered;
- Air force training and joint exercises and cooperation in aeronautics, including fighter pilots and qualified flying instructors exchange programs;
- Exchange of training delegations, which could identify areas for training attachments;
- Mutual visits to defense establishments and industries connected with defense production. This would help in identifying possible areas of cooperation, like shipbuilding, land systems, communication, electronics, multipurpose helicopter, LCA etc;
- Potential for RoK companies' investment in the defense sector. As FDI up to 26 percent is now permitted in the Indian defense sector to private industries, Korean companies can consider investing in Indian defense industries;
- Joint projects in ship construction and allied fields; and
- Regular interaction in regional forums and conferences on security matters.

The importance of protecting sea lanes of communication (SLOCs) in the Indian Ocean to the economic and trade security of India and Korea and the entire Asia-Pacific region needs our attention.[14] That is, the role the Indian Navy can play in SLOC protection can be easily recognized and it will continue to grow in importance. Therefore, our two nations will continue to exchange high-ranking military leadership including service chiefs and defense ministers, take CBMs by paying port calls, exchange of petroleum, oil and lubricant (POL), equipment and spare parts.

Bilateral and multilateral naval training and exercises, and mine-clearing operations, in coordination with the US Navy, will be on the list of our security and military cooperation. Training for PKO and employing special operation forces can also be pursued. Furthermore, one day after North Korea's second nuclear weapon test on May 25, 2009, South Korea announced that it would fully participate in the US-led Proliferation Security Initiative (PSI). And as a result of the recent sinking of the South Korean Navy corvette, *Cheonan*, it appears quite likely that Seoul will expand the scope of its activities in the PSI. Likewise, South Korea has been active in implementing the Container Security Initiative (CSI). It will further its efforts to turn the momentum into a more efficient mechanism in which many other countries, including India, will find the value of protecting common security interests.

In addition, cybersecurity, that is, security against, among other things, cyberhacking primarily by a third country, can also be an excellent candidate for our security cooperation in the years to come.[15] Even though some critics argue that "India does not have technical resources and expertise as well as legal framework to tackle terrorism and cyber terrorism,"[16] our two nations may achieve a lot of accomplishments in our cybersecurity not long after the implementation of our MOUs. For example, we can share our experiences in responding to current Chinese attackers and develop our joint strategy in fighting more efficiently against future Chinese hackers. In fact, "it is widely believed that the DPRK routes

14. Singh (2008).
15. See Segal (2010a).
16. Prasad (2008).

attacks, both criminal and political, through Chinese network."[17] And so-called voice phishing has been rampant in South Korea, as the so-called electronic or cyber fraud *(furigome sagi)* has become a major social problem in Japan. It deserves our special attention and interest on both sides so that Indian Defense Minister A.K. Antony called for a "crisis management action plan" and MP Sachin Pilot, Minister of State in the Ministry of Communications and Technology, proposed stronger ties with Washington in cybersecurity. South Korea has such a plan of its own and is making stronger ties with the US in preserving cybersecurity.

Cooperation on Utilizing Evolving Security Environment and Resolving Regional Security Issues

Today's changing security environments are notably characterized by terrorism, proliferation of weapons of mass destruction and ballistic missiles, and newly emerging and growing transnational security threats. For example, Washington and Tokyo agreed on 15 areas of cooperation at their "2+2" meetings in 2005. These include ballistic missile defense, counter-proliferation operations, counter-terrorism, search and rescue operations, humanitarian relief operations, reconstruction assistance operations, peacekeeping operations and capacity building for other nations' peacekeeping efforts. Japan, in fact, has promoted security cooperation with Australia and India in recent years. Thus, trilateral and even quadrilateral security cooperation has been increasingly sought in Tokyo's security and defense framework. This new form of regional cooperation has been viewed as functional cooperation for common concerns and Tokyo's counterparts were found in Canberra and New Delhi. The recent formation of an official US-Japan-Australia trilateral security cooperation mechanism and those of the proposed US-Japan-Australia-India security cooperation is a case in point.[18]

---

17. See Segal (2010b).

18. Japan's defense policy in 2007 showed noticeable developments such as its security cooperation with Australia and India, and the enlargement of the JSDF's primary mission to include international peace cooperation activities. For details on Japan's expanded security cooperation in the Asia-Pacific region, including security cooperation on non-traditional security issues, such as securing maritime security in navy-to-navy cooperation and anti-piracy operations, refer to NIDS (2008).

Existing Multilateral Security Mechanisms and Plus

Looking back to what has transpired in the security area among major players in East Asia, one would be overwhelmed by a multitude of initiatives and mechanisms for trilateral and other multilateral security dialogue and cooperation. First, with regard to managing various security issues directly and indirectly related to North Korea, there have been many active, and sometimes assertive, formulas among, for example, the United States, Japan and South Korea.

South Korea has sought CBMs with many regional countries in bilateral, trilateral, and multilateral settings. It has maintained bilateral CBMs with North Korea and such regional players as China, Japan, Russia and the United States. In addition, it has maintained a trilateral policy mechanism with the United States and Japan, as in KEDO and the Trilateral Coordination and Oversight Group (TCOG).[19] South Korea, moreover, has been engaged in various multilateral CBMs in East Asia, including the ASEAN Regional Forum (ARF), the ASEAN+3 regional community, the APEC forum, and both the Four-Party Talks and Six-Party Talks in Beijing at the track-one level. Added to these efforts, officials from the RoK foreign and defense ministries have routinely participated in international arms control regimes, such as the Conference on Disarmament (CD), the International Atomic Energy Agency (IAEA), the Missile Technology Control Regime (MTCR), the Chemical Weapons Convention (CWC), and the Convention on Conventional Weapons (CCW).

The RoK government will continue to pursue multilateral security dialogue and cooperation with all major regional powers including India, in addition to the existing bilateral and trilateral ones. It will need to request their assistance for a peaceful unification and convince them that a unified Korea will not pose any threat. Also, it will need to stress that the new regional security alliance with the US does not target any other regional powers and that a modest presence of US troops on the Korean Peninsula will make great contributions to regional security. After all, the changing nature of the RoK-US strategic alliance and the changing roles and missions of the USFK will have tremendous impact on Asian security as a

---

19. See Carlin (2007); The Stanley Foundation (2007).

whole. These issues can and should be put on the agenda of any major multilateral security dialogue and cooperation in the years to come. Keeping a balance between bilateral alliance and multilateral regional cooperation is the beginning of our search for a new paradigm of regional cooperation for a peaceful unification of the Korean Peninsula. Again, there is ample potential for India's positive contributions to achieving a peaceful reunification of the two Koreas in this increasingly globalized world.

Another area for security and military cooperation between our two nations would concern the North Korean missile issue,[20] which is composed of three elements of long-range missile development, short- and medium-range missile export, and deployed missiles. For instance, Egypt obtained Scud-Bs from the former Soviet Union in the 1970s, transferred them to North Korea, who reverse-engineered, including the Rodong 1 (1,300 km, 1993), the Taepodong 1 (2,500 km, 1998), and the Taepodong 2 (6,700 km, 2009). Their missile proliferation activities have attained much of the world media coverage. Recipients of their missiles have been mostly in the Middle East and South Asia such as Egypt, Iran, Iraq, Libya, Syria, and Pakistan, which are commonly referred to as "secondary proliferators." These countries and North Korea have traded missiles, their parts and technologies as part of their bilateral military cooperation. In particular, the so-called missile-nuclear trade among these countries has fostered regional instability and raised tensions. It is worth noting here that New Delhi has been cooperative with Washington, Tokyo, Seoul and Tel Aviv in sharing intelligence and information about these missile networks. Our continued cooperation and coordination over the North Korean missile issue should be a part of our broader vision for the future.

Related to this, India can join the US-led Proliferation Security Initiative (PSI) at a proper point in the future and South Korea can expand its PSI efforts with India in the Indian Ocean and at the global level, because North Korea's proliferation of ballistic missiles will continue to pose threats to East Asia, South Asia, and the Middle East.

20. Pattnaik (2006).

Responding Jointly to Non-traditional, Transnational Security Challenges

Our security cooperation in the early part of the 21st century should not be focused on countering a single security challenge. Instead, security cooperation should be implemented in such a way as to maximize respective capacities and contributions to preserving regional stability. If our security cooperation and coordination is organized in such a way as to maximize capacity to respond to multiple threats and is embedded in a broader politically-based partnership designed to respond to various security needs in East Asia and beyond, it will be harder for our neighbors to object to such efforts.

Our interest-based security cooperation might lay the foundation for security cooperation on missions that serve common interests in East Asia and beyond. Such an approach would allow for some flexibility to develop bilateral, trilateral and multilateral regional response capabilities in the event of natural disasters and humanitarian missions such as earthquake and tsunami relief, energy and environmental security,[21] public health security, international peace cooperation activities and other forms of activities to respond to non-traditional security threats. Such cooperation might form the core of an eventual mechanism for multilateral security cooperation that would more effectively respond to common regional and global threats.

Other challenges lie ahead. They include, first, designing a grand strategic initiative for our nations that goes beyond conventional regional security threats and contributes to peace in the Asia-Pacific and, to a lesser degree, the global community. Second, formulating and implementing regional and global financial relief and other assistance programs will prove to be another challenge for our security cooperation. Third, effective and efficient military operations including anti-terror and anti-piracy operations and those in response to other forms of non-traditional and transnational security threats are another type of immediate challenge facing our two

21. As one of the five pathways to dealing with eight global trends driving tomorrow's complex security environment, energy and environmental security over oil and gas, other minerals, and water have reached a tipping point, according to the Institute for National Strategic Studies' *Strategic Global Assessment 2008*. For its summary discussion, see Cronin (2008).

nations. Fourth and finally, facilitation and mediation of multilateral security dialogue and cooperation in the Asia-Pacific and beyond can be another challenge.[22]

Multilateral security cooperation has been actively promoted in recent years initially in the form of Track 2 dialogues. These forms of multilateral security cooperation are overlapping and have many commonalities, that is, a search for collective wisdom to effectively meet the new security challenges and diverse contingencies that are looming large in the 21st century. These non-traditional, transnational security challenges, including terrorism, natural disaster, pandemic diseases, climate change and global warming, and resource depletion are indeed the driving force behind the otherwise conflicting national interests of major powers, both advanced and emerging.[23]

A joint study by the Korea Institute for Defense Analyses (KIDA) in Seoul and the Institute for Defence Studies and Analyses (IDSA) in New Delhi can be an excellent starter to explore the visions of our security cooperation and roadmaps for implementation as discussed above. An MOU conclusion can be a starting point and we can proceed with an agreement on objectives and vision (to obtain required funding from our respective defense ministries) and to establish a detailed roadmap adhering to the agreed planning.

Concluding Remarks

India and South Korea have gained increasing prominence on the international stage in recent years and they have sufficient potential to continue to do so in the foreseeable future. The two nations have valuable pools of strategic partnerships with many major powers in the region and elsewhere on the globe. Their relations with the US, China, Japan, Russia,

---

22. See *Meeting Complex Challenges Through National Security Reform*. IISS Proceedings, October 16-17, 2008. Although this report aimed to offer options for national security reform of the United States, it provided other countries with many useful insights as well. It concludes that "Responses to natural disasters, shifting power centers, and nontraditional transnational threats require more integrated responses from inside and outside of government."
23. For further discussions on new security threats and security assistance, see Patrick *et al.* (2007).

Australia, and the EU, for example, will continue to prove that they have more common security interests than differences. In particular, their shared experiences in maintaining their relations with their giant neighbor, a rising China, will continue to provide them with unique opportunities in advancing their status in the international community as well as challenges.

This year marks the 60th anniversary of the beginning of the Korean War in 1950, and many South Koreans still remember and appreciate the assistance rendered by India when their nation was in desperate need. Our common experiences in fighting Communist aggressors during the Korean War bode well for our future cooperation in security, defense, and military fields, in addition to our economic, trade and investment efforts.

This paper has focused on laying out visions for our future security, defense, and military cooperation and some ways and means to implement them. It also has appreciated our potential for deterring and defeating many non-traditional, transnational threats primarily through naval cooperation, including the protection of SLOCs, exchanges of defense ministers, navy chiefs and high-ranking officers and security experts, port calls, search and rescue, other training and exercises, anti-piracy operations and PKOs, etc. And given the growing strategic significance of the Indian Ocean, our navies can and should expand their cooperation. There is little doubt that our defense industrial cooperation can and should be further pursued, and other areas such as international peace cooperation, energy security, cybersecurity will also prove to be excellent drivers in our strategic partnership.

Finally, in an era of globalization and networking, we can and should use the existing and emerging multilateral security dialogues and cooperative activities among major regional powers in the Asia-Pacific, including the US, Japan, Korea, China, India, and Australia.

References

Abdul Kalam, A.P.J. and Y.S. Rajan (1998). *India 2020: A Vision for the New Millennium*. Penguin Books.

Carlin, Robert (2007). *Notes from KEDO's Experience*. November 2007 and The Stanley Foundation (2007). *What Did We Learn from KEDO?*. May.

Cronin, Patrick M. (2008). "Barack Obama Faces 8 Global National Security Challenges", *US News and World Report*. Posted December 15.

Harding, Harry (2008). "The Asian Challenges Revisited", Available at *http://www.rsis.edu.sg/short%20reports/Harry_Harding_The%20Asian%20Challenge%20Revisited.pdf*

Kalyanaraman, S. (2010). *India's Security Policy in the Post-Cold War Era*. Institute for Defence Studies and Analyses. April 30.

Kim, Changsu (2005). "Which Powers will Rise in the Asia-Pacific?", in Jae-doo Kim, Changsu Kim and Tae-woo Kim *et al.* (eds.), *Future Predictions for 2020* [in Korean]. KIDA Press. pp.37-57.

Kim, Tong (2008). "Four Power Diplomacy", *The Korea Times*. October 5.

NIDS (2008). *East Asian Strategic Review 2008*. Japan: NIDS. pp.214-22.

Pradhan, Mahmood and Olaf Unteroberdoerster (2010). *Asia-Pacific Regional Economic Outlook: Does Asia Need Balancing?*. New Delhi: Asia and Pacific Department, International Monetary Fund. May 12.

Pattnaik, Rohit (2006). *India-South Korea: The State of Affairs*. Institute for Defence Studies and Analyses, September 22. Available at *http://www.idsa.in/idsastrategiccomments/IndiaSouthKoreaTheStateofAffairs_RPattnaik_220906?q=print/354*

Prasad, Shayam (2008). "National Security and ICT Policy of India", *Amerinews*. December 13.

Patrick, Stewart, James Schear and Mark Wong (2007). *Integrating 21st Century Development and Security Assistance*. Washington, DC: CSIS, December.

Segal, Adam (2010a). *India's Push on Cybersecurity*. Council on Foreign Relations. Posted on May 12.

———. (2010b). *More from the (Cyber) Road: Korea*. Council on Foreign Relations. Posted on March 13.

Singh, Lakhvinder (2008). "India-Korea Naval Cooperation", *The Korea Times*, June 2.

Singh, Lakhvinder and Changsu Kim (2005). "India's Recent Foreign Policy Initiatives and Implications for East Asian Security", *Korean Journal of Defense Analysis* 17(3): 129-50 (Winter).

Subrahmanyam, K. (2005). "Not just about F-16s!", *rediff.com/news*, March 31.